Call Centres and Human Resource Management

Call Centres and Human Resource Management

A Cross-National Perspective

Edited by

Stephen Deery

and

Nicholas Kinnie

Selection, editorial matter and Chapter 1 © Stephen Deery
and Nicholas Kinnie 2004
Individual chapters © the contributors 2004

All rights reserved. No reproduction, copy or transmission of this
publication may be made without written permission.

No paragraph of this publication may be reproduced, copied or transmitted
save with written permission or in accordance with the provisions of the
Copyright, Designs and Patents Act 1988, or under the terms of any licence
permitting limited copying issued by the Copyright Licensing Agency,
90 Tottenham Court Road, London W1T 4LP.

Any person who does any unauthorized act in relation to this publication
may be liable to criminal prosecution and civil claims for damages.

The authors have asserted their rights to be identified
as the authors of this work in accordance with the Copyright,
Designs and Patents Act 1988.

First published 2004 by
PALGRAVE MACMILLAN
Houndmills, Basingstoke, Hampshire RG21 6XS and
175 Fifth Avenue, New York, N.Y. 10010
Companies and representatives throughout the world

PALGRAVE MACMILLAN is the global academic imprint of the Palgrave
Macmillan division of St. Martin's Press, LLC and of Palgrave Macmillan Ltd.
Macmillan® is a registered trademark in the United States, United Kingdom
and other countries. Palgrave is a registered trademark in the European
Union and other countries.

ISBN 1–4039–1304–8

This book is printed on paper suitable for recycling and made from fully
managed and sustained forest sources.

A catalogue record for this book is available from the British Library.

Library of Congress Cataloging-in-Publication Data
Call centres and human resource management : a cross-national
perspective / edited by Stephen Deery and Nicholas Kinnie.
   p. cm.
"The material is drawn principally from a conference held at King's
College London in November 2001"—Introd.
Includes bibliographical references and index.
ISBN 1–4039–1304–8 (cloth)
1. Call centers—Great Britain—Personnel management. 2. Customer
services—Great Britain—Management. 3. Call centers—Australia—
Personnel management. 4. Customer services—Australia—
Management. 5. Call centers—United States—Personnel management.
6. Customer services—United States—Management. I. Deery, Stephen
II. Kinnie, Nicholas, 1955–
HE8789.G7C35 2004
658.8′12—dc22   2003059603

10 9 8 7 6 5 4 3 2 1
13 12 11 10 09 08 07 06 05 04

Printed and bound in Great Britain by
Antony Rowe Ltd, Chippenham and Eastbourne

Contents

List of Figures	vii
List of Tables	viii
Notes on the Contributors	ix
Acknowledgements	xi

1 Introduction: The Nature and Management
of Call Centre Work   1
Stephen Deery and Nicholas Kinnie

Part I   Managerial Strategies and Employment Practices

2 The Viability of Alternative Call Centre Production Models   25
Rosemary Batt and Lisa Moynihan

3 Call Centre HRM and Performance Outcomes: Does
Workplace Governance Matter?   54
Sue Fernie

4 Tensions and Variations in Call Centre Management
Strategies   75
Maeve Houlihan

5 Managing Client, Employee and Customer Relations:
Constrained Strategic Choice in the Management
of Human Resources in a Commercial Call Centre   102
Nicholas Kinnie and Jon Parsons

Part II   Characteristics and Organizational Features of Call Centre Work

6 Keeping Up Appearances: Recruitment, Skills and Normative
Control in Call Centres   129
Paul Thompson, George Callaghan and Diane van den Broek

v

vi *Contents*

7 Professionals at Work: A Study of Autonomy and Skill
   Utilization in Nurse Call Centres in England and Canada 153
   Caroline Collin-Jacques

8 A Female Ghetto? Women's Careers in Telephone
   Call Centres 174
   Vicki Belt

Part III   Effects of Call Centre Work on Employees

9 The Effect of Customer Service Encounters
   on Job Satisfaction and Emotional Exhaustion 201
   Stephen Deery, Roderick Iverson and Janet Walsh

10 Employee Well-being in Call Centres 223
    David Holman

11 All Talk But No Voice: Non-union Employee
    Representation in Call Centre Work 245
    Paul J. Gollan

12 Call to Arms? Collective and Individual Responses
    to Call Centre Labour Management 267
    Diane van den Broek

Name Index 285

Subject Index 291

List of Figures

4.1 Towards a typology of low-discretion
high-commitment (LDHC)   78

5.1 Client, employee and customer relations in Contact 24   123

8.1 An ideal-typical call centre organizational hierarchy   181

List of Tables

2.1	Mean characteristics of call centres by customer segment and HR practices	39
2.2	Bi-variate correlations of management practices, knowledge-sharing and performance	44
3.1	Characteristics of the call centres	62
3.2	Summary of means	69
3.3	Workplace governance and performance outcomes	70
4.1	Overview of LDHC Patterns at the case sites	84
8.1	Percentage of females in supervisory and management positions in the case study call centres	182
9.1	Work attitudes and demographic characteristics	210
9.2	Correlation matrix	213
9.3	Multiple regression for job satisfaction and emotional exhaustion	214
10.1	Expected relationships between the main study variables	228
10.2	Means, standard deviations and intercorrelations	232
10.3	Hierarchical multiple regressions: initial analysis of independent effects of main study variables on well-being variables	235
10.4	Hierarchical multiple regressions: unique effects of main study variables on well-being variables	236
10.5	Means and standard deviations for each call centre and for clerical and shop floor manufacturing work	237
11.1	Pay rates for Eurotunnel call centre staff, 1999 and 2000	253
11.2	Most important call centre issues	255
11.3	Satisfaction with management information	256
11.4	The amount of information given on workplace issues	256
11.5	The importance of the company council in communicating on workplace issues	258
11.6	Type of representation on workplace issues	259
11.7	Trade unions would improve the following workplace issues	261
11.8	The role of the company council if trade unions were recognized	262

Notes on the Contributors

Rosemary Batt is Alice Cook Professor of Women and Work, Cornell University.

Vicki Belt is a Lecturer in Management, University of Newcastle upon Tyne Business School.

George Callaghan is a Lecturer, Open University Business School.

Caroline Collin-Jacques, School of Management, Royal Holloway, University of London.

Stephen Deery is a Professor of Human Resource and Public Sector Management, King's College London.

Sue Fernie is a Lecturer, Department of Industrial Relations, London School of Economics.

Paul J. Gollan is a Lecturer, Department of Industrial Relations, London School of Economics.

David Holman is a Senior Research Fellow, Institute of Work Psychology, Sheffield University.

Maeve Houlihan is a Lecturer in Organizational Behaviour, Business Administration Department, University College, Dublin.

Roderick Iverson is Professor of Human Resource Management, Faculty of Business Administration, Simon Fraser University, Vancouver.

Nicholas Kinnie is Senior Lecturer in Human Resource Management, School of Management, University of Bath.

Lisa Moynihan is Assistant Professor of Organizational Behaviour, London Business School.

Jon Parsons is Director of Giocoso Ltd.

x   *Notes on the Contributors*

Paul Thompson is a Professor of Organizational Analysis, University of Strathclyde.

Diane van den Broek is a Lecturer in Work and Organizational Studies, University of Sydney.

Janet Walsh is a Reader in Human Resource Management, King's College London.

Acknowledgements

The editors would like to convey their grateful thanks to the individual. Virtually all of them contributed to the conference at King's College London in November 2001 which provided an excellent foundation for this collection. We would also like to thank the *Human Resource Management Journal*, especially its editor, John Purcell, for his encouragement and financial support for the conference.

Our thanks also go to the staff at Palgrave Macmillan for their support and patience, especially Jacky Kippenberger and her predecessor Caitlin Cornish. Any mistakes or errors remain our responsibility. Finally, we would like to thank Cathy Aubin at the University of Bath for her help with the manuscript and expert coordination.

STEPHEN DEERY
King's College London
NICHOLAS KINNIE
School of Management, University of Bath

1
Introduction: The Nature and Management of Call Centre Work[*]

Stephen Deery and Nicholas Kinnie

Introduction

There has been a substantial growth of employment in telephone call centres over the last five years. It is now estimated that around two workers in every 100 in the United Kingdom have jobs in call centres (Income Data Services, 2001, p. 11; Key Note, 2002, p. 19). In the USA they employ about 3 per cent of the workforce while in Europe the figure is just over 1 per cent (Datamonitor, 1998; 1999). Call centres are said to be the most rapidly growing form of employment in Europe today (Paul and Huws, 2002, p. 19). The number of call centres in France and Germany has more than doubled since 1997 (*Key Note*, 2002, p. 79). These developments reflect a more general shift in economic activity from goods production to service provision. Call centres epitomize many of the characteristics of service work that have come to dominate developed economies. Like most customer service organizations they provide an intangible, perishable product, which is highly variable and engages the customer in its production (Korczynski, 2002). However, distinctively, call centres require their employees to be skilled at interacting directly with customers while simultaneously working with sophisticated computer-based systems which dictate both the pace of their work and monitor its quality.

The servicing of customers through telephone call centres has delivered substantial financial benefits to organizations. Call centres engage staff to work interactively with customers on either inbound or outbound calls on activities as diverse as sales and telemarketing, product and service information and customer queries and bookings. The use of

---

[*]Parts of this chapter originally appeared in *Human Resource Management Journal*, 124, pp. 3–13.

2 Introduction

modern telephony and computer-automated equipment has radically altered the transportability of services (Miozzo and Ramirez, 2003). By switching customer contact from locations that were proximate to the customer to locations that consolidated service providers, organizations have been able to reduce the need for costly high street outlets and expensive branch networks. Moreover, the centralization of service provision has enabled firms to rationalize the work process through the extensive use of information and communication technologies thereby maximizing the use of service workers' time. The standardization of service encounters with customers and the use of functionally equivalent and interchangeable service providers has also helped call centres to achieve great speed and efficiency in the delivery of their services (Gutek, 1995). This, however, can carry costs for organizations. An emphasis on service throughput to the detriment of service quality can erode customer loyalty and damage an organization's reputation for competence in service delivery. This is particularly the case where organizations have made the call centre their principal source of interaction with the customer. The competing pressures of high productivity and customer service have often proved difficult to reconcile (Korczynski, 2002; Mulholland, 2002; Taylor *et al.*, 2002). Nor has the related issue of managing the labour process been an easy task to execute. Tight control can deliver efficient task completion but it is unlikely to elicit high-quality performance from employees. Control workers too completely, as Fuller and Smith (1996, p. 76) observe and management will 'extinguish exactly those sparks of worker self-direction and spontaneity' that are so critical for service quality.

The purpose of this book is to examine the nature and management of call centre work and its employment relations outcomes. The material is drawn principally from a conference held at King's College London, in November 2001, sponsored by the *Human Resource Management Journal*, that sought to explore the human resource implications of call centre work. The chapters in this volume explore a number of interrelated issues: the different management strategies and models of service delivery in call centres and the policies and practices that are used to manage employees; questions relating to the development and utilization of skills amongst call centre workers and to the opportunities for career progression and advancement for women; the effects of call centre work regimes and management practices on worker well-being and finally, the growth and development of employee voice in call centres. The purpose of our introduction is to locate these chapters within the context of the wider literature on call centres. We have arranged our discussion around four themes: first, the nature of call centre work; second, the choices and strategies that are available to manage the work; third, the effects of this form of work on employees; and finally, the responses and reactions of call centre staff to their work experiences.

The nature of call centre work

A number of research studies have explored the organizational characteristics and employment arrangements of call centres. In general they have not provided a flattering picture. Telephone call centres have variously been described as 'electronic sweatshops' (Garson, 1988), 'twentieth-century panopticons' (Fernie and Metcalf, 1998) and 'assembly lines in the head' (Taylor and Bain, 1999). The jobs have been characterized as 'dead-end' with low status, poor pay and few career prospects. Moreover, the research has shown that much of the work is closely monitored, tightly controlled and highly routinized. Computer technology plays a critical part in this process; work can automatically be allocated to telephone operators to minimize waiting time, the speed of work and level of downtime can continuously be measured and the quality of the interaction between the service provider and the customer can be assessed remotely and at management's discretion. This 'information panopticon' is said to continuously remind workers that 'although no manager may be physically present, every aspect of their performance may be... constantly measured' (Macdonald and Sirianni, 1996). Not surprisingly, it has been suggested that this form of service delivery bears the hallmarks of an engineering model (Herzenberg, Alic and Wial, 1998). Tasks have been simplified, services must conform to predetermined design specifications and the production process has been constructed to minimize labour costs. Indeed, one writer raised the prospect that 'a combination of twentieth-century technology and nineteenth-century scientific management is turning the office of the future into the factory of the past' (Garson, 1988, p. 10).

Other studies, however, present quite a different image of call centre work. Frenkel *et al.* (1998), for example, point to a greater diversity in call centre work revealing environments where jobs provide challenge and interest and where the skills of front-line workers are acknowledged and valued. They suggest that there are clear limitations to the engineering model and to the standardization of work procedures. Indeed there are a number of factors that may act to constrain the use of the Taylorized engineering model. First, where service work requires subjective interpretation and where employees must exercise judgement to meet

4 *Introduction*

customer needs it is clearly inappropriate to adopt methods of simple control to manage employees (Leidner, 1996). This type of work typically requires discretion. In these circumstances it is said that employees should be armed with information rather than instructions (Macdonald and Sirianni, 1996). Second, service work cannot be disembodied from the supplier. Customers care how services are delivered. The way in which employees display their feelings towards customers can have an important effect on the perceived quality of the interaction (Ashforth and Humphrey, 1993). Thus the attitudes of the employee are critical to the quality of the interaction, and tightly scripted dialogue and routinized responses can impair the service that is provided to the customer. Third, the involvement of the customer as a third party brings a greater degree of complexity and uncertainty to the labour process. Although management may wish to standardize the behaviour of customers and limit their options it is not always possible to achieve predictability and compliance in the service exchange. Where customers' requirements cannot easily be standardized workers will require some degree of flexibility and discretion in negotiating their interactions with customers.

Korczynski (2002) has argued that call centre work is infused with two logics: a need to be cost-efficient and a desire to be customer-orientated. He suggests that these twin objectives are fundamentally contradictory. On the one hand organizations seek to reduce costs per customer transaction by increasing the speed with which calls are processed, yet on the other hand they extol the virtues of customer service and encourage their employees to be quality-orientated. Mulholland (2002) refers to this as an attempt to combine a lean production model with a soft discourse of caring and quality. Her research, however, fails to find a genuine and sustained commitment to this language of quality. In contrast, Shire, Holtgrewe and Kerst (2002) believe that the need to be customer-orientated does impose real limits on the degree of service standardization. The tensions and contradictions of these two logics are clearly evident in the marketplace. Customers are seeking to obtain services that are adapted to their needs and requirements yet at the same time are inexpensive and can be supplied efficiently. Firms are attempting to personalize their service, perhaps as part of a customer relationship management programme, while at the same time seeking to reduce the cost per transaction. The type of work organization and employment practices that are adopted will be affected by the way in which these competing demands are balanced or reconciled (Hutchinson, Purcell and Kinnie, 2000). There are at least two different ways of managing these pressures.

Approaches to managing the employment relationship

Call centre work can be designed to maximize discretion and autonomy or it can be turned into a set of repetitive, routinized and highly scripted tasks. The human resource system can build an investment in training and development and establish supportive supervision and teamwork or it can rely on individualized pay systems, insecure jobs and workplace discipline. The decisions that are made in these areas will be influenced by the organization's business objectives, by the customer or market segment that is being serviced and by the conditions in the labour market. Should the firm want to maximize call volume and minimize costs it is more likely to design information systems that limit customer discretion and standardize the service and design jobs that limit employee discretion and make little use of their skills. In these circumstances electronic monitoring will be used as the primary means of ensuring minimum service standards for customers (Batt, 2001). By contrast, those firms that choose to compete on the quality of their service are more likely to use information systems that enable customers to satisfy complex enquiries or requests for information and to construct jobs that provide employees with greater autonomy and enable them to display wider skills and utilize discretion to meet their customers' demands. These two different models of managing the labour process have been termed the production-line approach and the empowerment approach (Bowen and Lawler, 1992).

Batt (2002) has noted, however, that there appears to be an emerging division between the service and manufacturing sectors in terms of the use of these two different models. At the very time that many manufacturing organizations are moving away from scientific management and the production-line approach to workforce management service organizations and especially call centres seem to be eagerly embracing this model. Jobs are narrowly constructed, contingent labour is extensively used and work is mentally and physically demanding.

Miozzo and Ramirez (2003) point to the role of technology in facilitating this process. Innovations such as automatic call distribution switches (ACDs), for example, have allowed organizations to re-route calls between different centres enabling them to create specialist operations especially designed to deliver a very narrow set of services. This, they argue can considerably reduce the tasks that each operator performs, drive down their skill levels and reduce the overall headcount. Systems designers then tend to focus on reducing call handling time and simplifying procedures and routines. This can yield significant financial benefits

6 Introduction

to the organization. Miozzo and Ramirez (2003, p. 70) report that a one-second fall in the handling time of 192 operator calls in the UK can save the business £2 million. Taylor and Bain (1999) have also drawn attention to the intensive control systems that are applied in most call centres. They have pointed to the widespread electronic monitoring and measurement of calls and the scripting and standardization of customer service. The use of target-setting is another pervasive feature of the work. This includes not only quantitative measures of customer throughput but qualitative assessments of the quality of customer interactions (Bain *et al.*, 2002).

It would be a mistake, however, to view these monitoring and measurement systems as the only form of control of call centre work. Tightly specified work regimes are often not sufficient to secure quality service delivery. Consequently, most organizations have sought to instil values of good customer service in their staff by way of cultural or normative control. Leidner (1993, p. 37) describes this as 'transforming workers' characters and personalities'. The aim is to develop an internalized commitment to quality service. This may be done through induction, training and performance appraisals. Callaghan and Thompson (2002) also point to the importance of recruitment with call centres focusing on personality traits and service-orientated attitudes. Korczynski *et al.* (2000, p. 676) have noted the way in which induction and training are used to promote self-control through an identification with customers: an active 'self-as-customer orientation'. Furthermore, they show how this form of normative control can be used as a means of obtaining acceptance of management's measurement and monitoring procedures. In training sessions employees are told, for example, that the company's control mechanisms (*viz.* call monitoring) are merely created to achieve a shared objective: customer satisfaction and good service.

Fernie and Metcalf (1998) suggest that these forms of control amount to an exercise of power over virtually every aspect of employee behaviour. According to them the control systems mean that 'the supervisor's power has indeed been "rendered perfect" – via the computer monitoring screen – and therefore its actual use is unnecessary' (Fernie and Metcalf, 1998, p. 9). Frenkel *et al.* (1999) take a different view. They argue that the increasing complexity of work and the need to be more customer-focused represents a direct challenge to the control model of workforce management. The research team found evidence that a hybrid form of managing call centres had emerged which they termed 'mass customized bureaucracy'. Korczynski (2002) refers to this approach as 'customeroriented bureaucracy' and suggests that human resource management (HRM) can assume a central role by promoting the 'dual focused, efficient, committed customer-oriented worker behaviour' that is required 'to cope with the inevitable tensions' (2002, p. 66). Although this approach retains a strong control component it includes elements of professional or knowledge-intensive work and techniques which have been referred to as high-commitment management (HCM) practices (Purcell, 1999; Wood and de Menezes, 1998). These include 'more exacting hiring criteria, training for job proficiency and limited career opportunities' (Frenkel *et al.*, 1998, p. 976). The role for HRM may involve developing explicit links with the business strategy and training programmes in stress and emotion management as well as the adoption of a more relaxed work environment.

Kinnie, Purcell and Hutchinson (2000a) discuss the use of HCM practices and contrast this with the relatively low-discretion jobs that tend to exist in the industry. They refer to this combination as 'fun and surveillance.' In the two cases that they studied this approach evolved as managers sought to reconcile the internal demands for efficiency and cost savings, the service expectations of customers and the pressures of increasingly tight labour markets. Crucially, in one case, RAC, the changes went beyond the superficial adoption of fun practices. More profound changes were made to the structure of the organization including a reduction in the number of layers in the hierarchy, the introduction of team leaders and team working and a move towards a multi-functional customer advisor role. These changes were complemented by alterations to recruitment and selection, training and development and remuneration and reward systems (Hutchinson, Purcell and Kinnie, 2000). Callaghan and Thompson (2002) also examined the contradiction between extensive and sophisticated selection and training and the routine nature of call centre work and found that employees were aware of these tensions which not infrequently led to labour turnover.

Wallace, Eagleson and Waldersee (2000) have argued that one way of resolving the tension between service and efficiency is to adopt what they refer to as the 'sacrificial HR strategy'. Rather than resolving this tension by improving employee morale, organizational commitment or job satisfaction, employers deliberately sacrifice the well-being of staff accepting 'high levels of stress and emotional burnout of the front-line staff, accompanied by high turnover' as the price for maintaining high levels of service at low cost (Wallace, Eagleson and Waldersee, 2000, p. 182). However, in order to achieve this result call centre managers must have access to a pool of skilled labour, jobs that require minimal organizational knowledge and the ability to closely monitor job performance.

8 *Introduction*

Variations in human resource practices may also take place within a single organization as a result of product market segmentation; a practice used to identify customers with different market characteristics. According to Batt (2000, p. 543) this approach 'allows companies to match the demand characteristics and potential value of the customer to the characteristics of the workforce and to human resource systems that shape the customer–worker interface'. She found clear evidence of a matching of market segment and human resource strategies amongst telecommunications companies in the United States. Employees servicing high-value customers were managed quite differently from those dealing with low-value customers in terms of the number and length of calls, the extent to which their work was controlled and monitored, the skills required to do the job, and the amount of discretion they could exercise.

Call centre work and its effects on employees

Call centre staff play a critical role in the management of customer relationships. As Belt, Richardson and Webster (1999, p. 18) observed they present the 'personality of the firm to the customer over the telephone'. Approximately two-thirds of all customer interactions with organizations now occur through call centres (Barker, 1998). The manner in which employees express their feelings towards customers can have an important effect on the perceived quality of that service transaction (Peccei and Rosenthal, 1997). As a consequence, organizations have placed a strong emphasis on recruiting and selecting employees with the appropriate skills and abilities to perform this work. Thompson, Warhurst and Callaghan (2001) found that the most critical skills were not technical but social. Even in call centres with highly routine tasks an individual's social skills and personality were seen as the most important and valued requirements. They noted: 'Management want people who can continually communicate with energy and enthusiasm, who can recognise nuances in conversations with customers and vary their voice accordingly' (2001, p. 935).

Frenkel *et al.* (1998) have also identified the importance of customer-related or social skills in recruitment and selection. These skills include 'the ability to remain calm under pressure . . . having a friendly, positive and tactful attitude . . . active listening . . . [and] being patient and empathetic . . . particularly when customers are upset' (1998, p. 963). In terms of staff recruitment, it would appear that call centre managers prefer women to men because they are perceived 'naturally' to possess those social skills and competencies. Belt, Richardson and Webster (2002) found that women were viewed as being more comfortable with the ethos of customer service and were seen as being more skilled at listening to and empathizing with customers. They were also perceived as having a greater ability to maintain a 'positive attitude' to customers despite the constant flow and pressure of work. As one female team leader commented to the research team: 'It's a "natural instinct" for women – looking after people, men are more aggressive, more likely to take people to task rather than encourage them' (Belt, Richardson and Webster, 2002, p. 28).

It is clear, therefore, that call centre workers are not simply expected to execute their physical tasks competently and efficiently and to display a knowledge of their organization's products, procedures or practices. They are held accountable for their emotions (Hochschild, 1983). Rather than exerting physical labour to manufacture a product the service labour process involves the use of emotional labour to manufacture relationships (Macdonald and Sirianni, 1996). Employees are expected to display emotions that help create a desired 'state of mind' in the customer. In order to achieve this result call centres have increasingly sought to specify and control the way in which employees presented themselves to customers.

Explicit norms are often embodied in recruitment strategies or included in job descriptions (Ashkanasy and Daus, 2002). In many service exchanges 'workers' moods, facial expressions and words are subject to supervision' (Leidner, 1996, p. 30). Employees are frequently supplied with tightly scripted dialogue and are required to follow highly detailed instructions when interacting with customers. The use of scripts has been described by Taylor and Bain (1999, p. 109) as an attempt to structure the 'speech of workers into a series of predictable, regulated and routinised queries and responses'. In their interaction with customers, employees are often forced to express emotions they do not feel (such as being friendly or happy) or suppress emotions that they genuinely do feel (such as anger or frustration). This can lead to feelings of inauthenticity and emotional dissonance and result in anxiety and burnout. Moreover as Ashforth and Humphrey (1993, p. 96) point out:

> customer perceptions of good service hinge on more than mechanical conformity with display rules. They hinge on the extent to which the service agent conveys a sense of genuine interpersonal sensitivity and concern. The establishment of this emotional rapport or resonance cannot simply be mandated by the organization.

10 *Introduction*

The negative effects of call centre work may be greater for some types of workers than for others and be more evident in some types of work situations (Deery, Iverson and Walsh, 2002). Women, for example, may be more likely to suffer negative effects of emotional labour than men because they are less protected from poor treatment of their feelings on the job (Hochschild, 1983). Macdonald and Sirianni (1996) argue that women are expected to be more empathetic than men and to tolerate more offensive behaviour from customers. Moreover, those who perform a 'second shift' of emotional work at home may be more vulnerable to the negative effects of call centre work. Sustained contact with customers with few opportunities either to vary the pace of work or the nature of the tasks can also result in greater stress and burnout (Morris and Feldman, 1996). Employees who have greater job autonomy could be expected to find emotional labour significantly less stressful. Enhanced responsibility over their expressive behaviour allows employees to avoid those display rules that cause tension and distress. There is evidence to indicate, for example, that the non-expression of negative emotions can have quite adverse psychological effects and that opportunities to interact more naturally with customers can reduce burnout (Wharton, 1993).

Issues relating to working time arrangements and work–life balance also affect the well-being of call centre workers. Many service providers, as Paul and Hews (2002, p. 21) note, are under pressure to maximize availability and operate into the night or round the clock to meet demand or respond to customers in different time zones. This can affect both the work and personal lives of employees. In the UK call centres are said to have some of the longest opening hours in Europe (Call Centres, 2002, p. 44). Indeed, a survey found that almost a third of all call centres operated 24 hours a day. Of those, more than three-quarters were open 365 days a year. Surprisingly, few offered staff flexibility to balance their working and caring responsibilities. Only a third of organizations offered staff some choice over shift arrangements; a quarter offered flexitime and 20 per cent provided some choice over starting and finishing times. Paradoxically, the survey disclosed that the organizations recognized that improvements in work–life balance would improve staff retention, minimize absenteeism and reduce stress (Call Centres, 2002, p. 52).

Service sector organizations have also increased the pressure on call centre workers by raising the expectations of customers about the service they can expect to receive (Ashforth and Humphrey, 1993). Many openly compete on the rhetoric of service quality. A study conducted by Reed Employment Services of more than 500 organizations in the United Kingdom found that almost two-thirds of the respondents claimed that phone rage – people losing their temper over the telephone – had increased in the past five years (*The Guardian*, 1997). The survey attributed the trend in part to the belief by customers that their problems would be resolved speedily over the telephone. The study found that the primary reason for phone rage was an apparent 'insincere tone of voice from the person handling the query'. Within this context Taylor (1998, p. 87) has suggested that customers are now more able to discern the difference between genuine 'quality service' and 'feigned quality service'. Of course, where employees are required to express emotions that they do not feel or where they attempt to change their mood to match the organization's rules they may sound 'insincere' to the customer.

An employee's emotional state will affect the quality of the emotional labour that is displayed during the service encounter. Fatigue, stress or depression will be transmitted to the customer. Ashkanasy and Daus (2002, p. 79) have noted that people 'catch' or are 'infected' by the feelings or emotions of others; a result that has become known as emotional contagion. Positive expressions of emotion by employees can create favourable impressions in customer's minds while negative attitudes expressed by employees can similarly create unfavourable impressions. The way in which employees are managed will ultimately affect the service recipient. What employees experience at work will thus be passed onto the customer (Schneider and Bowen, 1993). By implication, therefore, call centre managers are shaping the experiences of their customers by the way in which they are managing the experiences of their employees. Indeed, there is evidence to indicate that there is an association between the way employees are managed and the performance of the organization (Batt, 1999).

In this context it is interesting to note that customers' attitudes towards call centres in the UK appear to be rather negative. In a nationwide survey conducted by NOP in 2002, on behalf of Key Note, the majority of respondents were found to be critical of the time they had to wait for service; almost a half had a preference to speak to someone who was familiar or local and over a third believed that the organization benefited from call centres more than the customer did (Key Note, 2002, p. 105). In terms of service encounters between staff and customers 43 per cent of respondents admitted to 'not always being polite to call centre staff' (*Key Note*, 2002, p. 114). Tellingly, almost three in ten respondents believed that call centres reduced customer loyalty by providing an impersonal service (*Key Note*, 2002, p. 117).

12 *Introduction*

Responses and reactions of employees to call centre work

The responses of employees to call centre work vary considerably. There is evidence, for example, that some employees find this form of service work greatly rewarding and enjoy the social interaction and peer support that can exist in many centres. For others, the work is a tiring, stressful and emotionally exhausting experience. The cross-national studies conducted by Frenkel *et al.* (1998; 1999) and also reported in Korczynski (2002) suggest quite high levels of overall job satisfaction, with nearly three-quarters of their respondents reporting some satisfaction with their job (Korczynski, 2002, p. 95). The greatest satisfaction appears to be derived from customers ('helping people') and from the camaraderie and social support that develops in the work environment. Furthermore, performance monitoring seemed to be fairly widely accepted, although that acceptance was contingent upon the style of supervision. Over half were satisfied or very satisfied with the methods of control used and three-quarters said the controls helped them to work better (Frenkel *et al.*, 1998, p. 967). On the other hand, levels of job stress among the staff were quite high, with just over two-thirds of employees reporting a degree of stress (Korczyniski, 2002, p. 95).

Deery, Iverson and Walsh (2002) also found a relatively high incidence of stress amongst call centre staff in Australia. Using survey data from almost 500 telephone service operators in five call centres in the telecommunications industry they found that emotional exhaustion was associated with high workloads and pressure from management to maximize customer throughput at the expense of customer service. Moreover, the longer employees worked in call centres the more burnt out they became. In contrast employees who spent longer with customers on calls experienced lower levels of burnout. The study also found that higher levels of emotional exhaustion were associated with higher rates of absenteeism.

Employee withdrawal, either in a temporary or permanent form, is a pervasive feature of call centre work. For example, a nationwide survey in Britain found annual average turnover rates in 2002 of over 30 per cent (Call Centres, 2002). In the financial services sector almost half of the centres surveyed experienced annual turnover rates of between 25 and 50 per cent and almost a fifth of outsourced operations had annual turnover in excess of 100 per cent (Call Centres, 2002, pp. 34–5). Both turnover and absenteeism can be seen as a form of 'exit' involving an effort to escape from working conditions that are viewed as unpleasant. There are other ways of responding to an uncongenial or unsatisfactory work environment. Although strike action is rare and unionism still somewhat embryonic, employees do contest and challenge management decision-making and resist unfair treatment and unacceptable customer behaviour. However, in interactive service, as Macdonald and Sirianni (1996, p. 4) note, 'contests over control of the labor process are often more implicit than explicit'. Such contests may occur in a number of ways. Rosenthal (2002), for example, shows how workers can use management's forms of normative control – the language of consumer service – and direct control – the monitoring and measurement systems – to turn the tables on management and defend their rights and protect their interests. She argues that the espoused values of service quality invariably emphasize respect for employees, as well as for customers, and that the language of such programmes can supply workers with an effective means of enforcing standards of fair treatment. In this context, Lankshear *et al.* (2001, p. 605) found that tensions between service throughput and service quality often forced managers to compromise on quality measures and allowed the creation of 'organizational spaces in which employees could develop and defend their own definitions of professionalism and good performance'.

Call centre workers may confront management in other ways as well. Mulholland (2002), for example, has reported that call centre agents often challenge management's discourse about care, quality and teamwork by subjecting it to derision. She argues that 'making fun of a management style is a form of resistance' (2002, p. 299). Call centre workers may also disregard the organization's scripted conversational rules. They may search for weaknesses in the organization's control systems and construct free spaces for themselves 'which provide an amnesty from normal emotional labours' (Sturdy and Fineman, 2001, p. 146). In addition, they may deliberately redirect calls to other service operators, enter misleading activity codes into the system or simply hang up on offensive customers (Knights and McCabe, 1998).

Sturdy and Fineman (2001) have suggested that resistance amongst service workers is most likely to be covert, individual and temporary. However, there is evidence that collective representation in Britain is growing and that union claims for improvements in working conditions are proving effective (Call Centre, 2001; Taylor and Bain, 1999). In their survey of 108 Scottish call centres Taylor and Bain (1999) found that more than half of them had a trade union or staff association. Indeed, they pointed to a number of financial services organizations where more than three-quarters of the employees belonged to a union. There was also evidence of high levels of inter-union co-operation. Of course,

14   *Introduction*

collective resistance need not be organized through trade unions. Callaghan and Thompson (2001) show how collective responses by employees help individuals cope with the pressures and tensions of call centre work. They demonstrate in particular how 'CSRs [customer service representatives] use the loose framework of "teams" or other collective contexts to create and reproduce the same kind of informal group dynamics and mutual support found in previous generations of industries' (Callaghan and Thompson, 2001, p. 33).

The content of the book

The chapters in this book draw upon a number of the themes that we have outlined. In Chapter 2 Batt and Moynihan examine the relationship between employment practices and service market strategies. They explore the question of whether particular human resource practices are contingent upon the customer market segment that is served or whether certain types of practices can have a universalistic and beneficial effect on both workers and organizations irrespective of the market segment. The authors distinguish between three different models of service delivery: the mass-production model which seeks to maximize customer throughput and to minimize costs through Taylorized work methods; the mass customization model which seeks to incorporate the gains of mechanisation with some level of attention to service quality and customer loyalty, and the professional services model which seeks to provide high-quality individualized services through a well-trained and knowledgeable workforce. They find that there is a general conformity between the market segment served and the human resource practices that are pursued but that centres that adopted a high-involvement strategy (high skill levels, teamwork, training, employment security) had lower staff turnover and faster sales growth irrespective of the customer segment that was served. The mass-production model carried much higher turnover rates and more sluggish sales growth. The authors also show that high-involvement practices and team working are positively associated with more knowledge-sharing amongst employees and with higher-quality customer service.

The impact of workplace governance on call centre HRM and performance outcomes is the subject of Chapter 3. Fernie explores the nature of human resource practices at three different call centres owned by the same organization in order to identify whether different workplace governance arrangements affect particular organizational outcomes. Each of the call centres had a different form of governance. One practised an authoritarian form of management and was union-free. Another, in quite stark contrast, had a highly collaborative relationship with organized labour, while the third call centre practised a more sophisticated form of high-involvement HRM. It was also unionized. Fernie administered a large-scale survey to employees in the three centres to ascertain their responses to a range of questions relating to service performance (customer focus, empathy) and their attitudes and feelings about their organization and their job (organizational commitment, job satisfaction, anxiety). She found that the authoritarian non-union call centre had significantly poorer performance on a range of customer-service and employee-related outcomes.

In Chapter 4 Houlihan looks at the approaches used by managers to resolve the tensions they face in designing the labour process. She draws on detailed empirical research to examine the emergence of what she refers to as the low-discretion high-Commitment (LDHC) approach which involves the use of high-commitment management (HCM) techniques in what remain essentially low-discretion jobs. Using a model based on the orientation to HCM and on job design implementation, Houlihan identifies four variations of this LDHC approach. However, close inspection of the cases reveals very little evidence of a systematic and in-depth adoption of these HCM practices. Indeed, the data suggest, in three of the cases at least, that the HCM practices are little more than a veneer to offset some of the more unpleasant work experiences. The fragility of the LDHC approach is also revealed, as Houlihan identifies the persistent tendency of call centres to revert to a control approach to workforce management.

Chapter 5 by Kinnie and Parsons discusses the influences on the management of human resources in a commercial call centre which provides services for other businesses. It argues that managers of human resources (HR) in these organizations operate within a highly unpredictable and dynamic environment which is characterized by three sets of pressures, which at times conflict. They need to maintain relations with a variety of business clients, to provide a service to retail customers and to pay close attention to the volatile internal and external labour markets which they face.

Particular attention is paid to the ways in which commercial clients seek to influence HR policies and practices. This influence may directly affect the HR practices for managers and employees in areas such as recruitment, selection, training, career progression and reward. Indirect client influences are felt through the award and management of contracts. HR practices are affected by the terms of the contract, changes in

16 *Introduction*

business strategy, the amount of client contact and performance monitoring. Commercial call centre managers are not, however, simply at the mercy of these influences. During the period of the research they sought to manage the direct influence by making changes to their HR policies and practices and the indirect influence by modifying their business strategy and structure.

The case charts the dynamic interplay between managers' initiatives and responses and the pressures that they encounter over time. These managers exercise strategic choice over the management of HR but this is constrained by the need to balance the interests of clients, employees and customers. Indeed, the company illustrates some of the problems of achieving a 'best fit' of HR policies and practices when the pressures in the external environment are complex and fast changing, a situation which is likely to become increasingly common.

In Chapter 6 Thompson, Callaghan and van den Broek draw on research in two call centres (Telebank in Scotland and Servo in Australia) to examine how recruitment and socialization techniques influence employee skill formation. It argues that the identification and shaping of social competencies is integral to interactive service work.

The authors pursue their theme under four headings: recruitment and selection techniques; the tensions and constraints resulting from these techniques; socialization and training; and the limits to normative control. They draw attention to the elaborate recruitment and selection techniques and link these to the emphasis placed on customer service skills. However, the attention given to these activities, especially induction, contrasts markedly with the routine and mundane nature of many of these jobs and creates tensions in the minds of many employees. They go on to look at the techniques used for training and socialization and examine in particular the recreational activities developed and the extent to which these, too, are controlled and monitored. Towards the end they discuss the limits of these forms of normative control, picking out instances of employee reluctance and disenchantment with these measures. The employee strategy of satisficing is discussed especially in the context of their attempts at managing the emotional effort bargain.

In conclusion they return to the basic paradox identified in their two cases – why do the companies invest so heavily in recruitment, selection, training and related activities for jobs that are mostly routine and monitored with limited career opportunities and a high likelihood of employee burnout. They conclude that this combination is seen as essential if managers are to achieve their goals of high volume and consistent service needed to be successful in the marketplace.

Collin-Jacques' chapter makes a unique contribution to the study of call centre work, first, by examining the labour process from a comparative perspective and, second, by exploring the work activities of professional – as distinct from clerical – call centre staff. In Chapter 7 she compares the work organization of nurses employed in tele-health call centres in England and Quebec. Her principal objective is to identify whether a credential-based occupational group with distinctive professional qualifications and a strong consciousness of work practices is able to shape the way work is conducted and infuse its knowledge into the labour process. The findings suggest distinct differences between England and Quebec in terms of the extent to which nurses and a 'nursing methodology' affect the labour process. The tele-nursing process in England is more rigid and automated than in Quebec where nurses appear to have greater influence over their work methods. Collin-Jacques advances a number of historical, cultural and linguistic explanations for these differences.

Call centres have been characterized as 'female ghettos' with few opportunities for promotion and career development. In Chapter 8 Belt looks specifically at the female call centre labour market drawing data from 11 separate organizations in the United Kingdom and Ireland. She finds that call centres do provide opportunities for advancement for women and that their representation amongst team leaders and managers is strong in the organizations that she studied. Moreover, her interviews revealed that the staff themselves believed that women faced no distinct promotional disadvantage because career mobility tended to rely on social skills and interpersonal abilities, qualities that women seemed more likely to possess. Despite this encouraging picture, Belt also found many women who remained on the bottom rung of the career ladder often combining childcare commitments with part-time jobs. Furthermore, those women who did proceed to managerial roles tended to be single and not have dependent children. Moreover, the roles they occupied often necessitated long hours and geographical mobility.

The next two chapters look at the impact of call centre work on employee well-being. In Chapter 9 Deery, Iverson and Walsh explore the effect of different work systems and employment arrangements on workers' job satisfaction and levels of emotional exhaustion. They examine two call centres involved in quite different types of service encounters with their customers: one that seeks to deliver service according to a predetermined design and routine and the other that seeks to emphasize more specialized and customized relationships.

18 *Introduction*

They found that variations in the way that the call centres rendered their services and effected their transactions affected not only the design of their work systems but also the job satisfaction and stress levels of their staff. In the centre that chose to maximize service quality and construct more customized relationships, workers reported significantly lower workloads and emotional exhaustion and significantly higher levels of job satisfaction and social interaction as well as greater skill utilization and job autonomy.

The theme of worker well-being is examined further in Chapter 10. Here Holman seeks to discover the effects on employees of certain management practices commonly found in call centres. He examines the impact of job design, performance monitoring, team leader support and other human resource practices on anxiety and depression as well as job satisfaction. The chapter also compares levels of well-being in call centres with those in other industry sectors. A number of important findings emerge. Anxiety, depression and a lack of job satisfaction in call centre work tends to be associated with low job control, high levels of monitoring as well as inadequate training. On the other hand, supportive and helpful team leaders significantly improve worker well-being. This is an important finding because it resonates with the results obtained by Deery, Iverson and Walsh (2002) and Frenkel *et al.* (1998; 1999) and seems to confirm the important effect of supervisory style on employee attitudes and behaviour. Finally, Holman's research reveals that worker well-being in call centres compares favourably with shop floor manufacturing and clerical work. This, he suggests, challenges the stereotypical image of call centres as 'electronic sweatshops'.

In the last two chapters the book turns its attention to the question of employee representation in telephone call centres. In Chapter 11 Gollan assesses the effectiveness of non-union employee consultation and representation at the Eurotunnel call centre in the UK. The consultative structures had been erected by management to facilitate information-sharing and communication rather than as a mechanism for negotiation or collective bargaining. Their principal aim had been to increase productivity and enhance efficiency rather than to provide a robust form of interest representation for employees. Overall Gollan found that the call centre workers were dissatisfied with the form of consultation and information-sharing provided by the company council and expressed the view that a trade union would offer far stronger representation of their interests particularly in the critical areas of pay, grievances and discipline. Indeed the staff subsequently achieved this objective when a union recognition agreement was signed with the Transport and General Workers union (T&GWU).

The theme of employee representation is developed further by van den Broek in Chapter 12 in her analysis of the responses of customer service agents to the management of call centre work in the telecommunications industry in Australia. She examines not only the individual responses of withdrawal – such as absenteeism and turnover – but the collective alliances and joint worker responses that have led to a growing union presence in the call centre sector. Although union representation is shown to be quite uneven and certainly difficult to effect in greenfield sites, van den Broek detects an emerging trend of resistance to authoritarian management styles, high workloads and inflexible rosters. In other settings employees have historically reacted to workplace grievances by forming trade unions and responding collectively to their shared problems. An important question therefore is whether call centres will become a new and significant site for trade union membership and collective activity.

References

Ashforth, B. and R. Humphrey (1993) 'Emotional labor in service roles: the influence of identity', *Academy of Management Journal*, 18, pp. 88–115.

Ashkanasy, N. and C. Daus (2002) 'Emotion in the workplace: the new challenge for managers', *The Academy of Management Executive*, 16(1), pp. 76–86.

Bain, P. and P. Taylor (2000) 'Entrapped by the "electronic panoptican"? Worker resistance in the call centre', *New Technology, Work and Employment*, 15(1), pp. 2–18.

Bain, P., A. Watson, G. Mulvey, P. Taylor and G. Gall (2002) 'Taylorism, targets and the pursuit of quantity and quality by call centre management', *New Technology, Work and Employment*, 17(3), pp. 170–85.

Barker, G. (1998) 'Factories of the future', *The Age*, 24 February.

Batt, R. (2000) 'Strategic segmentation in front-line services: matching customers, employees and human resource systems', *International Journal of Human Resource Management*, 11(3) pp. 540–61.

Batt, R. (2001) 'Explaining wage inequality in telecommunications services: customer segmentation, human resource practices, and union decline', *Industrial and Labor Relations Review*, 54, pp. 425–59.

Batt, R. (2002) 'Managing Customer Services: Human resource practices, quit rates and sales growth', *Academy of Management Journal*, 45(3), pp. 587–97.

Belt, V., R. Richardson and J. Webster (1999) 'Smiling down the phone: women's work in Telephone call centres', workshop on call centres, March, London School of Economics.

Belt, V., R. Richardson and J. Webster (2002) 'Women, social skill and interactive service work in telephone call centres', *New Technology, Work and Employment*, 17(1), pp. 20–34.

Bowen, D. and E. Lawler (1992) 'The empowerment of service workers: what, why, how, and when', *Sloan Management Review*, Summer, pp. 73–84.

20 Introduction

Call Centres (2001) *Reward and Retention Strategies*, a joint report from the Call Centre Association Research Institute and Industrial Relations Services, London: Industrial Relations Services.

Call Centres (2002) *Reward and Work-life Strategies*, Philip Pearson and Michael Thewlis, London: Industrial Relations Services.

Callaghan, G. and P. Thompson (2001) 'Edwards revisited: technical control and call centres', *Economic and Industrial Democracy*, 22(1), pp. 13–37.

Callaghan, G. and P. Thompson (2002) '"We Recruit Attitude": the selection and shaping of routine call centre labour', *Journal of Management Studies*, 39(2), pp. 233–54.

Datamonitor (1998) *Call Centres in Europe 1996–2001: Vertical market opportunities*, London: Datamonitor.

Datamonitor (1999) *Opportunities in US and Canadian Call Centre Markets*, New York: Datamonitor.

Deery, S., R. Iverson and J. Walsh (2002) 'Work relationships in telephone call centres: Understanding emotional exhaustion and employee withdrawal', *Journal of Management Studies*, 39(4), pp. 471–96.

Edwards, R. (1979)*Contested Terrain: The Transformation of the Workplace in the Twentieth Century*, London: Heinemann.

Fernie, S. and D. Metcalf (1998) '(Not) Hanging on the Telephone: payment systems in the new sweatshops', Discussion Paper No. 390, Centre for Economic Performance.

Frenkel, S., M. Korczynski, L. Donoghue and K. Shire (1995) 'Re-constituting Work: Trends towards Knowledge Work and Info-normative Control', *Work, Employment and Society*, 9(4), pp. 773–96.

Frenkel, S., M. Korczynski, K. Shire and M. Tam (1998) 'Beyond Bureaucracy? Work organization in call centres', *International Journal of Human Resource Management*, 9(6), pp. 957–79.

Frenkel, S., M. Korczynski, K. Shire and M. Tam (1999) *On the Front Line: Organization of work in the information economy*, Ithaca, NY: Cornell University Press.

Fuller, L. and V. Smith (1996) 'Consumers' reports: management by customers in a changing economy', in C. L. Macdonald and C. Sirianni (eds), *Working in the Service Society*, Philadelphia: Temple University Press.

Garson, B. (1988) *The Electronic Sweatshop: How Computers are Transforming the Office of the Future into the Factory of the Past*, New York: Simon & Schuster.

The Guardian (1997) 'Telephone users take an ever more aggressive line', 28 August.

Gutek, B. (1995)*The Dynamics of Service: Reflections on the Changing Nature of Customer/Provider Interactions*, San Francisco Jossey-Bass.

Herzenberg, S., J. Alic and H. Wial (1998) *New Rules for a New Economy: Employment and Opportunity in Postindustrial America*, Ithaca, NY: Cornell University Press.

Hochschild, A. (1983)*The Managed Heart: Commercialization of Human Feeling*, Berkeley: University of California Press.

Hutchinson, S., J. Purcell and N. Kinnie (2000) 'Evolving high commitment management and the experience of the RAC call centre', *Human Resource Management Journal*, 10(1), pp. 63–78.

Income Data Services (IDS) (2001) *Pay and Conditions in Call Centres*, London: Income Data Services.

Key Note (2002) 'Call Centres: 2002 Market Assessment', Hampton: Key Note.

Kinnie, N. (2000) 'Rules of Engagement', *People Management*, 8 June.

Kinnie, N. J., J. Purcell and S. Hutchinson (2000a) '"Fun and Surveillance": the paradox of high commitment management in call centres', *International Journal of Human Resource Management*, 11(5), pp. 967–85.

Kinnie, N. J., J. Purcell and S. Hutchinson (2000b) 'Managing the Employment Relationship in Telephone Call Centres', in K. Purcell (ed.), *Changing Boundaries in Employment*, Bristol: Bristol Academic Press.

Knights, D. and D. McCabe (1998) 'What happens when the phone goes wild? Staff, stress and spaces for escape in a BPR telephone banking work regime', *Journal of Management Studies*, 35(2), pp. 163–94.

Korczynski, M. (2001) 'The contradictions of service work: call centre as customer-oriented bureaucracy', in A. Sturdy, I. Grugulis and H. Willmott (eds), *Customer Service: Empowerment and Entrapment*, Basingstoke: Palgrave.

Korczynski, M. (2002) *Human Resource Management in Service Work: The Fragile Social Order*, Basingstoke: Palgrave.

Korczynski, M., K. Shire, S. Frenkel and M. Tam (1996) 'Front line work in the "new model service firm": Australian and Japanese comparisons', *Human Resource Management Journal*, 6(2), pp. 72–87.

Korczynski, M., K. Shire, S. Frenkel and M. Tam (2000). 'Service work in customer capitalism: customers, control and contradictions', *Work, Employment and Society*, 14(4), pp. 669–88.

Lankshear, G., P. Cook, D. Mason, S. Coates and G. Button (2001) 'Call centre employees' responses to electronic monitoring: some research findings', *Work, Employment and Society*, 15(3), pp. 595–605.

Leidner, R. (1993) *Fast Food, Fast Talk: Service Work and the Routinization of Everyday Life*, Berkeley: University of California Press.

Leidner, R. (1996) 'Rethinking questions of control: lessons from McDonald's', in C. L. MacDonald and C. Sirianni *Working in the Service Society*, (eds), Philadelphia: Temple University Press, pp. 29–49.

Macdonald, C. L. and C. Sirianni (eds) (1996)*Working in the Service Society*, Philadelphia: Temple University Press.

Marshall, J. N. and R. Richardson (1996) 'The impact of telemediated service on corporate structures: the example of"branchless" retail banking in Britain', *Environment and Planning*, 28, pp. 1843–58.

Miozzo, M. and M. Ramirez (2003) 'Services innovation and the transformation of work: the case of UK telecommunications', *New Technology, Work and Employment*, 18(1), pp. 62–79.

Morris, J. and D. Feldman (1996) 'Managing emotions in the workplace', *Journal of Managerial Issues*, 9(3), pp. 257–74.

Mulholland, K. (2002) 'Gender, emotional labour and teamworking in a call centre', *Personnel Review*, 31(3), pp. 283–303.

Paul, J. and U. Huws (2002) *How Can We Help? Good Practice in Call-Centre Employment*, Brussels: European Trade Union Confederation.

Peccei, R. and P. Rosenthal (1997) 'The antecedents of employee commitment to customer service: evidence from a UK service context', *International Journal of Human Resource Management*, 8(1), pp. 66–86.

Purcell, J. (1999) 'The Search for Best Practice and Best Fit in HR Management: Chimera or cul-de-sac?', *Human Resource Management Journal*, 9(3), pp. 26–41.

22 Introduction

Richardson, R. and J. N. Marshall (1996) 'The growth of telephone call centres in peripheral areas of Britain: evidence from Tyne and Wear', *Area*, 28, pp. 308–17.

Rosenthal, P. (2002) 'Management control as an employee resource: the case of front-line service workers', Research Paper no. 009, The Management Centre, King's College, London.

Rosenthal, P., S. Hill and R. Peccei (1997) 'Checking Out Service: Evaluating Excellence, HRM and TQM in retailing', *Work, Employment and Society*, 11(3), pp. 481–503.

Schneider, B. and D. E. Bowen (1993) 'The service organization: human resource management is crucial', *Organizational Dynamics*, 21(4), pp. 39–53.

Sewell, G. (1998) 'The Discipline of Teams: The Control of Team-Based Industrial Work Through Electronic and Peer Surveillance', *Administrative Science Quarterly*, 43, pp. 406–69.

Shire, K., U. Holtgrewe and C. Kerst (2002) 'Re-organising customer service work: an introduction' in U. Holtgrewe, C. Kerst and K. Shire (eds), *Re-Organising Service Work: Call Centres in Germany and Britain*, Aldershot: Ashgate.

Sturdy, A. and S. Fineman (2001) 'Struggles for the control of affect – resistance as politics and emotion', in A. Sturdy, A. Gruglis and H. Willmott (eds), *Customer Service*, Basingstoke: Palgrave.

Taylor, S. (1998) 'Emotional labour and the new workplace', in P. Thompson and C. Warhurst (eds), *Workplaces of the Future*, London: Macmillan.

Taylor, P. and P. Bain (1999) "An assembly line in the head": Work and employment relations in the call centre', *Industrial Relations Journal*, 30(2), pp. 101–17.

Taylor, P., G. Mulvey, J. Hyman and P. Bain (2002). 'Work organization, control and the experience of work in call centres', *Work, Employment and Society*, 16(1), pp. 133–50.

Thompson, P., C. Warhurst and G. Callaghan (2001) 'Ignorant theory and knowledgeable workers: interrogating the connection between knowledge, skills and services', *Journal of Management Studies*, 38 (7), pp. 923–42.

Wallace, C. M., G. Eagleson and R. Waldersee (2000) 'The Sacrificial HR Strategy in Call Centres', *International Journal of Service Industry Management*, 11 (2), pp. 174–84.

Wharton, A. (1993) 'The affective consequences of service work', *Work and Occupations*, 20, pp. 205–32.

Wood, S. and L. de Menezes (1998) 'High Commitment Management in the UK: Evidence from the Workplace Industrial Relations Surveys and Employers' Manpower and Skills Practices Survey', *Human Relations*, 51(4), pp. 485–515.

Part I

Managerial Strategies and Employment Practices

2
The Viability of Alternative Call Centre Production Models*

Rosemary Batt and Lisa Moynihan

Introduction

Advances in information technologies and marketing techniques have led to a revolution in service delivery systems over the last decade. Whereas service delivery historically was decentralized and personal and service labour markets were local, advanced information systems and marketing techniques have made centralized remote servicing via technology-mediated call centres the preferred mode of customer – provider interaction for many firms. While data on call centres is difficult to procure, estimates are that call centres employ about 3 per cent of the workforce in the US, 2 per cent in the UK and 1.3 per cent in Europe (Datamonitor, 1998; 1999). US call centres were growing at an estimated annual rate of 15–20 per cent annually in the 1990s (Purdue University, 1999).

To manage call centre operations, firms have introduced industrial engineering models into customer services for the first time, mechanizing and routinizing work processes that historically were varied and complex. For these firms, the economic benefits of shifting service delivery to call centres include enormous scale economies achieved through office consolidation, service automation and process rationalization. For consumers, there are trade-offs: lower prices but also lower service quality as self-service menus shift labour costs to consumers and mechanized systems limit their choices. At the same time, the majority of workers

---

*This chapter originally appeared in *Human Resource Management Journal*, 12(4), pp. 14–34.

25

in these types of call centres experience a degradation in working conditions, with increased machine-pacing of work, routinization of work processes, boredom and increased stress associated with speed-up of job cycle times. Thus, this call centre production model creates a classic conflict that pits workers against employers. Here, with conflict built into the production system, the primary role of unions is to fight against oppressive working conditions and low wages, as exemplified in recent research on call centre unionization (Taylor and Bain, 2001).

Alternative strategies based on high-quality professional service also exist, but they are costly and characterize a minority of transactions generally reserved for business and elite clients. The open question is whether some form of mass customization is viable for serving large numbers of consumers. The business strategy under mass customization is to compete on quality and customer loyalty as well as price. To do so, firms would logically invest in new technology to complement, rather than substitute, for labour. They would adopt a set of management practices that invest in the skills and abilities of the workforce, design work so that employees have opportunities to use those skills effectively, and create incentives that reward effort and commitment. In this paper, we refer to these practices as 'high-involvement practices'. They may be viewed as a means to quasi-professionalize production-level work. Compared to a mass-production approach, this alternative should create better jobs for workers, better service for consumers and better organizational performance. Under this alternative, unions are likely to spend less time in workplace grievances and more time on initiatives such as joint training programmes. Yet, at a time when many manufacturing enterprises have moved away from a strict adherence to a mass-production model to adopt high-involvement work practices, many service firms have moved in the opposite direction. Production-line call centres proliferate.

The central question of this chapter is whether a mass-customization strategy coupled with high-involvement work practices is an economically viable model for service and sales call centres. If so, under what conditions and why? To answer these questions, in the next section, we describe alternative models of call centre management. In the third section of this chapter, we present a conceptual framework for understanding the relationship between management practices, workers' reactions to those practices and performance outcomes. We then review empirical evidence on these relationships, focusing primarily on studies of call centres or related service workplaces. In the fourth section, we draw on evidence from two recent quantitative studies of call centres to examine the performance outcomes of high-involvement practices in this context. We close with a discussion and critique of existing evidence and suggestions for future research.

Alternative models of service delivery

A useful way of distinguishing production models is along four dimensions: the use of technology; the skill requirements of jobs; the organization of work; and the use of other human resource (HR) incentives to reward effort. In this section, we outline three alternative models, which may be thought of as varying on a continuum in terms of investment in human capital and human resource incentives. At the low end is the classic mass-production model, while at the high end is the professional service model. Between the two extremes is a range of hybrid models that we describe as mass customization.

The spread of mass production in services

Under classic mass production, the goal is to maximize volume and minimize costs. To achieve that goal, firms have used a combination of mechanization and Taylorism to rationalize the production. Technology is used to mechanize and automate production where possible. It is viewed as a substitute for labour; and labour is a residual cost to be minimized. Jobs are designed along the principles of Taylorism, with detailed functional specialization and time and motion studies to standardize work. Taylorist work organization minimizes skill requirements, discretion and job cycle time. Learning is limited to repetition of simple rationalized tasks ('practice makes perfect'). Human resource practices to induce effort are built on fear of job loss and/or piece rate pay systems (or in call centres, individual commission pay). The approach assumes that jobs can be designed to be turnover-proof, with workers as replaceable parts.

The application of mass-production principles in service activities has been uneven for at least two reasons: first, the intangible nature of services limits the use of machine-pacing and, second, one party to the production process – the consumer – is not under the control of management. In clerical work, for example, machine-pacing was not possible, but the application of Taylorist principles was effective in creating clerical typing pools with efficient, standardized output. In customer-contact work, however, variation in consumer preferences introduces uncertainty into the production process. As a result, service managers also use work rules and norms to standardize work behaviours – what Leidner (1993) refers to as 'routinization'. To rationalize service

28 *The Viability of Alternative Call Centre Production Models*

production, therefore, firms have typically relied less on mechanization and more on Taylorist principles and routinization of behaviours.

Call centres, however, represent an exceptional case in which mechanization has spread into customer-contact work. For purposes of understanding today's call centres, an instructive case is the evolution of operator services in the large telephone bureaucracies such as AT&T and British Telecom. A hundred years ago, operator service jobs were considered highly skilled jobs in the 'high-tech' telephone industry. They were complex and varied, requiring physical manipulation of cords, social interaction skills and diagnostic assessments of faulty telephone circuits. From 1900 on, AT&T adopted Taylorist principles to standardize work methods. It also developed personnel policies to control work behaviour, including the recruitment of white middle-class women with a diploma or high school degree – because they matched the characteristics of the middle- and upper-class people who could afford telephones. Selection procedures required women to pass extensive entrance examinations; training covered rules of behaviour, speaking and scripts; and intensive monitoring and discipline was reflected in the ratio of supervisors to workers, which was typically 1:6 (Schacht, 1985).

From the 1920s on, however, the company began to mechanize operations, fragmenting once varied jobs. Mechanical switching made it possible for customers to dial their own local calls by the 1920s, and long-distance calls by the 1950s. In the 1970s, digital systems further eliminated operator work by letting customers use credit cards to direct-dial long-distance calls. Each new technological advance eliminated large numbers of operator jobs, while reducing the variety and complexity of the remaining jobs: eliminating the physical side of the job, reducing the types of calls and eliminating the diagnostic work (Kohl, 1993, p. 104). In the 1980s and 1990s, job fragmentation and displacement continued through the use of automated response and voice-recognition systems (Kohl, 1993, p. 105). In 2000, the typical telephone operator handles 1000 calls per day, a job cycle time of about 21 seconds per call, significantly lower than the average 60-second job cycle time of auto assembly workers.

AT&T's mechanization strategy produced dramatic improvements in productivity, with operators constituting 60 per cent of the telephone workforce in 1920, 44 per cent in 1950, 14 per cent in 1980 and 4 per cent in 1996. Automation spread to back office jobs (clerical, data processing) over the course of the last century, but most customer-contact operations resisted rationalization because of the variety and uncertainty introduced by the consumer. Research in operations management in the 1960s and

1970s attempted to solve that problem by limiting customer variation through standardized options (Levitt, 1972; Chase, 1978) – for example, in fast food or retail sales operations (Leidner, 1993). Telephone operator call centres provide a model of efficiency that managers in today's diverse call centres seek to emulate. The goal is to apply industrial engineering techniques to more complex service and sales interactions in order to increase volumes and reduce call handling time. The dramatic spread of call centres over the last decade or so has occurred because of advances in front-office automation. Automatic call distribution and routing systems, voice-recognition systems and other innovations made it possible to consolidate local service and sales centres into remote, centralized distribution channels serving much wider geographic areas. Large centres achieve scale economies through greater labour flexibility and by spreading call loads over larger numbers of workers.

The professional service model

At the opposite end of the spectrum from mass-produced services is the professional service model, with the goal of providing quality service. To do so, technology is used as a complement to labour, the formal education and specialized skills of employees are very high, the design of work builds on the independent discretion of professional employees who collaborate as needed with other specialists to provide service and who are rewarded with high relative pay, benefits and employment security. The professional model – exemplified by lawyers, healthcare professionals and others – is based on the idea of building long-term personal relationships of trust between professionals and their clients, what management theorists refer to as relationship management (Gutek, 1995). Clients are willing to pay a price premium for quality, customized services. Variations of this model now cover a much wider range of service occupations in, for example, high-tech specialities and business services. Recent interpretations of this model reject the idea of the individual professional working alone in favour of the idea that professional service depends on, and is embedded in, communities of practice – informal relationships between professionals that serve as a basis for learning, problem solving and sharing of contextually specific tacit knowledge (Brown and Duguid, 1991; Orr, 1996).

In the context of customer service and sales operations, the professional model would include the use of college-educated account executives, who are dedicated representatives serving particular business clients. They provide high-quality services through a combination of high general skills (formal education) coupled with firm specific skills (their deep tacit knowledge of the firm's products, work processes and customer characteristics). They provide a complete range of services and generally draw on other teams of experts in their company to meet customers' demands. Thus, firm-specific *social* capital is also valuable, which is defined by the personal relationships of trust among professionals in the firm and between professionals and their clients. The competitive performance advantage for firms that adopt the professional model is that their services are valuable, rare and hard to imitate (Barney, 1995). The longer a client stays with one provider, the more difficult it is to shift to another provider not only because of personal relations of trust, but because of the wide variety and complexity of services that are provided and the negotiating power and flexibility that come from long-term relations.

Mass customization models

Between the mass-production and professional service models are various hybrid models that may be generally classified as mass customization. The goal is to compete on quality and customization as well as price. To do so, firms would adopt some level of automation and process re-engineering found in mass-production models coupled with some level of attention to service quality and customer loyalty found in the professional model. This approach may be more economically viable than a classic mass-production model because consumers in today's mass markets demand quality, customization and innovation as well as reasonable prices (Pine, 1993). For this reason, many manufacturing firms have shifted from classic mass production to adopt some level of high-involvement work practices, and a reasonable number of empirical studies show that these practices lead to better performance in that setting (Ichniowski *et al.*, 1996; Becker and Gerhart, 1996; Appelbaum *et al.*, 2000). It is reasonable, then, to examine whether they produce better performance in call centres, which typically have been designed along a classic mass-production model. If companies compete on the basis of quality, customization and price, then call centre workers need the skills, discretion and incentives to handle relatively complex interactions with customers. A recent qualitative case study describes what a high-involvement strategy in a call centre might look like (Hutchinson, Purcell and Kinnie, 2000).

In this paper, we define high-involvement practices to include: a) technology used as a complement rather than substitute for labour; b) high relative skill requirements of jobs; c) work designed to provide opportunities for discretion and worker collaboration; and d) incentives such as high relative pay and employment security to reward effort. Our definition is consistent with much of the prior literature on high-involvement or high-performance work systems (MacDuffie, 1995; Huselid, 1995; Delery and Doty, 1996; Appelbaum *et al*., 2000). While there are several criticisms of this literature (see Wood, 1999; Wright *et al*., 1999), we use this framework in order to relate the discussion of call centre models to the literature on manufacturing, where the high-involvement model has been widely discussed.

However, we view the concept of high involvement along a continuum, from low levels in the classic mass-production model to high levels in the professional model. In other words, these management practices provide a vehicle to quasi-professionalize the employment of production-level service workers. We also view it as a relative concept: high relative to what? For example, in an industry where the norm is a classic mass-production model, then firms may realize improvements with only modest additional investments in training, technology and work redesign. In business services, by contrast, a professional or high-involvement model may be the price of entry, and variation in management practices may produce only small relative gains.

Alternative performance models: theory and evidence

The high-involvement and high-performance literatures are theoretically undeveloped, and researchers have questioned what is in 'the black box' linking management practices to performance outcomes. However, implicit in these paradigms are micro-level theories of organizational behaviour (for example, Lawler, 1986). One line of argument is that management practices influence employee attitudes and motivation, which in turns affects their performance. A second line of argument is cognitive: management practices influence employee skills and their ability to learn and solve problems on the job. In this section, we draw on research from organizational behaviour and human resource studies to discuss the empirical evidence for these arguments, focusing primarily on studies of service workplaces.

Management practices, affective reactions and performance

The idea that management can influence the performance of workers via an effect on their attitudes has a long history in organizational behaviour. The large literature on work design showed that enhanced job characteristics (for example, autonomy, variety, ability to complete a whole task; Hackman and Oldham, 1980) are significant predictors of worker satisfaction (Cotton, 1993). Reviews of the literature on self-managed teams provide similar conclusions (Cotton, 1993; Cohen and Bailey, 1997). However, these studies failed to find that happier workers are more productive (Locke and Schweiger, 1979). More recent studies have examined a fuller range of high-involvement practices and also report little evidence that better performance works through better employee affective outcomes. For example, Godard (2001) analyzed survey data from 500 Canadian workers and found that high-involvement practices were associated with greater intrinsic rewards (such as satisfaction and commitment), but also greater reported stress (Godard, 2001). Ramsay, Scholarios and Harley (2000) analyzed the 1998 UK Workplace Employee Relations Survey and found significant positive relationships between high-involvement work practices and several performance outcomes as reported by managers. However, they found only mixed support for the idea that employee perceptions mediate the relationship between management practices and performance. Neither of these studies differentiated between manufacturing and service organizations, however.

Nonetheless, several researchers in service management have pursued this line of thinking based on the idea that worker attitudes are likely to be more important in customer-contact jobs because workers' dissatisfaction can more readily spill over into customer interactions, leading to poor service. The most elaborate theory (the service profit chain) links human resource practices to employee satisfaction and loyalty, which in turn inspires customer satisfaction and loyalty, ultimately resulting in higher profits (Heskett, Sasser and Schlesinger, 1997). The HR practices discussed in this literature are similar to those found in the high-involvement literature. A more recent incarnation of this idea develops a set of performance metrics ('the balanced scorecard') that capture all of the links in the service profit chain (Kaplan and Norton, 1996).

Some empirical support for these arguments comes from Schlesinger and Zornitsky (1991), Tornow and Wiley (1991) and Wiley (1991), who found a positive correlation between employee job satisfaction and customer service ratings. Ulrich *et al.* (1991) found that at Sears, negative customer service ratings were correlated with higher levels of employee turnover and higher use of part-time staff; at Ryder Truck, negative customer ratings were significantly correlated with high employee turnover and high Workers' Compensation claims. Loveman (1998) is the first to test correlations along a series of links (internal service quality → employee satisfaction → employee loyalty → external service quality → customer satisfaction→ customer loyalty). Based on employee and customer data from 479 branches of a multi-site regional bank, he found significant correlations between many of the variables measuring relationships along the chain.

A similar line of argument is found in the 'service climate' literature, developed by Schneider and his colleagues. They have used worker surveys to capture whether management creates a positive 'service climate' – an overall environment or organizational culture that supports quality service. This approach differs from the high-involvement literature in that the latter attempts to measure specific management practices, such as training or the use of teams, rather than perceptions of the environment. Several researchers have used Schneider's framework and have found significant positive relationships between worker perceptions of service climate, worker attitudes and customer satisfaction (Schneider and Bowen, 1985; Schneider, Wheeler and Cox, 1992; Schneider, White and Paul, 1998; Schmit and Allscheid, 1995; Johnson, 1996). Sargent and Frenkel (2000) also found that support from supervisors, teams, technology and other departments led to higher worker satisfaction, commitment and self-reported service quality. However, the causal relationships are not entirely clear in this line of research, as some researchers have found that customer satisfaction leads to worker satisfaction (Ryan, Schmit and Johnson, 1996).

Another emerging line of research, set primarily in call centres, focuses on various measures of individual well-being, including stress, anxiety, depression, emotional exhaustion and burnout in call centres (Holman 2001; Holman, Chissick, and Totterdell 2001; Deery, Iverson and Walsh 2002; Singh, Goolsby and Rhoads 1994; Singh, Berbeke and Rhoads 1996; Singh 2000). Holman and colleagues found significant relationships between HR practices such as job design and electronic monitoring and worker well-being and satisfaction. Deery, Iverson and Walsh (2002) found that characteristics of call centre work, including customer interactions, scripts, routinization, workloads and managerial emphasis on quantity, were associated with emotional exhaustion, which in turn predicted absenteeism. Singh and colleagues have focused on the relationship between stress and burnout on the one hand, and performance on the other. Singh (2000), for example, found that worker burnout with customers is associated with lower self-reported service quality. He also found that task control, a construct similar to autonomy or discretion over work, was the most important source for reducing burnout. A particularly promising series of studies conducted at the University of Michigan has shown that electronic monitoring is significantly associated with worker disaffection and stress (Carayon, 1993).

There are several limitations to these studies. First, most do not incorporate measures of technology into their analyses of other management practices. Second, most examine a limited number of management practices, focusing instead on particular facets of work, such as work design or electronic monitoring. Third, they typically focus on individual workers rather than workers in the context of work groups and their social relationships. Fourth, they do not link worker outcomes to objective performance measures. Fifth, they do not deal with the critique of reverse causality. Sixth, they do not explore the conditionality of their findings. For simple transactions, for example, customers may prefer efficient, anonymous and impersonal exchanges, as Sutton and Rafaeli (1988) found. In their study of convenience stores, customers wanted speed; employee use of more positive affect or personal interaction was negatively related to store profitability. In sum, while there is promising research linking management practices to workers' attitudes and emotional state, there is much work to be done in explaining the relationship between affective or emotional outcomes and work performance.

The cognitive argument

Research on the cognitive argument linking management practices to performance has received less attention than the affective one. The cognitive argument has individual and group-level dimensions. The individual-level argument is similar to the logic of total quality management (TQM): individual workers closest to the point of production have the tacit knowledge to solve problems, so that providing workers with greater discretion should allow them to solve problems and continuously improve production. While there is some evidence that TQM methods are associated with better quality, there is little research regarding the actual mechanisms through which this occurs – for example, how individual learning or knowledge-sharing occurs in these settings.

A second line of reasoning is that organizing work into self-managed or semi-autonomous work groups leads to better performance because workers with interdependent tasks can solve problems collectively. This is a basic premise in the socio-technical systems and group-effectiveness research. While research in manufacturing settings has shown considerable support for this idea (Cohen and Bailey, 1997), empirical studies in service settings have provided mixed results. For example, Gladstein (1984) found a significant positive relationship between team processes and self-reported effectiveness, but not with objective sales, in a study of 100 sales teams in telecommunications. Yammarino and Dubinsky (1990) found that group autonomy was positively related to managerial ratings of sales workers in retail sales, but not insurance. A study of 100 matched pairs of self-managed and traditionally supervised work groups in telecommunications (Cohen and Ledford, 1994; Cohen, Ledford and Spreitzer, 1996) reported that team and manager evaluations (but not supervisor evaluations) of craft and administrative support teams were higher; but those for customer service and sales workers were not. Campion and his colleagues tested Hackman and Oldham's (1980) model of job characteristics, measured at the work-group level; they found it predicted significantly better objective performance among teams of clerical workers (Campion, Medsker and Higgs, 1993) and knowledge workers (Campion, Papper and Medsker, 1996) in a large financial services firm.

These studies, however, do not explore why teams are associated with better performance. In manufacturing settings, the benefits of teams are more obvious because workers on a production line have interdependent tasks; job rotation and cross-training provide labour flexibility (filling in for absences, and so on). In customer-contact settings such as call centres, by contrast, workers interact with customers to complete a transaction, not with other workers. The customer is assumed to get better service if one employee completes the transaction, as opposed to multiple hand-offs or consultation among employees. Computer technology also reinforces the independence of workers, each of whom has his or her own computer. In these settings, a cognitive explanation for better performance in teams is more plausible. For example, Batt (1999) studied self-directed teams in call centres and found that, compared to traditionally supervised groups, the teams had significantly higher self-reported quality and 9 per cent higher objective sales revenues. More importantly, the interactive effect of self-directed teams and new information technology increased sales by an additional 18 per cent. This result indicates that teams learned to use the new technology faster than traditionally organized groups, suggesting a cognitive explanation.

Interest in cognitive explanations of group effectiveness has grown recently, with researchers beginning to focus on information-processing and knowledge-sharing in groups as sources of performance gains (Hinsz, Tindale and Vollrath, 1997). Theories of group knowledge transfer and group memory consider the extent to which individual group members know the domains of expertise of other members and are able to access and/or utilize that information for the benefit of the group. Some researchers have conceptualized shared knowledge as a collective good, with each team member working from the same set of premises or team mental model (for example, Cannon-Bowers, Salas and Converse, 1993). Others have viewed shared knowledge as a complementary process, with each member contributing his or her unique expertise to the group (for example, Stasser, 1992). Three main theoretical approaches to group knowledge are team mental models theory (Cannon-Bowers, Salas and Converse, 1993; Klimoski and Mohammed, 1994; Mathieu *et al.*, 2000), group information-sharing theory (Stasser and Titus, 1985) and transactive memory (Wegner, 1987; Liang, Moreland and Argote, 1995). To date, however, this literature is at an early developmental stage. Most of it is conceptual or based on lab studies, and measures of central constructs such as group knowledge, knowledge-sharing, information exchange and learning are yet to be developed.

Recent studies of call centre performance

In this section, we draw on data from two recent studies of call centres to elaborate upon the meaning of high-involvement work systems in this context. In the first study we explore the affective explanation for the relationship between management practices and performance, by examining the relationship between high-involvement practices, quit rates and sales growth in a sample of 354 call centres. In the second study, we probe the cognitive explanation by moving to the work-group level of analysis. We use a survey of 419 workers in four call centres and match their responses to objective measures of call quality. We focus particularly on the relationship between team-based work, knowledge-sharing among workers and performance outcomes.

High-involvement practices, quit rates and sales growth

This study was based on a multi-year qualitative and quantitative research project on call centres in the US telecommunications industry. The quantitative data are based on a nationally representative survey of managers of 354 call centres. Prior analyses of these data revealed that production models varied significantly by the customer segment served (Batt, 2000). At the low end, telephone operator centres conformed to the classic mass-production model discussed above. Centres providing services to residential customers also followed a mass-production model, but with the rigidities of the production system somewhat relaxed. Centres serving large businesses, by contrast, were more likely to adopt a professional service model, while those dealing with small businesses adopted an intermediate model between mass production and professional service. In this paper, we analyze the data in a new way, by considering the range of variation in management practices within each segment and its relationship to performance outcomes.

Methods

The call centres in this study provide service and sales of telecommunications services to residential and business customers. The sample is a stratified random sample drawn from the Dun and Bradstreet listing of establishments. Establishments were stratified by size (10–99 employees, 100-plus employees), by industry segment (cellular, wireline, cable and Internet) and by state location. A 52-minute telephone survey, administered to the general manager at each call centre, covered questions related to basic industry characteristics, management strategies and work and HR practices. The response rate was 53 per cent. See Batt (2002) for a fuller description of methods and measures.

To measure-high involvement work practices, we used ten survey questions that captured skill levels, work design and HR incentives. The skill requirements of jobs were measured by two variables: a) years of formal education of the typical (median) core employee; and b) the months of formal and on-the-job training needed for a new employee to become proficient. For work design, we used two measures for individual discretion and two for employee collaboration in teams. The individual discretion scales use a one to five Likert response format, where one is little or no control and five is complete control. Discretion over work methods included eight questions adapted from MacDuffie (1995) (degree of influence over tasks, tools, work methods, pace of work, schedules, vacations and technology design, Cronbach's alpha = .79). Discretion over customer interactions was measured by two questions developed for this study: control over handling non-routine requests and control over the pace of serving customers (Cronbach's alpha = .60). Team participation includes the percentage of employees that participate in regular off-line problem-solving groups and the percentage that participate in self-directed teams.

Human resource incentives are of four types: ongoing training, employment security, pay level and electronic performance monitoring. Ongoing training indicates a firm's commitment to employee development employee receives each year. Pay is the natural log of the median annual base pay of the core workforce. Employment security is the percentage of the core workforce that is permanent and full-time, as opposed to part-time or contingent. Employers use part-time and contingent workers to cut costs (Houseman, 2001), and under these circumstances, full-time workers worry that their jobs will be turned into part-time or contingent ones, with lower pay and benefits. Electronic monitoring is measured by the percentage of work time that is typically electronically monitored

38 *The Viability of Alternative Call Centre Production Models*

(reverse coded). To create an additive index of high-involvement practices, we transformed all ten variables to z scores (mean zero, standard deviation one) and took their mean value. To make the index more transparent, we translated it into a 0–100 scale.

Performance outcomes included the average annual quit rate and the percentage change in sales in the prior two-year period. The measure of quits excludes discharges, retirements, transfers and promotions. The measure of sales growth is the natural log of the percentage change in the *value* of sales to the particular customer base served by the centre.

Results

For an initial analysis of the data, we divided call centres into those that fell below the mean of the high-involvement index for each customer segment and those that fell above the mean (see Table 2.1). On average the telephone operator centres scored 27.5 (the sample was too small to meaningfully divide it). For residential centres, the bottom half of the distribution scored an average of 32.6 points, while the top half scored 53.1 points. For small business centres, the scores were 36.5 points and 58.5 points respectively; and for large businesses, 48.8 and 72.3 points. In sum, taking a simple split-half comparison, we found large and significant differences in management practices within each market segment.

These differences in management practices translated into large and significant differences in quit rates and sales growth. Within the residential mass market, centres that adopted a lower-involvement strategy had over twice the employee quit rates as their counterparts that adopted a higher-involvement strategy (21 per cent versus 9 per cent). A similar pattern exists for the small and large business centres, although the size effects are not as large. Similarly, with respect to sales growth, those centres adopting a higher-involvement approach to serving residential customers had more than twice the rate of sales growth compared to their counterparts adopting a lower-involvement model (36.8 per cent versus 16 per cent). Again the effects are similar but not as large for the small and large business segments.

In further analyses, we analyzed the data using multivariate models, with controls for product market characteristics organizational characteristics and customer segment. We found that the high-involvement index significantly predicted quit rates and sales growth, and that the quit rates partially explained the relationship between management practices and sales growth (see Batt, 2002). That is, quit rates are not only detrimental because of the added costs of employee recruitment and training, but new workers have a learning curve that makes them

Table 2.1 Mean characteristics of call centres by customer segment and HR practices

	Operators	Residential		Small business		Large business	
		Lower*	Higher**	Lower	Higher	Lower	Higher
High-involvement index score (0–100)	27.53	32.66	53.12	36.51	58.49	48.76	72.29
Outcomes							
Annual quit rate	20.31	20.98	9.20	16.36	12.45	18.66	11.79
% change in sales	10.80	16.05	36.78	25.79	58.18	34.76	39.76
Average call handling time	0.52	5.47	6.43	4.88	9.59	10.55	12.17
Average customers/employee/day	460	127	72	88	39	19	42
Specific management practices							
Skill requirements of jobs							
Years of education	12.21	12.52	13.52	13.07	14.51	14.39	15.91
Weeks to become proficient	11.15	13.71	20.32	12.33	32.34	19.57	35.18
Days of ongoing training/year	0.67	1.41	2.67	1.39	2.43	2.15	2.52
Technology use							
# software programs typically used	1.13	3.06	4.22	3.09	4.87	4.97	8.17
% of day electronically monitored	75.00	59.64	38.63	44.19	23.50	35.32	7.66
Work design							
% of workforce in problem-solving teams	48.87	27.96	61.61	36.20	60.98	45.72	68.86
% of workforce in self-directed teams	6.67	2.16	28.43	5.28	19.13	13.79	38.43

Table 2.1 (*Continued*)

	Operators	Residential		Small business		Large business	
		Lower*	Higher**	Lower	Higher	Lower	Higher
HR incentives, rewards							
Employment security							
% workforce permanent and full-time	79.66	80.02	91.81	81.15	95.43	91.77	99.06
Compensation							
Annual base pay of median worker	16,353	20,440	25,291	22,908	23,400	26,988	48,069
Annual total pay of median worker	19,061	24,372	33,465	27,953	44,429	48,375	76,258
% of pay that is variable	11.67	10.61	16.84	14.74	41.26	34.68	34.83
Organizational characteristics							
% of establishments that are union	0.33	0.22	0.22	0.13	0.12	0.06	0.03
% workforce that is male	15.29	23.50	31.57	32.60	48.44	52.00	56.26
Sample size	15	52	54	45	41	32	35

Notes: *Lower refers to centres scoring less than the mean of the high-involvement index for the customer segment; **Higher refers to centres scoring more than the mean of the high-involvement index for the customer segment.

initially less productive – a period of time that managers estimate is about six months in residential service centres. We also found that the performance benefits were greater in magnitude for centres serving the residential market and to a lesser extent, those serving small business. We interpret this to mean that high-involvement practices are rare in more cost-conscious markets, but they confer value because employees are better able to meet the demand for customization and service bundling.

To translate the high-involvement index into more practical terms, we compared the centres in each segment above and below the mean of the high-involvement index along a range of specific management practices (Table 2.1). For example, the years of education of the typical call centre employee is an instructive indicator. For operators, it is 12 years (a high school diploma). For lower-involvement residential centres, it is 12.5 years, while for higher-involvement centres, it is 13.5 years. The formal educational qualifications of employees continue to rise in the small and large business centres, with lower-involvement centres in large business hiring workers with two years of college and higher-involvement centres hiring those with a four-year college degree.

Most of the indicators of management practices follow a similar pattern, with significant variation not only across different customer segments, but within them as well. However, some show only modest variation, as in ongoing training, which is low across the board.

For purposes of considering the viability of mass customization strategies in call centres, we want to focus this discussion on the residential call centre data (see Table 2.1). It is here that there is the greatest tendency is to adopt a mass-production model. These data suggest that a high-involvement approach would include hiring employees who have at least a year or so of formal education over a diploma (secondary or high school) degree. The job is defined as relatively complex, requiring initial training of five weeks on average coupled with on-the-job learning of about five months before employees are fully proficient. While electronic monitoring is used, it is not pervasive during the entire day (in this case, less than 40 per cent of work time is electronically monitored). This is due in part to the fact that workers do not spend 100 per cent of their day on-line (in this case they spend 70 per cent of their time on-line). Consistent with this picture, workers handle fewer customers per day – 72 as opposed to 127 in the lower-involvement centres – although the average call is only modestly longer (6.4 versus 5.4 minutes). Workers appear to be working smarter rather than longer, with work diversified through off-line tasks, including participation in problem-solving teams (on average, over 60 per cent of the workforce regularly participate in

42 *The Viability of Alternative Call Centre Production Models*

off-line teams in the higher-involvement centres). Also, on average almost 30 per cent of the workforce is organized into self-directed work groups. Moreover, the higher-involvement centres provide considerably greater opportunities for internal promotion and employment security. There also are remarkable differences in the use of layoffs, with the lower-involvement centres resorting to ongoing layoffs and hiring 20 per cent of the workforce into part-time or temporary positions. The higher-involvement centres, by contrast, made almost no use of layoffs and used part-time and contingent employment for less than 10 per cent of the workforce. Finally, base pay in the higher involvement centres is 24 per cent higher, and total pay is 37 per cent higher than in the lower involvement centres (notably, however, these differences are not as high as the differences in sales growth of 130 per cent between the lower- and higher-involvement centres).

It is also worth noting what this model is not. It is not a fully professional model. The higher-involvement residential call centres are still call centres that provide technology-mediated service, rely on electronic monitoring and allow modest opportunities for employees to use their independent discretion to serve customers. They use a limited number of contingent workers to provide labour market flexibility and have 16 per cent of pay that is variable or performance-based. They resemble the approach to management typically found in centres serving small and medium-sized business customers.

In sum, this nationally representative data on US call centres in telecommunications indicates that high-involvement work practices are associated with significantly lower quit rates and higher sales growth. Our analysis also provides a concrete idea of what types of management practices have been adopted to accomplish these results. It suggests that call centres serving the mass market may well do better economically if they adopt the kinds of management practices currently found in centres serving small business. It also suggests that small business centres should resist the temptation of shifting to a more production-line approach to service.

Team-based work systems, knowledge-sharing and performance

In our second study, we sought to understand more fully how the organization of work and incentives influence workers' ability to serve customers. As indicated in our review of the literature, most researchers assume that group-based work organization is only appropriate when work tasks are highly interdependent, a condition not met in customer service centres. However, the benefits of knowledge-sharing and learning found in prior research on teams in call centres (Batt, 1999) led us to examine this question empirically.

Methods

This study involved qualitative fieldwork and survey and archival data collection in four call centres in one company. Workers in these call centres serve employees in companies by answering service and billing questions regarding payroll, medical, pension and life insurance benefits. The company in this case administered the HR benefit plans for 100 companies. Workers were organized in teams, with each team dedicated to one (sometimes two or three) companies. We randomly sampled 50 per cent of the workers in each work group having more than two members and less than 25. Our final sample includes 333 workers in 78 teams. The response rate for the mail survey was 53 per cent. The respondent pool is 72 per cent female and 41 per cent married. The age of the participants ranged from 20 to 63 years, with a mean age of 30.2 years. We matched workers' survey responses to objective archival data on call quality.

In general, this non-union company adopted an approach to call centre management that, compared to a mass-production model, falls within the concept of a high-involvement model – with some features resembling those in the small and large business centres described in the telecommunications study. The formal education of workers is quite high (almost 60 per cent of the sample has a four-year college degree). Workers use an average of seven software programs, and typically spend 65 per cent of their day on the phone handling incoming calls and 35 per cent doing off-line follow-up. Work is organized into teams serving particular clients, and almost all employees are full-time permanent staff. However, average interaction time with customers is only 4.5 minutes and average annual salary in 2000 was relatively low, at $26,335.

Our survey questions captured three dimensions of the work system: the use of technology and skill level of jobs, work design and supportive HR practices.We measured the skill level of jobs by the number of software programs used and the frequency of program updates. Work design was measured by the extent of task interdependence, resource interdependence (shared information in computer data bases) and task variety. HR incentives included the extent to which work groups had shared goals and outcomes, shared training and group-based recognition and rewards. Knowledge-sharing was conceptualized along two dimensions: how much workers knew about each other's expertise and how much they actually used other workers' knowledge to solve work-related problems.

44 The Viability of Alternative Call Centre Production Models

Performance outcomes included the group's average call handling time, average call quality as determined by a company audit, perceived process loss (whether workers perceived knowledge-sharing as resulting in productivity losses), the extent to which workers relied on peer learning and the innovative problem-solving reported by group members (for a full description of methods and measures, see Moynihan and Batt, 2001).

Results

For our analysis, we examined variation in the implementation of work practices at the group level to assess what predicts better performance outcomes. Table 2.2 provides the results of bi-variate correlations between work practices and knowledge-sharing on the one hand, and knowledge-sharing and performance outcomes on the other. In general, we found that all three dimensions of the work system were significantly related to knowledge-sharing, with group-based work design and shared

Table 2.2 Bi-variate correlations of management practices, knowledge-sharing and performance

Dimensions of work system	Knowledge	Usage
Knowledge-sharing		
Knowledge of others' expertise	1.00	
Usage of others' expertise	.56**	1.00
Technology use and skill requirements		
Number of software programs	.20*	.10
Number of program updates	.27**	.22*
Work design		
Task interdependence	.52**	.30**
Resource interdependence	.33**	.27**
Task variety	.33**	.27**
Supportive HR practices		
Shared goals and outcomes	.08	.22*
Shared training	−.16	−.02
Group recognition	.32**	.42**
Worker actions and performance		
Call handling time	−.12	−.12
Objective call quality audit	.23*	.16
Perceived process loss	−.48**	−.29**
Perceived peer learning	.36**	.36**
Innovation and problem-solving	.24*	.59**
Self-reported job satisfaction	.37**	.20*

Notes: *Statistical relationship significant at p. < .05; **p. < .01.

outcomes and recognition providing the strongest correlations to knowledge-sharing. Knowledge-sharing, in turn, was significantly positively related to objective call quality and perceptions of innovative problem solving and peer learning. It was negatively related to process loss and not significantly related to call handling time, suggesting that the time that workers take to share their knowledge does not significantly interfere with their productivity.

In analyses using structural equation modelling, we found that these relationships held, with a single index of knowledge-sharing mediating the relationship between skill level, work design, and group-based incentives on the one hand, and the outcome variables on the other. Job satisfaction was also an outcome of knowledge-sharing. It did not explain the relationship between work practices and most outcomes, but did predict lower call handling time (Moynihan and Batt, 2001).

These findings suggest that team-based work systems in call centres have a somewhat different meaning than in manufacturing settings, where much of their value lies in job rotation, broadened job responsibilities, multi-tasking and labour flexibility. In call centres, being in a team does not alter the nature of the work itself, which consists of interacting individually with customers to respond to their enquiries. Almost all jobs are identical so, with the exception of team leader positions, there are few jobs to rotate. Moreover, collaborative structures are not 'technically required' by the technology, as in jointly producing a good along a machine-paced process. Rather, in call centres, collaborative structures must be self-consciously created by workers and supervisors. Those who are more successful in creating these collaborative structures are able to provide better service.

Thus, we found that the primary value of team-based work design is to provide an opportunity structure for employees to improve their skills and abilities. The primary value of group-based incentives (such as group-based goals, performance appraisal, recognition and rewards) is to motivate workers to continually learn from each other by sharing information, specific areas of expertise and innovative solutions to problems. The idea of emphasizing team-based work in call centres may appear counter-intuitive because the primary work task is individual employees interaction with customers. However, in order to serve customers well, employees need to be continually absorbing new information about customer services or new technologies and learning how to solve new customer enquiries. The information and knowledge needed to do the job effectively is constantly shifting. In this type of environment, workers with different areas of expertise are in the best position to assist each other. Supervisors are likely to be too removed from daily customer interactions to maintain high levels of expertise in the wide range of topic areas that are required.

Discussion and directions for future research

In this chapter we outlined three alternative production models and discussed their applicability to call centre management. We contrasted the classic mass-production model with the professional-service model and presented a hybrid mass customization model that incorporates the efficiency gains of mechanization and the attention to quality service found in the professional model. We then presented a conceptual framework that identifies potential links between management practices, workers' affective and cognitive reactions and performance outcomes. We used this framework to review literature on service workplaces in organizational behaviour and HR studies and to identify what empirical evidence we have regarding the causal links between management practices and performance outcomes. We then summarized two recent studies of call centres, one that examines the relationship between management practices, affective reactions (quit rates) and sales growth and one that assesses the relationship between management practices, cognitive reactions (knowledge-sharing) and performance. These studies provide two examples of recent quantitative research on call centre performance.

There are several limitations of existing research on call centre performance and studies of service workplaces more generally. Some of these criticisms also apply to the high-involvement literature more generally. A first critique concerns the performance measures that have been used. Most studies capture one or two context-specific outcome measures – such as productivity or quality – that do not adequately capture the economics of the production system. In our study of call centres in telecommunications described above, for example, we were not able to calculate the net effect of high-involvement practices on labour costs. Thus, while high-involvement practices were associated with lower quit rates and higher revenues, we were unable to assess the effect on net revenues, or profits, although we were able to examine wages. This is an important issue, because, in contrast to manufacturing where labour costs are now typically less than 25 per cent of total costs, in service operations they typically comprise the majority of costs. As Cappelli and Neumark (2001) point out, high-involvement work practices are costly due to high investments in training and high relative pay. Therefore, whether there is a net performance gain from high-involvement practices is an empirical question that is likely to vary with the relative labour intensity of an activity. The labour-intensive nature of services coupled with tight profit margins may limit the utility of high-involvement practices in mass markets.

A related issue is that our empirical studies do not examine the tradeoffs among different types of outcomes. In our study, we were able to measure sales growth, but not customer service ratings. Of particular importance in call centres is whether quality service and sales may be jointly maximized. In manufacturing contexts, researchers have demonstrated that improving quality and efficiency can be mutually reinforcing by eliminating defects and waste (MacDuffie, 1995; Appelbaum *et al.*, 2000). In customer services, however, the relationship between speed and efficiency and service quality are more ambiguous. In simple transactions, customers appear to want quick responses; but for many enquiries, quality of service is related to how long the service rep is willing to take to explain product features and answer enquiries. In the first case, quality and efficiency are complementary, while in the second, they appear not to be.

This observation leads to a second critique. In order to examine the relationship between quality and efficiency, we need to better understand the use of technology and operations management in call centres. Operations management research has focused on developing algorithms for efficient staffing patterns based on past patterns of call load volumes. The entire calculus focuses on increasing volume and minimizing labour costs. Human resource and industrial relations scholars, by contrast, have focused on understanding the organization of work and HR practices with little attention to understanding the logic of operations management, or the technology that underpins call centre operations. We have not, for example, developed effective measures of how technology use varies, especially in call centres and other service workplaces, and what implications that has for production outcomes. If we are to engage in debates over the relative merits of alternative production models, we must do a better job of understanding the assumptions and research findings in operations management.

Third, analysis of the causal relationships linking management practices to performance needs to move forward. The research on worker satisfaction has traditionally failed to show a link to performance, but studies linking workers' perceptions to actual customer satisfaction surveys is promising. As indicated above, however, this research should consider a much fuller range of performance outcomes. The research on emotional exhaustion and stress is particularly promising, but few studies have

48   *The Viability of Alternative Call Centre Production Models*

made the link to performance outcomes. The research on cognitive models is in its infancy, but is an important line of enquiry for the future. Given the firm-specific, tacit nature of knowledge and the ongoing change in information in customer service operations, knowledge-sharing and collaboration are likely to be important sources of performance gains that have been overlooked in the past.

In addition, we need to a more complete assessment of the implications of individual versus collaborative forms of work organization. Collaborative forms of work organization have the potential both to improve learning and problem solving and to reduce emotional exhaustion and stress. Yet, these effects on workers and their relationship to performance have not been tested in the current literature. Moreover, whether work is organized on an individual basis (typically coupled with commission pay) or a group model (perhaps accompanied by some form of group gainsharing) has other ramifications for workers and their unions. The individual sales model not only pits workers against each other and undermines co-operation and income security for many workers, it erodes the social fabric of the workplace and makes it harder to build solidarity and unionize or represent workers. For example, since the introduction of individual commission plans at US West in the mid-1990s, turnover has risen to 60 per cent annually and the Communication Workers of America (CWA) that represents workers has found it much more difficult to attract workers to assume union steward positions.

Fourth, we need to integrate a better understanding of marketing and consumer behaviour into our research on call centres. There are many market transactions in which customers want simplicity and speed, comparable to directory assistance operators or mass telemarketing. For these transactions, mass-production models are likely to be sufficient, and firms will continue to pursue automated solutions, as exemplified in the evolution of telephone operator jobs. The question is whether the production-line approach will continue to dominate a wider range of more complex service interactions, and how consumers will respond. Currently, consumer satisfaction with call centre service is notoriously low, at 54 per cent according to a recent US survey (Purdue University, 1999). Consumers are particularly dissatisfied with the *process* of service delivery – the length of time and alienation associated with automated voice-recognition systems, the frustration with finding their way through a maze of venues that often fail to connect the customer with the appropriate provider, the fragmented delivery of services requiring separate contacts for different types of service offerings and the confusion and complexity associated with ongoing changes in product and service features. However, there appearsg to be little open consumer action against companies. On the one hand, marketing researchers assume that customers can be trained to accept new service routines. They define customer satisfaction as the gap between expectations and actual service, so that if customer expectations can be manipulated, customer dissatisfaction can decline even if the actual service remains unchanged. Thus, arguably the recent rise in customer dissatisfaction is a temporary phenomenon that will disappear over time as consumers adjust to new standards of self-service. Historic examples of customer adaptation include self-service telephone dialling (as described above), petrol purchases, ATM machines and the like. On the other hand, if products and services continue to increase in complexity and consumers increasingly demand customization, then automated and self-service delivery models are unlikely to be effective. Under these circumstances, the business case for mass customization and high-involvement strategies may be more viable. In sum, our research on call centre performance models must address these issues, incorporating an understanding of marketing, consumer behaviour, technology and operations management into our models of human resources and industrial relations.

References

Appelbaum, E., T. Bailey, P. Berg and A. L. Kalleberg (2000) *Manufacturing Advantage*, Ithaca: Cornell University Press.

Barney, J. (1995) 'Looking inside for competitive advantage', *Academy of Management Executive*, 9(4), pp. 49–61.

Batt, R. (1999) 'Work organization, technology and performance in customer service and sales', *Industrial and Labour Relations Review*, 52(4), pp. 539–64.

Batt, R. (2000) 'Strategic segmentation and front-line services: matching customers, employees and human resource systems', *International Journal of Human Resource Management*, 11(3), pp. 540–61.

Batt, R. (2002) 'Managing Customer Services: Human resource practices, quit rates and sales growth', *Academy of Management Journal*, 45(3), pp. 587–97.

Becker, B. and B. Gerhart (1996) 'Special research forum: Human resource management and organizational performance', *Academy of Management Journal*, 39, pp. 779–801.

Brown, J. S. and P. Duguid (1991) 'Organizational learning and communities-of-practice: Toward a unified view of working, learning, and innovation', *Organization Science*, 2(1), pp. 40–57.

Campion, M. A., G. J. Medsker and C. A. Higgs (1993) 'Relations between work group characteristics and effectiveness: Implications for designing effective work groups', *Personnel Psychology*, 46, pp. 823–50.

50 The Viability of Alternative Call Centre Production Models

Campion, M. A., E. M. Papper and G. J. Medsker (1996) 'Relations between work team characteristics and effectiveness: A replication and extension', *Personnel Psychology*, 49(2), pp. 429–59.

Cannon-Bowers, J. A., E. Salas and S. A. Converse (1993) 'Shared mental models in expert decision making teams', in N. J. Castellan Jr (ed.), *Current Issues in Individual and Group Decision Making*, Hillsdale: Lawrence Erlbaum.

Cappelli, Peter and David Neumark (2001) 'Do "High-Performance" Work Practices Improve Establishment-Level Outcomes?', *Industrial and Labour Relations Review*, 54(4), pp. 737–75.

Carayon, P. (1993) 'Effect of electronic performance monitoring on job design and worker stress: Review of the literature and conceptual model', *Human Factors*, 35, pp. 385–95.

Chase, R. B. (1978) 'Where Does the Customer Fit in a Service Operation?', *Harvard Business Review*, 56(6), pp. 137–42.

Cohen, S. G. and D. Bailey (1997) 'What makes teams work: group effectiveness research from the shop floor to the executive suite', *Journal of Management*, 23, pp. 239–90.

Cohen, S. and G. Ledford (1994) 'The effectiveness of self-managing teams: A quasi-experiment', *Human Relations*, 47(1), pp. 13–43.

Cohen, S. G., G. E. Ledford and G. Spreitzer (1996) 'A predictive model of self-managing work team effectiveness', *Human Relations*, 49, pp. 643–76.

Cotton, J. L. (1993) *Employee Involvement: Methods for Improving Performance and Work Attitudes*, Newbury Park: Sage.

Datamonitor (1998) *Call Centres in Europe 1996–2001: Vertical market opportunities*, London: Datamonitor.

Datamonitor (1999) *Opportunities in US and Canadian Call Centre Markets*, New York: Datamonitor.

Deery, S., R. Iverson and J. Walsh (2002) 'Work relationships in telephone call centres: Understanding emotional exhaustion and employee withdrawal', *Journal of Management Studies*, 39(4), pp. 471–96.

Delery, J. and D. Doty (1996) 'Modes of theorizing in strategic human resource management: tests for universalistic, contingency and configurational performance predictions', *Academy of Management Journal*, 39(4), pp. 802–35.

Gladstein, D. L. (1984) 'Groups in context: A model of task group effectiveness', *Administrative Science Quarterly*, 29, pp. 499–517.

Godard, J. (2001) 'High performance and the transformation of work? The implications of alternative work practices for the experience and outcomes of work', *Industrial and Labour Relations Review*, 54(4), pp. 776–805.

Gutek, B. (1995) *The Dynamics of Service: Reflections on the Changing Nature of Customer/Provider Interactions*, San Francisco: Jossey-Bass.

Hackman, R. J. and G. R. Oldham (1980) *Work Redesign*, Reading, MA: Addison-Wesley.

Heskett, J., W. E. Sasser Jr and L. Schlesinger (1997) *The Service Profit Chain: How Leading Companies Link Profit and Growth to Loyalty, Satisfaction, and Value*, New York: Free Press.

Hinsz, V. R., S. Tindale and D. Vollrath (1997) 'The emerging conceptualization of groups as information processors', *Psychological Bulletin*, 121(1), pp. 43–64.

Holman, D. (2001) 'Employee Stress in Call Centres', Call Centres and Beyond: the Human Resource Management Implications, 6 November, Kings College London.

Holman, D., C. Chissick and P. Totterdell (2002), 'The effects of performance monitoring on emotional labour and well-being in call centres', *Motivation and Emotion*, 26(1), pp. 57–81.

Houseman, S. (2001) 'Why employers use flexible staffing arrangements: Evidence from an establishment survey', *Industrial and Labour Relations Review*, 55(1), pp. 149–70.

Huselid, M. (1995) 'The impact of human resource management practices on turnover, productivity and corporate financial performance', *Academy of Management Journal*, 38(3), pp. 635–72.

Hutchinson, S., J. Purcell and N. Kinnie (2000) 'Evolving high commitment management and the experience of the RAC call centre', *Human Resource Management Journal*, 10(1), pp. 63–78.

Ichniowski, C., T. Kochan D. Levine, C. Olson and G. Strauss (1996) 'What works at work: Overview and assessment', *Industrial Relations*, 35(3), pp. 299–334.

Johnson, J. (1996) 'Linking employee perceptions of service climate to customer satisfaction', *Personnel Psychology*, 49, pp. 833–51.

Kaplan, R. and D. Norton (1996) *The Balanced Scorecard: Translating Strategy into Action*, Boston: Harvard Business School Press.

Klimoski, R. and S. Mohammed (1994) 'Team mental model: Construct or metaphor?', *Journal of Management*, 20, pp. 403–37.

Kohl, G. (1993) 'Information technology and labour: A case study of telephone operators', *Workplace Topics*, 3(1), pp. 101–11.

Lawler, E. E. III (1986) *High-involvement Management: Participative Strategies for Improving Organizational Performance*, San Francisco: Jossey-Bass.

Leidner, R. (1993) *Fast Food, Fast Talk: Service Work and the Routinization of Everyday Life*, Berkeley: University of California Press.

Levitt, T. (1972) 'Production line approach to services', *Harvard Business Review*, 50(5), pp. 41–50.

Liang, D. W., R. Moreland and L. Argote (1995) 'Group versus individual training and group performance: the mediating factor of transactive memory', *Personality and Social Psychology Bulletin*, 21, pp. 384–93.

Locke, E. and D. M. Schweiger (1979) 'Participation in decision-making: One more look', *Research in Organizational Behavior*, 1, pp. 265–339.

Loveman, G. W. (1998) 'Employee satisfaction, customer loyalty, and financial performance: An empirical examination of the service profit chain in retail banking', *Journal of Service Research*, 1(1), pp. 18–31.

MacDuffie, J. P. (1995) 'Human resource bundles and manufacturing performance: Organizational logic and flexible production systems in the world auto industry', *Industrial and Labour Relations Review*, 48(2), pp. 197–221.

Mathieu, J. E., T. S. Heffner, G. F. Goodwin, E. Salas and J. A. Cannon-Bowers (2000) 'The influence of shared mental models on team processes and performance', *Journal of Applied Psychology*, 85, pp. 273–83.

Moynihan, L. and R. Batt (2001) 'Antecedents and consequences of Transactive Memory in Service Teams: Theory and Scale Development', Paper presented at the 2000 Academy of Management Meetings, Toronto, Ontario, August 6–9.

Orr, J. (1996) *Talking About Machines: An Ethnography of a Modern Job*, Ithaca: Cornell University ILR Press.

Pearce, J. A. and E. C. Ravlin (1987) 'The design and activation of self-regulating work groups', *Human Relations*, 40, pp. 751–82.

52 The Viability of Alternative Call Centre Production Models

Pine, B. J. (1993) *Mass Customization*, Cambridge: Harvard Business School Press.

Purdue University (1999) 'Call Centre Benchmarking Report'.

Ramsay, H., D. Scholarios and B. Harley (2000) 'Employees and high-performance work systems: Testing inside the black box', *British Journal of Industrial Relations*, 38(4), pp. 501–31.

Ryan, A. M., M. Schmit and R. Johnson (1996) 'Attitudes and effectiveness: Examining relations at an organizational level', *Personnel Psychology*, 49, pp. 853–81.

Sargent, A. and S. Frenkel (2000) 'When do customer contact employees satisfy customers?', *Journal of Service Research*, 3(1), pp. 18–34.

Schacht, J. (1985) *The Making of Telephone Unionism 1920–1947*, New Jersey: Rutgers University Press.

Schlesinger, L. and J. Zornitsky (1991) 'Job satisfaction, service capability, and customer satisfaction: An examination of linkages and management implications', *Human Resources Planning*, 14(2), pp. 141–9.

Schmit, M. and S. Allscheid (1995) 'Employee attitudes and customer satisfaction: Making theoretical and empirical connections', *Personnel Psychology*, 48, pp. 527–47.

Schneider, B. and D. E. Bowen (1985) 'Employee and customer perceptions of service in banks: Replication and extension', *Journal of Applied Psychology*, 70, pp. 423–33.

Schneider, B., J. Wheeler and J. Cox (1992) 'A passion for service: Using content analysis to explicate service climate themes', *Journal of Applied Psychology*, 77, pp. 705–16.

Schneider, B., S. White and M. Paul (1998) 'Linking service climate and customer perceptions of service quality: Test of a causal model', *Journal of Applied Psychology*, 83(2), pp. 150–63.

Singh, J. (2000) 'Performance, productivity, and quality of frontline employees in service organizations', *Journal of Marketing*, 64, April, pp. 15–34.

Singh, J., W. Berbeke and G. Rhoads (1996) 'Do organizational practices matter in role stress processes? A study of direct and moderating effects for marketing-oriented boundary spanners', *Journal of Marketing*, 60, July, pp. 69–86.

Singh, J., J. Goolsby and G. Rhoads (1994) 'Behavioral and psychological consequences of boundary spanning: Burnout for customer service representatives', *Journal of Marketing Research*, 31, November, pp. 558–69.

Stasser, G. (1992) 'Information salience and the discovery of hidden profiles by decision-making groups: A "thought experiment"', *Organizational Behavior and Human Decision Processes*, 52, pp. 156–81.

Stasser, G. and W. Titus (1985) 'Pooling of unshared information in group decision making: Biased information sampling during discussion', *Journal of Personality and Social Psychology*, 48, pp. 1467–78.

Sutton, R. I. and A. Rafaeli (1988) 'Untangling the relationship between displayed emotions and organizational sales: The case of convenience stores', *Academy of Management Journal*, 31(3), pp. 461–87.

Taylor, P. and P. Bain (2001) 'Trade unions, workers' rights, and the frontier of control in UK call centres', *Economic and Industrial Democracy*, 22, pp. 39–66.

Tornow, W. W. and J. W. Wiley (1991) 'Service quality and management practices: A look at employee attitudes, customer satisfaction, and bottom-line consequences', *Human Resource Planning*, 14(3), pp. 105–15.

Ulrich, D., R. Halbrook, D. Meder, M. Stuchlik and S. Thorpe (1991) 'Employee and customer attachment: Synergies for competitive advantage', *Human Resources Planning*, 14(3), pp. 89–103.

Wegner, D. M. (1987) 'Transactive memory: A contemporary analysis of the group mind', in B. Mullen and G. R. Goethals (eds), *Theories of group behavior*, New York: Springer-Verlag.

Wiley, J. W. (1991) 'Customer satisfaction: A supportive work environment and its financial costs', *Human Resources Planning*, 14(3), pp. 117–27.

Wood, S. (1999) 'Human Resource Management and Performance', *International Journal of Management Reviews*, 1(4), pp. 367–413.

Wright, P., L. Dyer, J. Boudreau and G. Milkovich (eds) (1999) *Research in Personnel and Human Resource Management: Strategic HRM in the 21st Century*, Supplement 4, Greenwich, CT: JAI Press.

Yammarino, F. J. and A. J. Dubinsky (1990) 'Salesperson performance and managerially controllable factors: An investigation of individual and work group effects', *Journal of Management*, 16, pp. 87–106.

3
Call Centre HRM and Performance Outcomes: Does Workplace Governance Matter?

Sue Fernie

Introduction

Links between different forms of workplace governance and economic and industrial relations performance outcomes have become an important focus of research in recent years. Most of this work has involved statistical analysis using nationally representative survey data (see, for example Fernie and Metcalf, 1995; Lasaosa, Wood and de Menezes, 2001). This chapter, by contrast, uses case studies and examines the effects of human resource management practices in three different workplaces (call centres) owned by the same firm.

Many of the newer service jobs involve voice-to-voice interactions with customers. During these interactions, employees are expected to display those values of the organization that create a desired 'state of mind' in the customer (Hochschild, 1979). The quality of the emotional labour performed by staff has an important effect on the quality of customer service delivered by the provider. Indeed, the quality of the service is usually the mechanism by which the service is differentiated – old notions of competing on cost alone are relegated to the lower end of the mass market. Call centre management, therefore, spend a great deal of effort managing employees' presentation of self. The most well-publicised aspect of this relates to the close monitoring of employee behaviour, the tight scripting of conversations and the enforced conformity to certain behaviours (Fernie and Metcalf, 1999). Of increasing significance in today's employment relationship is the role of the customer as a monitor and sometimes co-manager of the labour process (Leidner, 1996). People management practices help shape employees' attitudes, motivation and satisfaction at work. This in turn influences the customer satisfaction/workforce satisfaction mirror, which is seen by some authors as critical to the delivery of front-line service work. Schneider and Bowen (1993) remind us that 'what employees experience at work gets transmitted to the customer' and suggest that the key to managing customers' experiences of service quality is to manage employees' own experiences at work. Schneider and Bowen's (1985) study in the banking sector showed a positive association between employees' perceptions of HR practices and customers' perceptions of service quality. They also claimed that there was a correlation between those perceptions and a 'climate for employee well being'. Likewise, Guest and Conway (1999), using a 1997 Institute of Personnel and Development survey, find that a higher number of HR practices is associated with higher ratings of trust, fairness and management delivery of promises, job satisfaction and job security.

Previous studies of the effects of HRM on performance in both the UK and US demonstrate a link between certain HRM practices and positive organizational outcomes. But there is a need to shed light on why HRM has this positive link (Guest, 1997). It could be argued that, with interactive service work, nothing could be more important than those management methods which attempt to elicit 'correct' behaviours in order to cement the service delivery. It is therefore imperative to study the antecedents of employee well-being in call centres, and a start has been made to this (Deery, Iverson and Walsh 2002; Holman 2002 and this volume). What the present case study seeks to add to the debate is the comparison between call centres which are differentiated not only in terms of their product market but also in terms of their 'governance' arrangements.

Types of workplace 'governance'

Mahoney and Watson (1993) identify three forms of workplace governance along the continuum from the economic to the social relationship. At one extreme, the economic exchange assumes the individual's pursuit of self-interest and a permanent difference between the parties. The form of governance found at this extreme – the authoritarian form – assumes adversarial relationships. The principal employs subordination to further his or her objectives. Decision-making is centralized, there is lack of trust and no performance beyond contract. In extreme cases, there is no employee voice: exit is the only option. This type of governance has been shown to have the worst industrial relations and economic outcomes (see, for example, Guest and Hoque, 1994) although others (for example, Guest and Conway, 1999) find that some employees report satisfaction in these workplaces.

The second type of relationship – collective bargaining – continues the tradition of the economic exchange but major aspects of the employment relationship are negotiated. The exchange is between the collective workforce and the employer. Unions may be a constraint upon performance, but participation of unions in the design of policies provides a voice and therefore contributes to perceptions of justice. Union–management partnerships best illustrate this type of governance. They imply co-operative rather than adversarial industrial relations with the aim of securing mutual gains. Recent examples of partnership agreements in private services include those at Barclays Bank (IPA, 2000a) and ASDA (IPA, 2000b). Very little empirical work has yet been done on the effects of partnership, although Guest and Peccei (2001) have found that partnership practices are positively associated with a range of employee- and employer-related outcomes including internal organizational performance (productivity, quality and innovation) and external performance (sales and profits). On the other hand, in a comparison of matched pairs of organizations with and without partnership agreements Badigannavar (2003) found mixed results concerning satisfaction, influence and organizational commitment.

The third form of governance – employee involvement – has direct participation as a central element. Mahoney and Watson (1993) believe that enhanced perceptions of distributive justice will result from the increase in procedural justice, and the reciprocity of trust and discretion will create a social exchange of obligations far in excess of those in the economic exchange. An important element of this social exchange is the link between leader–member relationships and the outcomes of greater organizational commitment and increased extra-role behaviour. Mahoney and Watson (1993) see this model as having the most benign impact on workplace performance Studies of the effects of high-involvement work practices abound (see, for example Huselid, 1995; Fernie and Metcalf, 1995; and Ichniowski *et al.*, 1996, for an overview). More recently, Metcalf (2003) has shown that, in private service sector workplaces, the HRM form of governance is associated with superior economic outcomes.

Call centre management types

Kinnie, Purcell and Hutchinson (2000) have pointed out much of the research on call centre work has treated it as if it were homogeneous. It is evident, however, that call centre work varies considerably with regard to skill and knowledge levels, job design, monitoring and HR practices (Batt and Moynihan, 2002; IDS, 1999; Knights and McCabe, 1998; Taylor and Bain, 1999; Frenkel *et al.*, 1998; Fernie and Metcalf, 1999). From this literature it is possible to categorize call centres into three types: the first could be described as 'mass production', the second characterized as 'empowered' and the third some hybrid form, sharing common characteristics of the other two types. Let us describe the features of the first two types of centres: mass-production and empowered.

In the 'mass-production centre' jobs are designed according to Taylorist principles and are usually unskilled, require little knowledge and are repetitive and monotonous. The agent is force-fed one call after another, calls are of a short duration and must be completed in a specified time. The call is conducted in accordance with a script that may specify the entire wording of the conversation. The agent has little control over the timing of her work and the methods she may use. Any problems must be handed over to a supervisor. In the 'empowered' call centre, the semi-professional agent is given much more control over her work and is required to combine her extensive product or service knowledge (often a complex product such as mortgages) with her IT and customer service skills to provide a service that is tailored to the needs of the customer (Winslow and Bramer, 1994; Frenkel *et al.*, 1998). Work tends to be more varied, with problems handled at source. Calls tend to be longer, although may still be force-fed and have scripted openings and closings. Agents may also spend a significant amount of time doing administrative duties.

The monitoring of agent behaviour in the mass-production centre is achieved in two ways. First, information on employees' activity can be derived from the call management system, enabling management to examine any number of quantitative indicators of performance – average handling time, number of calls taken, and so on. Second, supervisors can listen remotely to an agent's calls, with or without that agent's knowledge, in order to ascertain that the agent is conforming to technical and social performance standards. The emphasis is on disciplining and directly controlling agents rather than coaching them to improve their abilities. This has been compared to Bentham's panopticon (Fernie and Metcalf, 1999), although others emphasize that there are always ways in which

58   *Call Centre HRM and Performance Outcomes*

agents can cheat the system (Knights and McCabe, 1998). In the empowered call centre, although behaviour can be monitored just as closely as in the mass-production type, less weight is placed on call management systems and more emphasis is put on monitoring the quality of an agent's interactions with customers. Such monitoring is usually placed within a wider system of training, coaching and performance management whose aim is to develop the agent's skills.

Personnel management practices differ in both types of centres. Terms and conditions in the 'mass production' centre tend to be characterized by low pay, temporary contracts and flexible hours of working. This contrasts with the empowered call centre, where employees have better rates of pay, performance related pay, permanent contracts, relatively fixed hours of working and good benefits. Other differences relate to the nature and extent of training, the role of management and team leader support. However, it is important to emphasize that so-called high-involvement work practices are not necessarily confined to those employees who service higher-value-added customers (*cf.* Batt, 2000). Kinnie (2000) points out that both the labour market and the organization's wider HR policies can have a direct influence on call centre practices, and that many 'control'-type call centres use high-commitment practices to try to reduce stress, turnover and improve staff performance and loyalty. He notes the paradox of tightly controlled, heavily monitored and scripted work co-existing with high-involvement practices. (This paradox is further examined by Houlihan in this volume.)

Existing call centre research suggests that the level of employee well-being is related to job design, monitoring and HR variables (Knights and McCabe, 1998; Zapf *et al.*, 1999; Chalykoff and Kochan, 1989; Frenkel *et al.*, 1998; Batt and Appelbaum, 1995; Holman, 2002). The main thesis of this chapter is that workplace governance, as characterized by the authoritarian, union/partnership or HRM/union modes, will have an influence on HR practices and outcomes.

Our investigation: sample, method and preparation

The financial services market, deregulated by the 1986 Financial Services Act, experienced radical changes in a very short time period. In the drive to deal with increased competition, banks rapidly closed their high street branches and looked to a more cost-effective way of doing business – the call centre. This was the case for the particular high street bank looked at in this study. It combined all its call centres under one umbrella.

The main sample for this study consisted of call centre agents who were employed in three different call centres of this bank. Each call centre dealt with a different type of product, namely personal and business accounts, mortgages and loans. Furthermore, each approximated to the three ideal types described above. They are referred to as Bank-Call, Mortgage-Call and Loan-Call respectively. In addition, the call centres represented our three 'stylized' types of workplace governance – authoritarian, union partnership and union recognition/partnership plus advanced HR practices centred on teamworking. Characteristics of the call centres' governance are summarized below.

A questionnaire was administered on site to all employees (n = 724), together with extensive observation of working practices, analysis of internal documents and interviewing. Prior to the questionnaire administration, interviews with 40 agents and ten team leaders were conducted and the information obtained was used in the questionnaire design. One month before the administration of the questionnaire all employees received a ten-minute briefing and a handout describing the research and its aims. The survey took place during normal working hours – employees being released from the telephone for an hour each. Five hundred and fifty-seven questionnaires were returned: 221 from Bank-Call, 157 from Mortgage-Call and 179 from Loan-Call. This represented a response rate of 68 per cent, 88 per cent and 81 per cent respectively, giving an overall response rate of 79 per cent. Of the total sample, 57 per cent were full-time and 31 per cent were male. The mean age was 30 years and ten months. Twenty-one per cent of the sample had college- or university-level qualifications. Average job tenure was 19 months. In addition to the employee questionnaire, several in-depth interviews lasting half a day were held with call centre managers, personnel managers, trade union representatives and employees.

Statistical analyses were carried out to investigate two major issues. First, which forms of governance yielded superior organizational and employee outcomes? Second, what was the relative contribution of job design variables, monitoring variables and HRM variables on six outcome variables, as described below?

Description of variables

Dependent variables

- Production ownership was a seven-item scale ($\alpha = 0.85$) which asked respondents about the extent to which they would be concerned if the team did not pull its weight and service quality was adversely

60 *Call Centre HRM and Performance Outcomes*

affected. Responses were measured on a five-point scale from No Concern to Very Concerned.

- Organizational commitment was a six-item scale of statements designed to measure the extent to which employees felt loyal to the bank and were prepared to 'go the extra mile' (Mowday, Steers and Porter, 1979). Responses were measured on a five-point scale from Strongly Agree to Strongly Disagree.
- Empathy, persuasion, self-control and customer focus were four scales consisting of 26 items designed to gauge skills and knowledge as they related to customer service. Responses were on a five-point scale from Strongly Disagree to Strongly Agree.
- Job satisfaction consisted of two measures, intrinsic and extrinsic (Warr, Cook and Wall, 1979). Responses were measured on a seven-point response scale from Extremely Dissatisfied to Extremely Satisfied.
- Contentment/anxiety was a six-item measure (Warr, 1990). Questions pertained to the extent to which the individual had felt tense, calm, relaxed, worried, uneasy and contented at work in the last month ($\alpha = 0.82$).
- Enthusiasm/depression was a six-item scale which measured the extent to which the individual had felt miserable, depressed, optimistic, enthusiastic, gloomy and cheerful at work in the last month ($\alpha = 0.85$). Responses were scored so that higher values represented greater contentment or enthusiasm.

Independent variables

- Job characteristics: five main job characteristics were measured in the study, namely timing control (sample question: 'do you decide how long to spend with a customer?'); method control (for example, 'can you vary how you talk with customers?); attention demand (for example, 'do you have to switch quickly between products or systems?'); problem-solving demand (for example 'do you have to solve problems which have no obvious correct answer?') using adapted versions of the Jackson *et al.* (1993) scales; and role breadth, using a 22-item scale covering activities outside of the main task (Pepper *et al.*, 1999).
- Monitoring: monitoring of agents' performance was measured using two single-item measures: the extent to which agents felt they were monitored and the extent that agents thought monitoring was used to punish rather than develop them.
- Personnel practices: payment fairness was a two-item measure that asked about the extent to which agents thought the payment and

Sue Fernie 61

bonus system was fair. Performance appraisal was a one-item measure that asked whether agents found their appraisal useful. Training was a two-item measure that asked about the perceived adequacy of training and coaching received ($\alpha=0.81$). Team leader support (sample question: 'does you team leader inform you of changes that are to be made?') was a nine-item measure (Axtell *et al.*, 2000) which asked about support received from team leaders ($\alpha=0.89$). Management support (sample question: 'do managers praise you for doing a good job?') was an 11-item scale asking about management style, in particular openness and communication ($\alpha=0.78$).

Call centre governance

Bank-Call ('authoritarian')

This was one of three call centres within the bank dealing with tele-banking. It opened in 1997 on a greenfield site. Key features of personnel strategy were driven by a central unit, into which call centre managers could have an input. The main objective of management for the survey year was to recruit and retain staff in the face of 30 per cent turnover (at a recruitment cost of £500 per employee). Most common reasons for leaving were the monotony of the work and a dislike of the flexible hours. In addition, the (predominantly young) workers who left were attracted by higher pay in numerous other local call centres. In the previous year, improving service levels had been the objective, and this had been achieved by extra recruitment and conversion of agency staff. The imminent emphasis on cross-selling – turning every personal account enquiry call into an opportunity to sell a new product – meant that training had become an important issue. Bank-Call comes closest to the 'mass-production' type – the need to make cost savings and provide flexibility of opening hours are driving factors. Personnel policy was reactive – mainly the servant of the central planning unit which allowed little discretion in local issues. Three types of employment contract existed, and staff who transferred from the branches enjoyed better pay and conditions than newly appointed staff, who were on fully flexible shifts with no overtime premiums. Starting salaries were lower than other centres in the area: there were more than 50 other call centres situated in close proximity. Bank-Call did not recognize trade unions, even though local management were personally neutral. In addition, the landlord was extremely hostile to unions and would not allow trade union representatives on site. A recent employee survey showed a severe crisis in morale and disillusionment with management. The HR manager

Table 3.1 Characteristics of the call centres

	Bank-Call (authoritarian)	Mortgage-Call (partnership)	Loan-Call (HRM + partnership)
Nature of business			
Product	Personal and business accounts	Mortgages	Loans
Focus	Service	Service/sales	Sales
Site	Greenfield	Brownfield	Brownfield
Opening hours	7 days, 7–11	Mon.–Fri. 8.30–5.30, Sat. am	7 days, 7–11
Competition – product market	Intense	Intense	Intense
Competition – labour market	Intense	Moderate	Slight
Productivity *cf.* others	Same	Probably better	Same
Characteristics of employees			
Number	450	360	225
% part-time	20	15	20
Average age	19	34	33
Type of contract	3 types	Bank-wide	Bank-wide
Agency staff?	No	20%	20%
Staff recruited	Mainly external	Mainly internal	Both
Sick rate	4%	6%	4%
Attrition	30%	4%	6%
Characteristics of payment system			
Minimum pay	£9,500	£12,000	£12,000
Salary *cf.* local rates	Same	Higher	Higher
Any PRP?	Yes	Yes	Yes
Unsocial hours paid at premium	No	Yes	Yes
Employee representation			
Union recognition	No	Yes – partnership	Yes – partnership
Union density	Handful	40%	50%
Management attitude to union	Hostile	Keen	Receptive
Any industrial action?	No	No	Yes
Employee communication	Yes	Yes	Yes
Consultation	Some	Yes – extensive	Yes
Negotiation over terms and conditions	No – imposed	Yes – central + some local	Yes – central

People management

Initial training	3 weeks	4 weeks	4 weeks
Ongoing training	If promoted, yes	Coaching	Yes, extensive
Investors in People	Would like	Yes	Yes
ISO 9000	No	No	Yes
Seating	Random, hotdesking	Traditional	Snowflake
HR manager	HR trained	HR + Ops background	Ops background
Call centre manager	Specialist, recruited externally	Sales, ex-branch	Vacancy
Health and safety	Bank-wide counselling	Consultant	Consultant
Dealing with stress	Teamleader to pick up	Stress workshops, gym	Aerobics programme
Mission	To recruit, retain and train	To develop people	To be best call centre in the bank
Teamworking	Physically separate	Yes	Yes, extensive
Management report of climate of employment relations	Poor	Good	Excellent
General type	Controlling bureaucracy	Empowered	Hybrid
Specific governance	Authoritarian	Partnership	Visionary HRM

Source: Interviews and documentary sources.

felt that involvement was important, and the consultative committee, dealing with items such as car parking, was the main forum for this. Bank-Call employees saw themselves as poor relations compared to the other two telebanking centres owned by the bank, who enjoyed facilities such as gyms, restaurants and more acceptable working conditions such as fixed shifts. The layout of the office meant that staff were required to 'hotdesk' and designated 'teams' were administrative rather than coherent groups.

Mortgage-Call (union + partnership)

The 'collective bargaining' form of governance is most closely approximated by Mortgage-Call. Shortly before the study commenced, this

64 Call Centre HRM and Performance Outcomes

workplace was known as the Bank Home Finance Centre but had changed its name to the Leeds Call Centre to reflect the bank's new form of service delivery. However, staff saw themselves as home finance specialists, not call centre agents. At Mortgage-Call, the HR director was experienced in both HR and in operations (ops), and the new call centre manager post was filled by an ex-branch head of sales, not a call centre specialist. The HR director emphasized that the complexity of the product and the repositioning of the business from an autonomous business unit to a functional unit required a different focus from that of Bank-Call. Of his ten strategic objectives, the HR manager concentrated on that which emphasized the development of his staff – 'his most important asset'. He felt that his HR practices formed a coherent whole, and that HRM should be the responsibility of all management. However, he felt constrained by centralized bank decisions over pay and contracts, but at the same time praised the union for its negotiation skills. Both the HR manager and union representatives emphasized the partnership approach (indeed, a formal partnership agreement was signed shortly after our visit), and pointed out that the centre had a tradition of working in partnership, of management encouraging staff to join the union and of strong support for the union – as long as such a relationship added value. Human resources measured the extent of this value in staff surveys and productivity, as measured by unit costs, which the HR manager pointed out were falling year on year. In MORI employee satisfaction polls, this centre's management was consistently voted into one of the top three positions. Although terms and conditions were negotiated centrally, some issues were also discussed locally. There was consultation on performance management, information on growth plans was shared and union involvement in discussions on working time was encouraged. Management described its attitude to unions as keen, and met once a month in addition to *ad hoc* consultation sessions. Changes to the pay grading system in the previous year had led to industrial action in most bank branches, but not at Mortgage-Call. The HR manager and union representatives reported that the climate of employment relations was good.

In terms of its 'partnership' stance, Mortgage-Call most closely corresponded to the pluralistic form of partnership described by Guest and Peccei (2001), where differences of interest were clearly acknowledged and a representative system was a key feature. But management at Mortgage-Call appeared to take the notion of partnership even further with their insistence on providing job security and satisfaction for their employees. During his interview, the HR manager stated that he considered it to be morally wrong to recruit from outside of the bank if this meant redundancy for existing bank employees. Through choice, 40 per cent of the call centre employees were recruited from elsewhere in the bank, and a main aim for HR for the following year was to increase the numbers of disabled, ethnic minority and part-time staff. 'Developing our people' was the main tenor of the HR manager's message. Unit cost reduction should not be achieved at the expense of training or higher stress levels for agents.

Loan-Call ('visionary HRM')

The bank's only call centre for personal loans had been situated in purpose-built premises in Liverpool since 1988. The general manager at Loan-Call, in post since its inception, was the most 'visionary' of the three managers. His mission was to have the 'best call centre in the bank' and this was to be achieved via a strategy of employee involvement. He felt that the 'can-do' mentality always succeeds and had a negative view of Personnel as 'fluffy fluffy, theorizing and underestimating the need to be business focused'. He was seen as a role model and forward thinker when it came to quality issues within the bank. His senior staff had the call centre's mission and values printed on the back of their business cards in 1997, and a great amount of time was spent inculcating those values to staff, via orientations and ongoing team briefings. The general manager and his team had spent considerable time at Disney in the US, and had imported to the call centre those techniques that he believed would improve motivation and success. Although he described management's attitude to unions as receptive, only six lines were devoted to the union in a quality submission document of 73 pages. He believed that unionism led to split loyalties amongst the staff. Whilst he reported employment relations to be 'excellent', his staff did not always share this view. Staff had, for example, gone on strike during a pay dispute. The manager wanted to see less bank-wide influence over pay and conditions and more localized negotiations.

The attitude of Loan-Call management to partnership differed considerably from that at Mortgage-Call. 'Partnership' was referred to only in the context of staff training. Involvement and consultation was often cosmetic (by the manager's own admission), with staff having no real influence on matters already decided by management. The union was 'kept informed' very early on of any impending changes. Partnership in this case, then, corresponded more to the unitary model, with management attempting to integrate the employer's and employees' interests by maximizing commitment to the organization and a perceived involvement. Such involvement was often secured by recognition (not usually monetary) of an individual agent's work or suggestion – in other words, via direct

66 Call Centre HRM and Performance Outcomes

rather than representative ways. Leadership behaviour of team leaders and management was the most important aspect of management with extensive feedback and training given.

It should be noted that the categorization of authoritarian, partnership and visionary HRM was derived from the author's subjective view of management based on extensive interviews with staff, management, union representatives and documentary evidence. The governance regimes appear to arise from a mixture of labour market and organization-specific factors as well as product market considerations. It is interesting to point out that the centre with the most complex product knowledge requirement (Mortgage-Call) was not that with the most advanced HRM (Loan-Call).

Propositions

On the basis of the links between workplace governance and performance set out in the second section of this chapter, the descriptions of call centre management (in the third section) and the specific characteristics of the three call centres (in the fourth section) our propositions are as follows:

1. We would expect that the visionary HRM centre (Loan-Call) and the partnership centre (Mortgage-Call) would have superior service-orientated outcomes to the authoritarian centre (Bank-Call). In the introduction, it was noted that certain types of high-commitment work practices consistently yielded superior economic and industrial relations outcomes and in the second section of this chapter it was noted that partnership between unions and management was better than no partnership in terms of outcomes. The third section suggested that empowered call centres might be expected to yield better service performance than the mass-production type. This notion was reinforced by our description of the authoritarian centre emphasizing staff members as 'numbers' whereas the visionary HRM centre focused on staff development, teamwork and empowerment.

This proposition is tested by analyzing the whole sample of individuals – controlling for individual characteristics, job characteristics, monitoring and personnel practices – and then comparing the coefficients on call centre dummies for each of the nine service outcomes (Table 3.3).

2. We would expect the associations between the job characteristics, monitoring and personnel practices and the service outcomes to vary by governance type. For example:

- intense monitoring is disliked in both the authoritarian and empowered centre. One-quarter of all the calls taken by the TUC during its call centre workers campaign in two weeks in February 2001 were complaints about the extent of monitoring. In 1999 BT call centre workers struck over excessive monitoring in its most 'Tayloristic' centre in the north of England. If call centre managers monitor too much and use call monitoring punitively well-being is likely to be negatively affected – even if employees are provided with high job control, supportive managers and well-run personnel practices, characteristics we might expect to find in the empowered centre. But in partnership, this may not be so. Korczynski (1999) found that a partnership agreement in an Australian call centre had a significant impact on job design, nature of control and training/ career development. More specifically, a management–union working party had been established to investigate the job design of agents by enlarging discretion and delegation of more varied tasks. Monitoring of agents could only be done with their agreement, and both performance assessment and monitoring were conducted in a way to foster worker commitment, involving dialogue and participation.
- job characteristics such as method and timing control, role breadth and problem-solving demands will affect service outcomes (Spector, 1987; Terry and Jimmieson, 1999). Holman (this volume) shows that a high degree of control over method and timing are two factors highly associated with employee well-being. Given the restrictive nature of scripting, force-feeding of calls and lack of discretion when dealing with customers in many mass-production call centres, we would expect that these variables would have a more negative impact on job satisfaction, production ownership and organizational commitment than in the empowered type of call centre.
- Progressive personnel practices – or the lack thereof – will have an impact on outcomes such as job satisfaction, perceptions of fairness and perceptions of management support (Guest and Conway, 1999). In addition, we may expect that workplaces with no HRM strategy would report worse employee outcomes (Guest and Hoque, 1994).

These propositions are examined by dividing the sample up according to call centre location and then comparing the coefficients (for example, on problem-solving demands, level of influence, production ownership) among the three centres.

Results and discussion

A summary of variable means is given in Table 3.2. If we look first at the independent variables and at the job characteristics we see that agents at Mortgage-Call experience more timing and method control and problem-solving demands than the other two centres. This is not surprising: the technical nature of the mortgage business would dictate greater autonomy on method and timing. Monitoring was seen to be least excessive at Mortgage-Call. This was a result of union pressure. One of the aims of the union had been to decrease the amount of monitoring, and it had campaigned vigorously for this. As a result, the average handling time statistic had been dropped at Mortgage-Call, whereas it remained a standard measure at the other centres. On the other hand, almost half of respondents at Loan-Call agreed or strongly agreed that they were monitored too much at work, compared with only a third of those at Bank-Call, where we would expect high levels of monitoring to be most common. Agents at Loan-Call were also exposed to the greatest degree of quality monitoring – both electronic and by team leaders – of the three centres. Moreover, some of the initiatives at Loan-Call that were designed to engender team playing – for example, competitions of various kinds – were perceived by some agents as an example of management's 'big brother' approach.

On the other hand, respondents at Loan-Call had more positive perceptions of the fairness of their payment and performance appraisal systems. For example, two-thirds of agents at Loan-Call agreed or strongly agreed that their payment system was fair, compared with only one-fifth at Bank-Call. (The low level of pay at Bank-Call compared to its local competitors was a major source of dissatisfaction.) Loan-Call agents gave much more favourable responses to other items in this scale, such as the fairness of the bonus system, the effectiveness of that system to motivate, and the usefulness of performance appraisals than agents from the other two centres.

Responses from the employee questionnaire indicate that the average age of the agents at Bank-Call was 27 years. This was somewhat younger on average than employees at the two other sites, with an average age of 33. Ten months was the average tenure at Bank-Call compared with four years at Loan-Call and nearly six years at Mortgage-Call.

Links between call centre HR strategy, governance and various service-orientated performance outcomes were analyzed in two different ways. First, the sample was split by location (*viz.* Loan-Call, Mortgage-Call) and the coefficients on the independent variables (*viz.* timing control, method

Sue Fernie 69

Table 3.2 Summary of means

	Bank-Call	Mortgage-Call	Loan-Call
Dependent variables			
Production ownership	3.50	3.75	3.98
Organizational commitment	3.27	3.46	3.67
Empathy	3.98	3.98	4.16
Persuasion	3.57	3.60	3.77
Self-control	3.56	3.70	3.70
Customer focus	3.95	4.05	4.30
Job satisfaction	4.07	4.57	4.75
Contentment/anxiety	2.50	2.68	2.68
Enthusiasm/depression	2.71	2.64	2.36
Independent variables			
Timing control	2.06	3.07	2.28
Method control	2.63	3.32	2.74
Attention demands	3.3	3.76	3.99
Problem-solving demands	2.97	3.44	3.43
Role breadth	1.99	1.97	2.08
Monitoring	3.22	3.17	3.57
Payment system fairness	2.58	3.12	3.49
Performance appraisal	3.4	3.23	3.93
Training (asked at M-Call only)		3.38	
Team leader support	3.73	3.5	3.84
Management support	2.96	3.03	2.97
Implementation of suggestions	1.69	1.62	1.69
Controls			
Age	26.6	32.5	33
% female	50.8	67.5	86.9
Highest educational qualification	A level	NVQ	GCSE
% part-time	74	75	44
% agency or temp	0	14	10
Time in organization (months)	9.94	57.4	48.44
Time in current job (months)	8.48	20.8	30.2
Union membership (%)	0.05	42.9	64

Notes: 1. All dependent and independent variables measured on a five-point scale, averaged over the different items (for example, production ownership, seven items, each five-point scale).
2. In the statistical analysis the unit of observation is the individual, with his or her specific scale scores as the dependent or independent variables.
Source: Employee questionnaire.

control) were compared across locations. However, we found very few coefficients that were significant and as a consequence the results have not been reported. Second (see Table 3.3), the full sample of almost 500 individuals was examined together with a dummy variable representing

Loan-Call (visionary HRM) or Mortgage-Call (union recognition plus partnership) compared with Bank-Call (authoritarian).

The governance structure had a significant effect on many of the service performance and employee outcomes. The 'visionary HRM' call centre at Loan-Call had superior service-orientated outcomes to the authoritarian (Bank-Call) centre on all but two of the nine indicators. In turn the partnership centre scored significantly better than the authoritarian centre (Bank-Call) on four of the outcomes. It is clear that HRM governance yields a strong feeling of production ownership (at Loan-Call and Mortgage-Call) and organizational commitment (at Loan-Call). The individuals who worked at Loan-Call were more persuasive, had a greater focus on the customer and were more satisfied in their jobs than employees at Bank-Call. On the other hand, the most significant result for the partnership workplace, Mortgage-Call, is that employees at the centre were significantly more satisfied with their jobs than those at Bank-Call.

Table 3.3 Workplace governance and performance outcomes

Service performance outcome	Visionary HRM workplace (Loan-Call)	Union + partnership workplace (Mortgage-Call)	n	R^2
Production ownership scale	0.27***	0.12*	499	.35
Organizational commitment scale	0.29***	0.09	498	.35
Empathy	0.04	0.04	499	.19
Persuasion	0.30***	0.09	499	.17
Self-control	0.04	0.17*	498	.10
Customer focus	0.27***	0.11*	499	.19
Job satisfaction	0.27***	0.23***	498	.65
Enthusiasm/depression scale	0.16*	0.04	499	.39
Contentment/anxiety scale	0.14*	0.13	498	.19

Notes: 1. Coefficients are dummy variables by workplace (compared with excluded workplace at Bank-Call 'authoritarian'). 2. Controls (see also pp. 60–1).
Job characteristics: timing control, method control, attention demands, problem-solving demands. Monitoring: extent and purpose. HR practices: payment fairness, performance appraisal, training, team leader support, management support, participation. Individual: age, gender, highest educational qualification, part-time, temporary or agency contract, time in organization, time in current job, union membership. 3. ***, **, *significant at 1%, 5%, 10% respectively.

What might explain the impact of workplace governance on these outcomes? One factor could be leadership. Effective leadership is considered a critical factor in eliciting better performance from employees and encouraging them to improve performance. Fiedler (1996) notes that the effectiveness of leaders may account for up to 35–40 per cent of the variation in organizational performance. A charismatic leader able to motivate and communicate well directly with staff, with an employee-involvement style, and with an emphasis on service and sales can positively affect customer-service outcomes by raising the customer focus of the staff.

An analysis of the three call centres which were under the ownership of the same company showed that workplace location exerted a strong influence on a number of service and employee outcomes. One way of explaining the variations across the locations was by reference to the type of workplace 'governance', including the nature of leadership. The centre with the 'visionary HRM' outperformed the authoritarian centre on a range of customer-service and employee-related outcomes. The centre with the representative, pluralist partnership arrangements also outperformed the authoritarian centre. Indeed, Bank-Call with its 'mass-production' model of service delivery and its authoritarian style of management had the worst performance on most facets of employee well-being as well as areas such as customer focus that can have a significant effect on sales and service.

References

Axtell, C., D. Holman, T. Wall, P. Waterson, E. Harrington and K. Unsworth (2000) 'Shopfloor Innovation: facilitating the suggestion and implementation of ideas', *Journal of Occupational and Organizational Psychology*, 73(3), pp. 265–85.

Badigannavar, V. (2003) 'Social Partnership in NHS Trusts', Centre for Economic Performance, London School of Economics, *mimeo*.

Bass, B. M. (1981) *Stogdill's Handbook of Leadership: a survey of theory and research*, New York: Free Press.

Batt, R. (2000) 'Strategic segmentation in front-line services: matching customers, employees and human resource systems', *International Journal of Human Resource Management*, 11(3), pp. 540–61.

Batt, R. and E. Appelbaum (1995) 'Worker participation in diverse settings: does the form affect the outcome and, if so, who benefits?', *British Journal of Industrial Relations*, 33(3), pp. 353–78.

Batt, R. and L. Moynihan (2002) 'The viability of alternative call centre production models', *Human Resource Management Journal*, 12(4), pp. 14–34.

Belt, V., R. Richardson and J. Webster (1999) 'Smiling down the phone: women's work at telephone call centres', workshop on call centres, March, London School of Economics.

Cassar, V. (1999) 'Can leader direction and employee participation co-exist?', *Journal of Managerial Psychology*, 14(1), pp. 57–68.

Chalykoff, J. and T. Kochan (1989) 'Computer-aided monitoring: its influence on employee job satisfaction and turnover', *Personnel Psychology*, 42, pp. 807–4.

Deery, S., R. Iverson and J. Walsh (2002) 'Work relationships in telephone call centres: Understanding emotional exhaustion and employee withdrawal', *Journal of Management Studies*, 39(4), pp. 471–96.

Fernie, S. and D. Metcalf (1995) 'Participation, Contingent Pay, Representation and Workplace Performance: Evidence from Great Britain', *British Journal of Industrial Relations*, 33(3), pp. 379–416.

Fernie, S. and D. Metcalf (1999) (Not) hanging on the telephone: payment systems in the new sweatshops', in D. Lewin and B. Kaufman (eds), *Advances in Industrial and Labor Relations*, Stamford, Conn.: JAI Press.

Fiedler, F. (1996) 'Research on leadership selection and training: one view of the future', *Administrative Science Quarterly*, 41, pp. 241–50.

Frenkel, S., M. Korczynski, K. Shire and M. Tam (1998) 'Beyond Bureaucracy? Work organization in call centres', *International Journal of Human Resource Management*, 9(6), pp. 957–79.

Guest, D. (1997) 'Human resource management and performance: a review and research agenda', *International Journal of Human Resource Management*, 8(3), pp. 263–76.

Guest, D. and N. Conway (1999) 'Peering into the black hole: the downside of the new employment relations in the UK', *British Journal of Industrial Relations*, 37(3), pp. 367–89.

Guest, D. and K. Hoque (1994) 'The Good, the Bad and the Ugly: Employment relations in new non-union workplaces', *Human Resource Management Journal*, 5(1), pp. 1–14.

Guest, D. and R. Peccei (2001) 'Partnership at Work: Mutuality and the balance of advantage', *British Journal of Industrial Relations*, 39(2), pp. 207–36.

Heery, E. (1999) 'Social Movement or Social Partner? Strategies for the Revitalisation of British Trade Unions', paper presented at ECSA Annual Conference, June, Pittsburgh.

Hochschild, A. (1979) 'Emotion work, feeling rules and social structure', *American Journal of Sociology*, 85, pp. 551–75.

Holman, D. (2002) 'Employee wellbeing in call centres', *Human Resource Management Journal*, 12(4), pp. 35–50 and this volume.

Huselid, M. (1995) 'The impact of human resource management practices on turnover, productivity, and corporate financial performance', *Academy of Management Journal*, 38(3), pp. 635–72.

Ichniowski, C., T. Kochan, D. Levine, C. Olson and G. Strauss (1996) 'What works at work: Overview and assessment', *Industrial Relations*, 35(3), pp. 299–334.

Income Data Services (IDS) (1999). *Pay and Conditions in Call Centres*, London: Income Data Services.

Involvement and Partnership Association (IPA) (2000a), *Partnership: Barclays Bank, sarah.dawson@partnership_at_work.com*

Involvement and Partnership Association (IPA) (2000b) *Consultation: Asda, sarah.dawson@partnership_at_work.com*

Jackson, P., T. D. Wall, R. Martin and K. Davids (2003) 'New measures of job control, cognitive demand and production responsibility', *Journal of Applied Psychology*, 78(5), pp. 753–62.

Kinnie, N. (2000) 'Rules of Engagement', *People Management*, 8 June.

Kinnie, N., S. Hutchinson and J. Purcell (2000) '"Fun and surveillance": the paradox of high commitment management in call centres', *International Journal of Human Resource Management*, 11(5), pp. 967–85.

Knights, D. and D. McCabe (1998) 'What happens when the phone goes wild? Staff, stress and spaces for escape in a BPR telephone banking work regime', *Journal of Management Studies*, 35(2), pp. 163–94.

Korczynski, M. (1999) 'What a difference a union makes: the impact of partnership unionism on the work organisation of call centres', workshop on call centres, March, London School of Economics.

Lasaosa, A., S. Wood and L. de Menezes (2001) 'High Involvement Management and Performance', CEP Working Paper, May.

Leidner, R. (1996) 'Rethinking questions of control: lessons from McDonalds', in C. L. Macdonald and C. Sirianni (eds), *Working in the Service Society*, Philadelphia: Temple University Press.

Mahoney, T. and M. Watson, (1993) 'Evolving modes of work force governance: an evaluation' in B. Kaufman and M. Kleiner (eds), *Employee Representation: Alternatives and Future Directions*. Ithaca, NY: ILR Press.

Metcalf, D. (2003) 'Unions and Productivity, Financial Performance and Investment: international evidence', chapter 5 in J. Addison and C. Schnabel (eds), *International Handbook of Trade Unions*, London: Edward Elgar.

Mowday, R., R. Steers, and L. Porter, (1979) 'The measurement of organizational commitment', *Journal of Vocational Behavior*, 14, pp. 223–47.

Pepper, K., C. M. Axtell, C. W. Clegg, P. H. Gardner and T. D. Wall (1999) *Measures of Role Breadth*, Sheffield: Institute of Work Psychology, University of Sheffield.

Schneider, B. and D. E. Bowen (1985) 'Employee and customer perceptions of service in banks: Replication and extention', *Journal of Applied Psychology*, 48, pp. 527–47.

Schneider, B. and D. E. Bowen (1993) 'The service organization: human resource management is crucial', *Organizational Dynamics*, 21(4), pp. 39–52.

Spector, P. E. (1987) 'Interactive effects of perceived control and job stressors on affective reactions and health outcomes for clerical workers', *Work and Stress*, 1(2), pp. 155–62.

Taylor, P. and P. Bain (1999) '"An assembly line in the head": work and employment relations in the call centre', *Industrial Relations Journal*, 30(2), pp. 101–17.

Trades Union Congress (TUC) (1998) 'Promoting Best Practice Through Workplace Partnership – Case Studies', briefing, 7 September.

Terry, D. And N. Jimmieson, (1999) 'Work control and well-being: a decade review', in C. Cooper and I. Robertson (eds), *International Review of Industrial and Organizational Psychology*, London: John Wiley & Sons.

Warr, P. (1990) 'The measurement of well-being and other aspects of mental health', *Journal of Occupational Psychology*, 63, pp. 193–210.

Warr, P., J. Cook and T. Wall (1979) 'Scales for the measurement of some work attitudes and aspects of psychological well-being', *Journal of Occupational Psychology*, 52, pp. 285–94.

Winslow, C. and W. Bramer (1994) *Futurework*, New York: Free Press.

Yukl, G. (1994) *Leadership in Organisations*, 3rd edition, Englewood Cliffs, NJ: Prentice Hall.

Zapf, D., C. Vogt, C. Seifert, H. Mertini and A. Isic (1999) 'Emotion work as a source of stress: the concept and development of an instrument', *European Journal of Work and Organizational Psychology*, 8(3), pp. 371–400.

4
Tensions and Variations in Call Centre Management Strategies*
Maeve Houlihan

Introduction

Call centres have become part of everyday experience and hold a grip on public imagination. Predominantly, the call centre reflects a 'mass production approach to customer service' (Batt, 1999; Cameron, 2000). Volume is managed through task routinization, scripting, and a sophisticated information and communication technology (ICT) architecture configured to distribute, manage and monitor calls. Service quality is managed through a mixture of behavioural management and HR strategies. By these means, call centres seek to balance the logics of efficiency and the customer. The tension between these goals is keenly felt due to heightened visibility of cost trade-offs (Korczynski, 2001, p. 83; Sturdy, 2001, p. 7; Wallace, Eagleson and Waldersee, 2000, p. 174). This tension unmasks a series of conflicts: between costs and quality; between flexibility and standardization; and between constraining and enabling job design.

The question of how these tensions are managed raises interest in the broader management strategies (see Batt, this volume). Recent papers by Frenkel *et al.*, 1998; 1999; Kinnie, Purcell and Hutchinson, 2000; Hutchinson, Purcell and Kinnie, 2000; Callaghan and Thompson, 2002; and Wallace, Eagleson and Waldersee, 2000 discussed the use of high-commitment management practices in call centres. Their use in the context of low-discretion job design adds a new and seemingly paradoxical

---

*This chapter originally appeared in the *Human Resource Management Journal*, 12(4), pp. 67–85.

dimension to normative interpretations of high-commitment management (HCM). Why are these practices adopted? Can this strategy thrive in a low-discretion environment? And in this context, how do the tensions between control and commitment manifest themselves?

This chapter uses empirical data from four British call centres to examine 'low-discretion high-commitment' (LDHC) in action. Each of these cases suggest, first, the deliberate but varied use of HCM strategies and, second, the tensions of combining elements of control with HCM. These cases suggest that LDHC is not homogeneous, but rather that it operates in a variety of forms. The paper thus proposes a typology of LDHC approaches and explores the conflicts underpinning them.

Previous research

There is growing evidence of the commingling of control and commitment strategies in the call centre. Frenkel and colleagues (1998; 1999) examined the linkages among work organization, employment relations and control relations in call centres, cross-nationally. They identified an emerging hybrid of control and empowerment, which they characterized as 'mass customized bureaucracy' (MCB). MCB supplements regimented work with 'info-normative control' and pockets of creativity and discretion, a model that 'remains primarily bureaucratic but includes elements associated with professional or knowledge-intensive settings' (1998, p. 958). While Frenkel *et al.* acknowledged the tensions invoked by greater work complexity and yet limited discretion, along with consequential contradictions of limited pay, training and career prospects (1999, p. 273), they view the MCB form as a significant adaptation of the control model.

Similarly, based on their CIPD research on lean-working environments in the UK, Kinnie, Purcell and Hutchinson (2000) and Hutchinson, Purcell and Kinnie (2000) challenged the view that HCM strategies are suited (and cost-effective) only to high-scope flexibility work environments, and incompatible with a control orientation. Specifically, they observed that HCM practices could be used 'to offset some of the worst features of call centre working' (Kinnie, Purcell and Hutchinson, 2000, p. 967). They viewed this as a new, pragmatic interpretation of the commitment model, reflecting greater alignment of HR practices and control systems with the demands of the labour market and high-quality customer service. An illustration of this is the paradoxical combination of 'fun and surveillance'.

However, other research highlights the tensions underlying commitment in a control context. Batt (1999) found significant evidence that the introduction of self-managed teams led to greater service quality and sales levels in Regional Bell Operating Companies, yet the organization subsequently suspended their team management and TQM initiatives in favour of a traditional mass-production model, driven by economies of scale and tensions between quality and quantity. Callaghan and Thompson (2002) explored the strategic use of elaborate selection and training procedures more traditionally associated with high-end, non-routine work, at Telebank. This was designed to recruit, mould and standardize 'attitude', reflected by social competencies such as teamwork, adaptability and tolerance of ambiguity. Seeking both 'survival as well as communication skills', Telebank used HCM techniques to elicit and transform discretionary behaviours and attitudes, appropriating emotional labour in order to absorb the tensions within the job design (Call aghan and Thompson, 2002, p. 251). Wallace, Eagleson and Waldersee (2000) found that some call centres consciously pushed these tensions onto front-line customer service agents, through a 'sacrificial HR strategy'. Rather than compromising between efficiency and service, they relied on the goodwill and enthusiasm of employees, and the reality that stress and burnout could be absorbed by a ready labour market and 'turnover-proof' job design.

An emerging typology of LDHC

It is clear that all call centres are not the same. Call centres can be distinguished by type (Hutchinson, Purcell and Kinnie, 2000; Callaghan and Thompson, 2002), relating both to organizational strategy (for example, low-cost or high-differentiation) and to task, ranging broadly from 'advice/solutions', to 'sales' and 'transactions' (Wallace, Eagleson and Waldersee, 2000). These criteria indicate a correlation between type, degree of routinization, and the depths of knowledge required by customer service representatives (CSRs) to carry out their work (Callaghan and Thompson, 2002, p. 237).

However despite variations in type and task objectives, there remains a strong uniformity to call centre rhythms and routines (Frenkel *et al.*, 1998, p. 976). The structuring influence of available call centre technologies partially accounts for this convergence (Taylor and Bain, 1999, p. 105; Wallace, Eagleson and Waldersee, 2000, p. 182). Notwithstanding strategic choice, these ICTs influence both potential work design and the social technology of relationships, communications and routines. Notably, this sets a context for low-interdependence work (Batt, 1999, p. 545) and the encoding of knowledge and procedures to support standardization.

This in turn enables use of relatively unskilled workers, minimized training investment, lower wage costs and insulation against 'churn'. Thus, while alternative models have been suggested, particularly at the 'high end' of knowledge-intensive firms (Frenkel *et al.*, 1999), the normative pattern of low-discretion work design is pervasive.

This normative pattern of low-discretion work design and associated technologies are evident across all four sites reported in this chapter, despite significant differences in the organizational strategy and task objectives. Equally, all four cases offer similarly contained pay levels and career opportunities, reflecting industry norms. However, despite these commonalities, approaches to people management and job design implementation in each of the four centres vary considerably. This suggests that rather than being a homogeneous concept, LDHC is approached to different degrees, and in a variety of forms.

To expand this perspective, a typology of call centre organizing is proposed (Figure 4.1). Its intention is to highlight differentiation in management approaches to LDHC. The emerging typology is based on the fit between HR strategy and work design. Thus it combines on one dimension the underlying assumptions of the HCM strategy deployed (broadly control or commitment), and on the other, the character of low-discretion work implementation (broadly coercive or enabling).

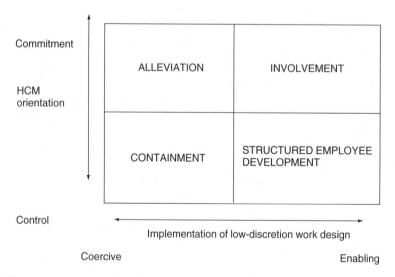

Figure 4.1 Towards a typology of low-discretion high-commitment (LDHC)

Organizational commitment and HCM

This chapter approaches organizational commitment as a managerial strategy aimed at mobilizing involvement and discretionary work effort among employees (Frenkel *et al.*, 1998, p. 959). In the workplace, commitment has become associated with HR strategy through the concept of high-commitment management (Wood, 1995; Purcell, 1999). HCM espouses an integrated, strategic approach to people management which typically incorporates strategies including high job scope, job security, strategic recruitment and selection, teamwork, performance-based pay, sophisticated training and career development policies and involvement initiatives (MacDuffie, 1995; Pfeffer, 1998; Hutchinson, Purcell and Kinnie, 2000). Such strategies are typically associated with high-discretion, 'knowledge work' environments. Clearly, the call centre seems a paradoxical site for HCM given its low-discretion construction of job design, and underlying costs orientation (Kinnie, Purcell and Hutchinson, 2000, p. 968).

However, as the empirical data serve to illustrate – commitment strategies can be implemented in comprehensive or superficial ways. HCM techniques adopted in a piecemeal fashion, rather than as part of a coherent strategy risk a culture of 'mixed messages' (Guest, 1992). Walton argued that control and commitment models are 'radically different from each other in conception and operation' (1985, p. 36). For Walton, and for Guest, the commitment model involves a paradigm shift in managerial assumptions about work, workers and the nature of the organization (Guest, 1992). Applying this perspective to the call centre: what are the underlying assumptions behind the adoption of HCM practices?

Low-discretion job design implementation

Adler and Borys (1996) present the terms 'enabling' and 'coercive' as contrasting modes of bureaucracy. This approach is useful because it emphasizes the ways in which low discretion and formalization are implemented. A key strength of Adler and Borys' approach is that it does not prejudge highly routinized or formalized work designs. As the authors describe, 'enabling procedures help committed employees do their jobs more effectively and reinforce their commitment' (1996, p. 93). Enabling procedures work *with* employees, notwithstanding a bureaucratic context, facilitating appropriate discretion and supporting them in the execution of their work. In contrast, coercive procedures work *on* employees, controlling what they do and how, and strongly undermine discretion and involvement. The authors use this typology as a way of theorizing employees' experiences of the differences between 'good' and 'bad' regimes.

This highlights that the experience of low-discretion work depends on how job design is implemented and supported, and how it fits/misfits with the demands of the task. Routinized work is clearly most appropriate in contexts where the task is simple. The surface configuration of call centre work as straightforward masks considerable complexity and may represent a misalignment between work design and task demands. This issue will be addressed in more detail later in this chapter.

Notwithstanding fit, job design implementation has clear implications for the degree to which, and the methods by which roles, rules and procedures are enforced. There is clear evidence that team leaders can have a significant ameliorative effect on work stress through supportive, relational management approaches (Wallace, Eagleson and Waldersee, 2000; Deery, Iverson and Walsh, 2002). Alternatively, an authoritarian, task-focused orientation can significantly entrench the demands of the task. Similarly, emotional support from peers serves as a primary sustaining force (Frenkel *et al.*, 1999; Cameron, 2000; Deery, Iverson and Walsh, 2002). While peer support can be heavily constrained by call centre work intensity, CSRs are generally innovative in creating 'space for escape' (Knights and McCabe, 1998). However, opportunities for interaction are further hindered when the job design is rigidly implemented. The key point here is that where coercive procedures restrict job performance they may in fact frustrate and alienate otherwise committed employees.

Undoubtedly the use of a two-by-two matrix introduces simplification at the cost of complexity. The variations of LDHC presented here are drawn from empirical examples, to highlight a range of strategies in use. This model is not exhaustive, and further variations and mixed forms are likely. However, by combining the elements of work design and HR strategy it becomes possible to characterize variations in management strategies. This opens up a more differentiated and fine-grained analysis of the LDHC construct and its potential operation and implications. The following account elaborates the four LDHC characterizations suggested by the typology.

First, combining control-orientated HCM and a coercive approach to task implementation, call centres may pursue a 'containment' model of LDHC. Under this approach, the standard features of the low-discretion model are supplemented by HCM techniques; however, the underlying ethos of control is discernable. Supervision is compliance-orientated as espoused values are constrained by overriding pressures to 'push calls through'. Echoing the 'sacrificial HR strategy', this approach relies on control to deliver productivity, and the emotional labour of CSRs to achieve a degree of service quality. Commitment interventions seek to elicit the sort of competencies and attitudes that produce creativity and discretionary effort, but in narrow terms (Callaghan and Thompson, 2002; Frenkel *et al.*, 1998). Containment seeks to overcome the resulting stress and motivation problems by utilizing a pragmatic mix of HCM initiatives such as teams, training and performance management. Such interventions risk superficiality as a containment approach fails to address underlying causes. At the heart of the containment model, espoused HCM is sacrificed to performance objectives 'weighted heavily towards numerical targets for efficiency and speed' (Wallace, Eagleson and Waldersee, 2000, p. 176). Thus LDHC by containment reflects a *managed* misalignment between work organization and task demands. It is likely that such a model depends on a lean employment market where employees have limited alternatives.

Alternatively, organizations may seek to distract from the stresses and problems of routinized, intensively managed work. LDHC by 'alleviation' retains a coercive approach to task implementation, but attempts to compensate for extreme routine and manage morale problems by significant investment in cultural support and symbols of commitment. Such investment may include 'big' statements such as state-of-the-art facilities, lifestyle benefits such as childcare, or a 'fun' environment (Kinnie, Purcell and Hutchinson, 2000). HCM approaches may also include explicit use of part-time workers, who may be more tolerant of the intensive work environment, given their interests outside of work. Nonetheless, alleviation policies are set within the context of highly formalized procedures, minimal discretion and task-focused supervision. Thus, while LDHC by alleviation is high-commitment orientated, it is fundamentally coercive in its job design. Such a model may be most associated with high-volume, low-cost business strategies seeking to minimize churn and retain staff goodwill in the interests of customer service quality. Such a model depends very much on person-fit, and may be associated with an 'employees' market or lifestyle choices.

In contrast, 'structured employee development' LDHC seeks to create an enabling context for the normative low-discretion job design, but retains a compliance-orientated HCM strategy. In this case, routine, bureaucratic work design is supplemented by initiatives to reduce ambiguity and support employees, for example through the use of teams for peer support and problem solving, and relations-orientated supervisory strategies (Frenkel *et al.*, 1999, p. 94; Batt, 1999, p. 557; Wallace, Eagleson and Waldersee, 2000, p. 179; Deery, Iverson and Walsh, 2002, p. 491). Training and development focuses on product and call handling skills, but also on psychological coping strategies (Leidner, 1993; Callaghan and Thompson, 2002). However, as Cameron's (2000) analysis of call centre training materials shows, interventions tend to focus on attitudes and 'fixes' rather than deeper levels of empowerment or career development. This approach is also likely to include a strong emphasis on cultural control and individualized psychological contracts. In terms of HCM, this version of LDHC reflects 'hard HR' (Storey, 1992), for example through extensive use of agency employment, single status contracts and a command approach to work allocation. Thus, while LDHC by structured development can be enabling, it is also control-orientated. Such a model suggests a fast-changing work context, where flexibility and responsiveness are key elements of the business strategy or where there is a relatively competitive employment market.

A more radical approach to LDHC challenges some of the normative assumptions about call centre work organization. Thus, LDHC by 'involvement' is both high-commitment-orientated and also strives to be enabling in job design implementation. In this case, the normative low-discretion work design is integrated with an engaged culture of support and participative problem solving. While the job design retains the hallmarks of routine and formalization, job discretion may be developed through a relational approach, either externally in the type of interaction with the customer, or internally with regard to organizational roles and relationships (Hutchinson, Purcell and Kinnie, 2000; Batt, this Volume). Here, HCM 'bundles' form part of a coherent strategy, rather than a piecemeal approach, for example through the planned and supported development of employees and their construction as skilled knowledge workers. LDHC by involvement suggests 'soft HR' (Storey, 1992) but also a radical reappraisal of HR strategy, job design, staffing levels, task mix and the type of behaviours offered by and expected from CSRs. In its best forms, this comes close to conventional understandings of HCM; however, the pervasive demands of quantitative measures and call volume exert considerable counter-pressure towards standardization and control. Such a model may be associated with higher-end knowledge-type call centre work (Frenkel *et al.*, 1998), less commercial environments such as helplines, or contexts where quality of service is at a premium. It may also be associated with more innovative, visionary or values-driven management styles. However its wider application is not precluded.

Methodology

The research for this chapter examines the management ethos, HR strategies and work processes of four call centres in the North of England carrying out routinized work in sales, customer service and advice provision. Data was collected between 1997 and 1999, in two forms. The first is a two-year participant ethnography during which the author worked as CSR at 'Quotes Direct', an insurance centre. This involved one year of undisclosed participation (20 hours per week) and one year of disclosed participation (eight hours per week).

Participant observation was adopted in order to engage with the nuances of call centre work, specifically from the perspective of CSRs and team leaders. This approach enabled full involvement in the work processes of the call centre and the relationships among CSRs, team leaders, customers and managers; ongoing dialogue with all these parties, and participation in induction, training, team meetings and performance coaching. In addition, a series of extended off-site interviews was conducted with eight team leaders and CSRs over the period of a year.

The second phase of data collection involved more traditional case investigation of five further call centres. This chapter will draw on three of these cases ('Shopping Direct', 'Call Centre Bureau' and 'Education Line'), to illustrate and explore the varied managerial ethos, HR strategies and work regimes adopted. In contrast to the ethnography, these case studies focused on extended dialogue with managers about their methods, choices and beliefs. Fifteen individuals were interviewed, ranging from team leaders to HR, operations and centre managers. This casework was supplemented with limited non-participant observation, attendance at induction and training sessions, and dialogue with 12 CSRs (in this case selected by management).

The intention of this research design was to establish and explore espoused theories, and theories in use (Argyris and Schon, 1974) in relation to call centre management. In particular it examined the tensions of LDHC though the experiences and perspectives of managers and CSRs. This form of data collection sought to understand the meaning of beliefs and behaviours within their natural context (van Maanen, 1979, p. 520). Analysis of the various theories espoused and practices observed has led to the conceptual framework presented in this chapter.

The LDHC models in action

An overview of the four call centres can be seen in Table 4.1, reflecting their work, employment and control relations (following Frenkel *et al.*,

Table 4.1 Overview of LDHC patterns at the case sites

	Quotes Direct (QD)	Shopping Direct (SD)	Call Centre Bureau (CCB)	Education Line (EL)
Activity	Direct home and motor insurance quotations and sales	Catalogue order taking and customer service	Third-party customer service contracts	Educational advice and information services
Size	200 of 600	1,200	600	60 and growing
Work organization	Routine, low discretion	High routine, low discretion	High routine, low discretion	Routine, part discretion
Employment relations: key HCM policies and practice	Structured performance management system. Teams and 'fun culture'	World-class facilities and lifestyle benefits. Strategic use of part-time staff, person-fit	Multi-tasking, secondment and cross-deployment. Individual 'development plans'	Deliberate use and development of skilled workers. Career progression: tiered roles
Control relations	Disciplinary use of targets and control orientated HCM	Coercive task implementation offset by HCM interventions	Enabling task implementation offset by control orientation	Enabling task implementation complemented by HCM
LDHC orientation	Containment	Alleviation	Development	Involvement

1998, p. 960). The chapter now turns to examine each case in action. These accounts highlight the HCM policies and practices in each centre, and examine evidence of tensions within each form of LDHC related to conflicts between commitment and control.

LDHC by containment: 'back to school' with Quotes Direct

Between 1997 and 1999, Quotes Direct (QD) employed approximately 600 staff. There were few other call centres in the locality. The call centre was divided into separate 'floors', respectively inbound and outbound telemarketing, customer services, claims and a helpline. The participant study focused on the inbound telemarketing floor of this call centre, a group of 200 people whose job was to generate quotations and sell policies for home and motor insurance.

Work design on the inbound floor was governed by a complex array of rules and changeable targets. These related to conversion rates, quality benchmarking, cross-reference data capture and sales 'asks'. Thus, job formalization was extremely high (underscored by the legal character of insurance contracts) and the job was intensive. Call length averaged four minutes, reflecting a range from instant turn-aways to complex quotations. Lean staffing meant a constant pressure on service levels and agent availability, emphasized by flashing leader boards. The explicit message was 'avoid deviation and special cases, just push the calls through'. As Colin, a 25-year-old full-time CSR reflected: 'Time is very important and it's a numbers game. The more calls you take, the more people that you get that are interested. It's sad but its true.'

QD espoused many of the policies associated with HCM including an elaborate recruitment and induction process, ongoing training and an integrated performance-management system. However in action, HCM implementation was uneven and its espoused values were regularly at odds with on-floor practice.

For example, the performance-management system incorporated explicit targets, monitoring and coaching, performance appraisal and performance-related pay. Individual bonuses related to 'sales' over the target, which for top sellers could account for 20 per cent of income. However, targets constantly shifted upwards and information on how bonuses were determined was changeable and ambiguous.

Target achievement was predicated on coaching and detailed performance management, yet monitoring was erratic, despite policy. Team leaders were regularly redeployed to take calls, making them unavailable to their team. This lack of support alongside and fast-paced yet dependent work design was keenly felt by all concerned:

How many times ... I know it happened to me a countless number of times ... How many times have you found yourself with red lights on the phone, you've had a major problem, you've taken the customer's phone number because you really can't keep this man any more, and you've tried to find help ... And there were 20 people to scream at you to get back into 'available' ... But there wasn't one that would help you ... and you really couldn't go back into 'available' because you really needed to ring this man, so you wind up standing there in such a turmoil ... thinking, 'God, should I go back on the phones? What button does my hand go for? Do I ring him back or think blow him? Do I go take another call, and leave him sitting at home waiting for my call ... ? Is it going to be half an hour or an hour by the time I get someone to help?'

> Helen, former CSR, now team leader, Quotes Direct

QD 'inbound' was organized into 15 teams, each comprising a team leader and approximately 12 CSRs, presenting an opportunity to create a sense of 'community' and enhance motivation. Yet, for QD, the use of teams was manifestly a co-ordinating device. Members had limited formal opportunities for interaction and work intensity meant, at most, snatched acknowledgements to neighbouring CSRs. Further, team membership was frequently changed to 'keep things fresh'.

Team meetings were regularly sacrificed due to 'inability to get off the phones', and teams leaders were under pressure to compete with each other through targets. Team members were primarily linked via their team leader rather than to each other, with little opportunity for meaningful input into team strategy or development.

At QD a control philosophy unconsciously expressed itself through a school-like approach to management. CSRs were teased into conformity, and performance was managed through a culture of 'naming and shaming'. Marker boards detailed individual weekly sales performance and awards were made to 'star of the week' and 'slowcoach of the week'. CSRs were threatened to be put 'on report' for deficient performance, while rewards were tellingly childish. As Diane comments:

I'm not in primary school. The way they set the teams up reminds me of being on red, blue and green tables – you know – red's the best and if you work really hard you might get on it. And if you want to draw some cartoon figures to give your team a bit of a rar-rar ... We're supposed to think it's a reward to get signed off the phones to colour something in – that just reinforces what I was saying about feeling like being back at school. I can't do it, not even for a break.

'Dress up' days and nights out were frequently organized, despite a low-key response by the staff. Many agents were sarcastic about the extensive focus on team themes, slogans and contests. Such measures were loosely devised to break up the work and create a lighthearted atmosphere, yet the cultural contradictions meant they were distrusted. This conveys something of the fragility of 'fun' in a control environment. Yet at times, many CSRs enjoyed the camaraderie and bluntness of this culture, and shared moans enabled catharsis. This was a coping mechanism in the context of limited alternatives although nonetheless, CSRs succeeded in exploiting the uneven enforcement of rules when they chose.

Turning to the LDHC framework, QD espoused elements of HCM, but clearly their operation was patchy. In all these ways the work design must be characterized as coercive, and the HCM approach as controlling and piecemeal. This combination of control and coercion with an overlay of HCM practices meant that the adopted model of call centre management at QD was strongly rooted in containment LDHC.

All of this is indicative of the dominance of control over commitment values and a culture of mixed messages, arising from a superficial approach to commitment. This culture undermined HCM interventions, causing CSRs to be sceptical about new initiatives. At QD the potential of HCM interventions was missed, and instead created frustration through falsely raised expectations and unkept promises. The problems lay not with the policies, but rather with how they were implemented and their fit with an already conflicting culture. As a result, the rhetoric of commitment barely masked the underlying control philosophy (Legge, 1995).

LDHC by alleviation: 'It's not a job, it's a lifestyle' at Shopping Direct

Shopping Direct (SD) was based in a large industrial city. As an established catalogue shopping business, its core activities were order lines, customer service and debt recovery. The centre supported a staff of 1,200. Ninety-seven per cent of CSRs were female – the conventional 'solution' to demanding customer service work (Frenkel *et al.*, 1999, p. 273). Two unusual features of the call centre were long length of service and the predominant use of part-time staff. There was also a steady turnover of casual and temporary staff employed through agencies.

SD was in the process of strategic business renewal to recover profit levels and become more market-led and contemporary in relation to

88 Tensions and Variations in Call Centre Management Strategies

products, customer relations and staff management. Both staff and customers had aged in profile, and this needed to change to survive in new markets. The new ethos was designed around a concept of 'work as lifestyle', intended to both convey commitment to staff, and to signal change. This was reflected in the commissioning of a 'world-class' new premises.

The impact of the physical workplace has received little attention in call centre research (for an exception see Baldry, Bain and Taylor, 1998). The standard features of call centres tend to create unforgiving working conditions (noise, heat and densely packed rooms), yet some centres seek to communicate 'people values' by creating state-of-the-art workplaces.

SD's new building projected an integrated focus on customer service excellence and employee well-being. It was a striking, open-plan glass structure, centred around swirling desk banks and water features. Workstations had three times more space than the industry norm and the centre was unusually 'noiseless'. The centre housed a gym, swimming pool, cafés, an in-company retail outlet and specially designed de-stress zones. An elaborate training suite overlooked the main floor.

Beyond physical re-engineering, a key change was the move from centralized command and control management, to team organizing. The main call centre housed 45 teams of up to 24 people. Teams were self-contained and semi-permanent. Performance management was devolved to team co-ordinators who worked closely with CSRs on a daily basis. Weekly monitoring focused on 'tone' of communications, call structure and the offer of structured cross-sells. An on-floor call centre management team liaised with team co-ordinators and provided forecasting and call routing.

However, in terms of job design, CSRs followed a strict script and very short job cycle, meaning minimal discretion. The order line process was straightforward and constant, with an average call length of less than two minutes. As a volume business, the dominant philosophy was 'just keep answering'. Customer service line calls tended to be longer and more unpredictable, but involved a constant exposure to dissatisfied customers.

SD sought to alleviate the monotony of this work process by training team co-ordinators to encourage positive thinking and product belief. A key strategy was the use of part-timers, and 80 per cent of order line staff worked four-hour shifts. CSRs were allocated 20 minutes per shift 'off-line time', which was generally taken as breaks between calls. Overtime was frequent, but optional. Business managers worked to predict demand and optimize staffing levels, but inevitably this was hard to get right. Certain times, particularly Christmas, were acknowledged as 'three weeks of hell'.

Reflecting its new focus on performance management, SD introduced a 'balanced scorecard' template focusing on quantitative and qualitative call performance, telemarketing targets, HR indicators and employee satisfaction. However, unusually, SD elected 'not to accentuate the numbers' to CSRs. There were no flashing leader boards, no motivational slogans and no explicit sales targets. New recruits were told: 'your place is to offer – let the sales look after themselves'. SD's approach was to avoid gimmicks. As floor manager Chris described:

> We don't pressurise people, so we don't say 'this is our top person, they've taken the most calls'. If people do a good job they are told it. But we don't put it on a board and give them a hat or anything.

There were no sales targets, and hence no bonus structures; however, detailed targets related to call structures, offer rates, idle time, call length, and attendance and timekeeping. Performance achievements were recognized through internal publications and prizes. Promotion opportunities were limited for CSRs, although new third-party services provided additional opportunities for development. These were staffed through internal recruitment utilizing interviews and assessment centres. All staff underwent two weeks of induction, and training was ongoing, relating to product, technology and customer service skills.

Cultural dynamics were strong at SD. Most had worked together for a long time and as one CSR commented, 'it's like a village really'. Many staff were related or came from the same communities. Recruitment through recommend-a-friend schemes added to this, and also ensured realistic job preview. Notably, most CSRs were also customers, and the discounted staff store generated substantial income for the company. SD provided activities such as beauty product demonstrations, dry cleaning collection and children's party organizing. These benefits were geared to appeal to the needs of the staff, the majority of whom were mothers balancing family demands.

Having made such a substantial investment, SD was disappointed when the gym, swimming pool and stress zones did not attract the utilization expected, and latterly the stress zones were re-designated. Managers admitted that the 'initial euphoria' was short-lived, yet remained positive about the results of the investment. SD learned that facilities alone were insufficient to change motivation and morale over time. They subsequently

90 *Tensions and Variations in Call Centre Management Strategies*

commenced a series of initiatives to tap into latent dissatisfactions and activate two-way communication: structured weekly time slots for team meetings, regular attitude surveys and centre-wide focus groups. An espoused tenet of SD's commitment strategy was to involve staff in the business, notwithstanding their limited job design. Yet, passing comments told a different story, such as this from Sue: 'If you think of something good, tell me and I'll pass it off as my idea. But I'll still get no recognition for it.'

When asked, CSRs were pragmatic about their work and their unusual working environment. While they talked positively about the building, in practice they paid it little attention, treating it much like the backdrop of a shopping mall. Comments about the work itself reflected job monotony and stress in rhythm with its peaks and troughs. Break-time conversations were mostly about products, customer anecdotes and 'getting on with it'. Yet, the reality is that for these CSRs, opportunities to 'slack off' were limited. Calls just kept coming and non-routine issues were automatically referred upwards.

Fundamentally, Shopping Direct utilized an extreme form of routinized low-discretion work. However, it attempted to manage this through a supportive culture and deliberate use of part-timers and person-fit strategies. It expressed its commitment to employees by 'knowing who they are and what their needs are'. SD sought to distract from routine and manage morale through an alleviating version of LDHC. This bought 'good enough' performance. However, as such the alleviation model remains a narrowly conceived status quo approach.

LDHC by structured employee development: snakes and ladders at Call Centre Bureau

Call Centre Bureau (CCB) was a modern, spacious, purpose-built call centre, in a suburban business park, surrounded by a number of other call centres. CCB provided high-routine customer services to third parties on a contract basis. As a result it operated a wide range of accounts, from short-term campaigns to insourced services, all with different processes and performance criteria. Typical contracts included a postcodes service, catalogue order lines and parcel delivery services.

Contracts were located in designated areas throughout the centre, each having their own 'identity', although CCB also strived for an integrated culture. Each zone had a local supervisor, who managed the 'stats' and co-ordinated through team leaders. CSRs were grouped in teams of 12 to 20. Typically, staff were recruited via an agency on short-term contracts, for the basic information lines. New starters received minimum training before commencing to take calls. Over time suitable candidates were encouraged to apply for direct CCB employment, and train for more complex contracts depending on their skills and objectives. The extreme routine of most contracts was countered in part by multi-tasking, with agents switching between screens and scripts depending on each call. Like Shopping Direct, CCB accepted repetition and low discretion as key features of the job; in fact most contracts had been outsourced precisely because they were so routine (Frenkel *et al.*, 1999, p. 273). However, CCB's distinctive approach to HCM took the form of focusing CSRs on 'personal development plans'. These involved CSRs undertaking NVQ training, and identifying learning objectives such as team skills, 'acting up', or adding more complex contracts to their skill set. Thus, CSRs moved through five categories of development, reflected in their pay structure. As a flat organization, these levels were the main means of advancement.

However, while development plans were used as a motivational tool, dependency on third-party clients meant that business demands came first. Thus, product-based training was prioritized but other training such as team building and communication skills were subject to cancellation at short notice:

> When it comes down to it with team meetings, training and one-to-one coaching, we have to establish a happy medium between service levels and development. So you have to do it reactively. If the service level is good, that is the time to say 'Right – I'm going to do your one-to-one now, and get it out of the way.' It can be hard at times when you see potential in someone and you can't get them off the phones.
>
> Joanne, training officer

A key feature of the development plan was the policy of 'acting up'. Thus, many CSRs worked as deputy team leader or were seconded to other work throughout the centre. As acting-up was unpaid for periods of less than a week, this relied on the message that such behaviour would help advancement. Most team leaders, and indeed HR and training officers, had 'worked their way up'. However, at CCB this policy worked both ways and many staff worked on conditional secondment, subject to reassignment to CSR according to business needs. For example, after two years in the role, the training officer was still contracted as a CSR. Even the HR manager, Maria, joked 'at any moment I could be back serving the chips'. She added: 'You have to remain very flexible. I like change so this type of environment suits me. But it's not for everybody.'

92 *Tensions and Variations in Call Centre Management Strategies*

At the time of this case study, the training department was being dismantled. Training was being 'cascaded' to team leaders, which enabled new opportunities for acting up. The former training team was redeployed to new business generation, reiterating the message that everybody was exposed.

The contract-based nature of CCB meant that it was fundamentally service level- and target-orientated. The fact that most of its work was 'owned' by third parties set a very clear context for managers, given the pressure to retain contracts and remain competitive. Clients managed these contracts with a strong quantitative focus. Like most call centres, CCB promised clients a 'service level' target of 85 per cent – a figure they generally strived to exceed, 'but not too much', lest they portray excessive slack. As John, a team leader, commented: 'If you achieve 100 per cent service levels people are going to say "why?" – and then they will cut your staff numbers.'

As a bureau, CCB's competitive advantage lay in remaining highly flexible and containing its costs; thus, CCB strived to achieve 100 per cent staff utilization across contracts. This led to an intensive focus on balancing service levels. Tensions arose between contracts as CSRs were cross-deployed for optimized utilization. Thus, it was particularly difficult to balance individual staff development plans and business demands, as all 'time off the phones' had an opportunity cost. In this sense development plans were a mixed blessing for team leaders, as they, in turn, were assessed on the service levels they achieved through their teams. Discussing a team member who has been seconded as a trainer, John observed:

> I bet we are going to lose her to them permanently, but for the moment I'm one person down and when numbers are down I can't get the calls answered. So do I go train someone else because she's been seconded? And at the end of the day I trained her and made her as good as she is and it's frustrating not to have her.

Although staff were relatively diverse in age and background, this was a youthful and open environment and CCB aspired to a 'can-do culture' among staff. In this regard team leaders played a key role in shaping CSR attitudes and helping CSRs reframe the negative aspects of routine work and develop upbeat coping strategies. Personal development plans were a key method. Some spoke with pride of the progressions they had made, other new entrants were motivated by the scope to increase their income and skills through their development plans. The open-plan building structure meant lots of community interaction, thus CSRs were aware of the pros and cons of different contracts and development options.

This structured employee development model is a particularly interesting packaging of LDHC. Development plans were effectively used to manage both the culture and behavioural commitment. The plans were presented to CSRs as an opportunity; however, they also strongly served CCB's wider business strategy by delivering flexibility. In reality, the development opportunities offered were fairly standard to the wider call centre community, yet they had been successfully repackaged to create an organizational focus-point. CCB risked demoralization among agents reaching the top of their tier and finding nowhere else to go. However, this must be seen in the context of a local environment with abundant call centre employment opportunities. CCB used the development plans to attract and motivate staff competitively but, the low-discretion routine structure of the work meant a steady level of turnover was absorbable. This reflects a combination of adapting to and 'living with' the problems of high-volume routine work (Callaghan and Thompson, 2002, p. 225).

LDHC by involvement: building a knowledge community at Education Line

Education Line (EL) was a young and growing national helpline providing information on training opportunities, and offering basic career guidance advice. Based in a busy city-centre office, EL was the result of a commercial tender by its parent, a charity with a long history in helpline services. This call centre differed to the previous cases because it had both social and business objectives. Its charter was to develop the participation of adults in career and learning opportunities. Reflecting this, it was committed to welfare, development and input of employees. As a publicly funded contract, it had demanding service level, ethical and development targets. Separately it had a mission to expand and develop its viability as a business. The method by which EL responded to these contrasting goals offers some insight into alternative models of call centre organizing.

Callers were assured of 'no scripts', and being listened to and helped with appropriate advice and information. This offered elements of job discretion, although call structures were used prompt dialogue, and the majority of enquiries had a structured response. Sixty per cent of calls were standard three-minute queries, the remainder averaging ten minutes. CSRs used a knowledge database and inputted demographic data on each call.

94 Tensions and Variations in Call Centre Management Strategies

The core processes at EL mirrored other call centres in relation to monitoring technology and pressure on service levels. However, EL was very clear that its primary goal was quality service provision. While this is part of the rhetoric of most call centres, EL's mandate in this regard facilitated decision-making in relation to quality/quantity and routine/discretion conflicts. While 'lost calls' were benchmarked, the normative pressure to rush calls through was explicitly resisted.

The centre was divided into teams of ten, each with their own targets and specialisms. Performance stats were managed locally within the team. Helpline co-ordinators were responsible for both the development and support of the staff's skills and knowledge, and the management of their efficient performance to quality standards. Statistics and performance targets remained important; however, monitoring largely focused on identifying training needs and caller profiles.

Staff backgrounds were intentionally diverse and EL relied on the expertise and experience of its CSRs. CSRs drew on a wide range of working knowledge including geography, fees and childcare resourcing and the full spectrum of education and career possibilities. Many staff had teaching or counselling experience, although some came from traditional call centres. EL saw the mix between these groups as synergistic. While staff had a broader-than-typical skill profile, the more distinctive feature was its deliberate strategy of enabling, utilizing and developing CSR knowledge. This contrasts with the familiar approach of containing CSR input and discretion. An express part of the job description was to 'think creatively about the service'. Despite its social ethos, this approach was driven by the business strategy:

> At the end of the day, with the subjects we deal with you can't store all that information in a database, and what you can store is really hard to keep current. So the bottom line is that we rely a lot on CSRs' own knowledge and experience.
>
> Brian, operations manager

Nonetheless routine information provision was a core part of the work, and EL had to find ways of balancing this with more open-ended activities. As the demand for its services grew, EL responded to call patterns by using a two-tier approach. All calls were answered by 'information advisors' who were qualified to handle straightforward enquires. More complex calls (about 40 per cent) were transferred to 'learning advisors', CSRs with more experience in the career guidance area. Staff were recruited as information advisors, and encouraged to build up their skill sets in order to progress to the learning advisor role. Information advisor roles mirrored national average call centre salaries, although without commission earnings, while learning advisors earned on average £2,000 more.

This segmented approach is adopted in many call centres (see Batt and Moynihan, this volume) and commonly associated with 'dumbing down' (Frenkel *et al.*, 1999, p. 273). However EL strived to minimize status differences and empower information advisors by integrating both groups, to allow shared learning. This had advantages and disadvantages, as information advisors learned to handle more complex work, but also 'sometimes tackled calls they shouldn't'. Learning advisors reverted to information line queries whenever calls were waiting.

Nonetheless, these designs presented EL with something of a cultural challenge. Like all call centres, CSRs were prone to dips in morale at times of high or very low call volume. While staff were generally very positive about their jobs, learning advisors sometimes complained that their work was monotonous compared to face-to-face work. They also tended to dislike targets and monitoring procedures. As a result, labour turnover was initially high, although many went on to applied roles in careers and education and remained useful to EL. Thus, recruitment procedures were adapted to include extensive job previewing. As Brian commented:

> We find that the majority of learning advisors are conscientious and they like helping people but there is no doubt about it, being stuck on information calls and answering the same type of calls over and over gets monotonous. It is a difficult thing, so the way we manage it is to set up a lot of other activities as well.

Creating and using opportunities for CSRs' involvement and development was a key part of EL's HCM strategy. All CSRs were involved in peer training and in working groups related to business, IT, or development. Additionally, learning advisors were given one hour a day 'off the phones' for research and preparation purposes. Finally, all staff were involved in the building and development of the live database, a massive ongoing exercise. All this serves to emphasize that relational work need not be confined to customer contact, but can also reflect a widening of the CSR's role and participation in the internal organization (Hutchinson, Purcell and Kinnie, 2000).

EL's main challenge was getting the balance right between its distinctive ethos, and being a commercial call centre. The culture it strived for

96   *Tensions and Variations in Call Centre Management Strategies*

(in contrast to Quotes Direct) was one of 'treating people as adults'. However, EL was not insulated from the tensions noted at other call centres. As a contracted service provider, the externally set targets were demanding, and did not always allow for the complexity of trade-offs between development time, business needs and service levels. Further, as part of its continued expansion, EL had begun to tender for other third-party speciality business. As it grew, EL faced the classic tensions and had to remind its empowered workers more and more that 'the numbers matter'. As Brian acknowledges:

> Yes [we] are going to have to answer a high volume of calls – otherwise some other service will do it cheaper, but if the client wants that quality there, they've got to accept trade-offs. And we have to be assertive with them about it.

Thus, while still constructed as a classic call centre, some characteristics made EL distinctive. These included a straightforward commitment philosophy and a work design that was, as far as possible, conciously enabling. This paints a picture of LDHC *by involvement*.

Discussion

The foregoing accounts have presented four cases that combine elements of both control and commitment strategies. These cases have many similarities, and also important differences. Each adopted elements of HCM, yet with varied underlying philosophies. Each has a similar work design yet differentiated approaches to its implementation. To summarize, the case of Quotes Direct suggested containment LDHC that primarily sought to absorb the problems of an intensive work environment. Shopping Direct's experience reflected an alleviation approach that strove to distract from severe routine by providing world-class facilities and matching employee lifestyles. Call Centre Bureau adopted structured employee development in order to manage employees' expectations and mould their experience of the work. Finally, Education Line offered involvement LDHC by featuring, utilizing and developing employee knowledge.

A key question arising from the cases is *why* these differentiated approaches have emerged. Each of the four call centres had different competitive contexts, both internally and externally, and their chosen or emergent LDHC reflected degrees of idiosyncratic fit (Hutchinson, Purcell and Kinnie, 1999).

For Quotes Direct, containment related to both low labour market competition and an overriding strategy of increasing market penetration. Its history of evolution from maverick start-up to major player had led to an emergent, business and HR strategy. New policies rested uneasily with earlier *ad hoc* approaches. Espoused service standards and employee commitment were easily compromised to on-floor pressures and vulnerable team leadership. Commitment in this context was a normative ideal, not a genuine aspiration (Turnbull and Wass, 1998, p. 109). Shopping Direct's emphasis on commitment was part of an integrated strategy for business renewal. SD's use of alleviation LDHC was iteratively a response to and a creation of its workforce profile, reflecting the company's dependence on – and yet, exposure due to – their particular characteristics and attributes. The size of the centre and its dependence on local labour markets meant staff retention was important. However, the starkly routine context meant that managing morale and motivation were key priorities, particularly as employees became long-serving. In part, LDHC was perceived to offer greater control over employees and potential antidotes to motivation, absenteeism and morale problems, reflecting a 'market-driven HRM' (Turnbull and Wass, 1998).

CCB's status as an outsourcing partner meant a heightened exposure to formalization and statistical control. Its LDHC strategy of structured employee development enabled an increased level of flexibility. It also offered differentiation in the context of a highly competitive local labour market. LDHC in this context was aligned with client and customer service quality, and to a degree with the needs of employees (Kinnie, Purcell and Hutchinson, 2000, p. 980).

Finally, the unique ethos of Education Line and the nature of its business made way for its approach to LDHC by involvement. Again, its recruitment policies both fed into and demanded its approach to knowledge use and involvement. Staff were orientated to development, and their management appropriately reflected this. EL was strongly influenced by its history and location within a helpline environment, providing a platform for re-imagining the call centre. However, this does not preclude the wider application of its approach.

More generally, all sites were influenced by their local employment contexts and the desire to be seen as a professional employer. A wider tendency towards strategic imitation and appropriate use of HRM language also plays a hand (Legge, 1995). Finally, actual implementation of the adopted approaches to commitment was strongly influenced by local managers, and their individual philosophies and styles were key to how these strategies were experienced.

98   Tensions and Variations in Call Centre Management Strategies

An interesting question is: what prevented more deep-reaching, comprehensive approaches to HCM? Commitment is potentially more effective, less costly and less inflexible than the traditional control model (Guest, 1992). Yet the orthodox design of the call centre is clearly rooted in a control paradigm. In simple terms, the use of commitment approaches in the call centre attempts to remedy the problems of control, by modifying that control. This does not suggest a fundamental paradigm shift (Walton, 1985).

The common theme to these cases was low discretion, routinized customer service. A variety of strategies were used to mediate its inherent tensions and conflicts. Can these conflicts be overcome? LDHC by involvement, illustrated by the Education Line case, represents the strongest prognosis, moving towards a fundamental redefinition of CSR roles, contributions and tasks.

LDHC: variations on a theme of control

While the LDHC models described here reflect actual practice among the four research sites, it is not intended that they be seen in a prescriptive light. The foregoing analysis suggests that HCM strategies *can* help offset *some* of the negative features of low-discretion work (Kinnie, Purcell and Hutchinson, 2000). However, the tensions experienced in each case indicate that low-discretion work environments can also *undermine* HCM – particularly where employees experience implementation as superficial or obstructive to their work. Further, these cases provide considerable evidence of 'leakage' of underlying control tendencies. This persistent pull to control reflects the fragility of combining control and commitment.

A key source of this leakage is the very nature of call centre work with its vulnerability to call volume pressures and highly visible, duly quantifiable performance dimensions. Call throughput and espoused behavioural targets were the dominant influences in each of the case sites, and with the exception of EL, there was a general reluctance to compromise perceived notions of efficiency for service quality or employee morale. As a result, the tensions emerging from the avoidance of this trade-off became a 'problem to be managed' (Wallace, Eagleson and Waldersee, 2000, p. 179). In this sense, these interventions present not as HCM, but as substitutes – 'low-discretion, high-commitment' strategies.

Evidence has been presented of opportunities for the use and misuse of these strategies. Much has come down to their fit with the prevailing culture and management style. At QD, they were used to ill effect when the wider mixed messages were not addressed. They were utilized at SD as a spectacular but benign cultural backdrop. At CCB, they were used to create a powerful, perhaps illusory, narrative of 'progress' and to reinforce the business priorities. They have been used at EL as an opportunity to reconceive some of the script of how a call centre can organize. In the final analysis, each case must be judged on its merits.

At their heart, LDHC approaches are underpinned by a series of conflicts: treating people as machines, while espousing that they are 'valued'; wanting control, while seeking contained initiative and flexibility; espousing an atmosphere of trust, while utilizing technologies of distrust. As a result, CSRs are left to absorb the contradictions and tensions, struggling to balance their own needs, their wish to help the customer, the customer needs, and the demands their organization places on them (Leidner, 1993; Korczynski, 2001).

Conclusion

This chapter has argued that the 'low-discretion high-commitment' model persists, although not without difficulty. It has suggested that this LDHC model can take a variety of forms. It has presented case findings from four call centres, which each reflect a different approach to LDHC. Based on these cases, a typology of LDHC approaches was proposed, reflecting the underlying assumptions of the HCM strategies adopted, and the character of the low-discretion work implementation. The four case accounts were presented to examine the realities of these LDHC strategies in action and reveal the tensions that they create.

These models and cases must ultimately be seen as piecemeal interpretations of HCM. In different measures their weaknesses and tensions have emerged. Thus, on the whole, concerns must be expressed about LDHC. However, it is clear that through it many call centres are on some level adopting broader, more humanistic HR strategies.

The LDHC typology proposed in this chapter offers a tentative platform for a more differentiated and precise analysis of contemporary HCM practices and ultimately, of their outcomes. Further research is needed to examine the performance outcomes of these various approaches, and test and potentially extend this typology based on evidence of LDHC strategies in other cases.

A final message is that the construction of call centre work as routine and low discretion masks deeper realities. There is clear evidence from field data and from the wider literature, of the increasing complexity of front-line work, even as it remains veiled in a routine, low-discretion construction (Frenkel *et al.*, 1999, p. 276; Wallace, Eagleson and Waldersee, 2000, p. 181). The persistent interpretation of customer service as production, rather than knowledge work disguises the emotional labour and discretionary work effort demanded of CSRs. A growing recognition of CSR skills in action is partially driving the field towards greater attempts to harvest CSR potential, and recover the ground lost by excessive routinization.

References

Adler, P. and B. Borys (1996) 'Two Types of Bureaucracy: Enabling and Coercive', *Administrative Science Quarterly*, 41, pp. 61–89.

Argyris, C. and D. Schon (1974) *Theory in Practice: Increasing Professional Effectiveness*, New York: Addison-Wesley.

Bain, P. and P. Taylor (2000) 'Entrapped by the "electronic panopticon"? Worker resistance in the call centre', *New Technology, Work and Employment*, 15(1), pp. 2–18.

Baldry, C., P. Bain and P. Taylor (1998) 'Bright Satanic Offices: Intensification, Control and Team Taylorism', in P. Thompson and C. Warhurst (eds), *Workplaces of the Future*, London: Macmillan.

Batt, R. (1999) 'Work organization, technology and performance in customer service and sales', *Industrial and Labour Relations Review*, 52(4), pp. 539–64.

Callaghan, G. and P. Thompson (2002) 'We Recruit Attitude: the selection and shaping of routine call centre labour', *Journal of Management Studies*, 39(2), pp. 233–54.

Cameron, D. (2000) *Good to Talk?*, London: Sage.

Deery, S., R. Iverson and J. Walsh (2002) 'Work relationships in telephone call centres: Understanding emotional exhaustion and employee withdrawal', *Journal of Management Studies*, 39(4), pp. 471–96.

Frenkel, S. J., M. Korczynski, K. Shire and M. Tam (1998) 'Beyond Bureaucracy? Work organization in call centres', *International Journal of Human Resource Management*, 9(6), pp. 957–79.

Frenkel, S., M. Korczynski, K. Shire and M. Tam (1999) *On the Front Line: Organization of work in the information economy*, Ithaca, NY: Cornell University Press.

Guest, D. E. (1992) 'Employee Commitment and Control', in J. F. Hartley and G. M. Stephenson, (eds), *Employment Relations: The Psychology of Influence and Control at Work*, Oxford: Blackwell.

Hutchinson, S., J. Purcell and N. Kinnie (2000) 'Evolving high commitment management and the experience of the RAC call centre', *Human Resource Management Journal*, 10(1), pp. 63–78.

Keenoy, T. (1990) 'HRM: A Case of the Wolf in Sheep's Clothing?', *Personnel Review*, 19(2), pp. 3–9.

Kinnie, N. (2000) 'Rules of Engagement', *People Management*, 8 June, pp. 34–8.

Kinnie, N., J. Purcell and S. Hutchinson (2000) 'Fun and Surveillance: the paradox of high commitment management in call centres', *International Journal of Human Resource Management*, 11(5), pp. 967–85.

Knights, D. and D. McCabe (1998) 'What happens when the phone goes wild? Staff, stress and spaces for escape in a BPR telephone banking work regime', *Journal of Management Studies*, 35(2), pp. 163–94.

Korczynski, M. (2001) 'The contradictions of service work: call centre as customer-oriented bureaucracy', in A. Sturdy, I. Grugulis and H. Willmott (eds), *Customer Service: Empowerment and Entrapment*, Basingstoke: Palgrave.

Legge, K. (1995) *Human Resource Management: Rhetorics and Realities*, London: Macmillan.

Leidner, R. (1993) *Fast Food, Fast Talk: Service Work and the Routinization of Everyday Life*, Berkeley: University of California Press

MacDuffie, J. P. (1995) 'Human resource bundles and manufacturing performance: Organizational logic and flexible production systems in the world auto industry', *Industrial and Labour Relations Review*, 48(2), pp. 197–221.

Pfeffer, J. (1998) *The Human Equation*, Boston: Harvard Business School Press.

Purcell, J. (1999) 'The Search for Best Practice and Best Fit in Human Resource Management: Chimera or Cul-de-Sac?', *Human Resource Management Journal*, 9(3), pp. 6–41.

Storey, J. (1992) *Developments in the Management of Human Resources*, Oxford: Blackwell.

Sturdy, A. (2001) 'Servicing Societies? – Colonisation, Control, Contradiction and Contestation', in A. Sturdy, I. Grugulis and H. Willmott (eds), *Customer Service: Empowerment and Entrapment*, Basingstoke: Palgrave.

Taylor, P. and Bain, P. (1999) ' "An assembly line in the head": work and employment relations in the call centre', *Industrial Relations Journal*, 30(4), pp. 101–17.

Taylor, S. (1998) 'Emotional labour and the new workplace', in P. Thompson and C. Warhurst (eds), *Workplaces of the Future*, London: Macmillan.

Turnbull, P. and Wass, V. (1998) 'Marksist Management: Sophisticated Human Relations in a High Street Retail Store', *Industrial Relations Journal*, 29(2), pp. 99–111.

van Maanen, J. (1979) 'The Fact of Fiction in Organizational Ethnography', *Administrative Science Quarterly*, 24, pp. 539–50.

Wallace, C. M. and G. Eagleson and R. Waldersee (2000) 'The Sacrificial HR Strategy in Call Centres', *International Journal of Service Industry Management*, 11(2), pp. 174–84.

Walton, R. E. (1985) 'Towards a Strategy of Eliciting Employee Commitment Based on Policies of Mutuality', in R. E.Walton and P. R. Lawrence (eds), *Human Resource Management, Trends and Challenges*, Boston: Harvard Business School Press.

Wood, S. (1995) 'Can We Speak of High Commitment Management on the Shop Floor?', *Journal of Management Studies*, 32(2), pp. 215–47.

5
Managing Client, Employee and Customer Relations: Constrained Strategic Choice in the Management of Human Resources in a Commercial Call Centre

Nicholas Kinnie and Jon Parsons

Introduction

Although research into call centres is growing fast most studies pay little attention to the context within which these organizations operate. This is surprising because it is essential to understand the environment of any organization if we are to explain the approach to the management of human resources (HR). The organizational context is especially important for commercial call centres which provide outsourced services for clients with whom they form relationships which vary in nature, depth and duration.[1]

This chapter draws on research in a single case to examine the influence of these clients on the management of HR and the actions that call centre managers take to manage this influence. It argues that the management of HR in these call centres can only be understood in the context of the need to be responsive to and maintain relations with clients, employees and customers. It highlights the constraints on the exercise of strategic choice in HR in organizations that form commercial relations which are of increasing importance to the economy, but have received relatively little attention.

The next section outlines the relevant research and describes the methods of data collection employed. The third section provides a detailed discussion of the case looking at the client influences and management actions. This is followed by an analysis of the competing pressures facing commercial call centre managers and a discussion of why these pressures exist. The final section examines the implications of this case for other organizations working in similar contexts.

Previous research

Although call centre research generally has paid little attention to the organizational context, Frenkel and his colleagues (1999) developed a model which identified the competing demands on the customer service representative (CSR). These are their immediate manager, their co-workers, team members and the external customer. This method of analysis is developed and extended here to take account of the different external environment. Whereas Frenkel *et al.* examined the retail customer, the focus here is, in addition, on the effect of the commercial relationships formed with clients on the management of HR.

There is a longstanding interest in the impact of external clients and customers on the management of HR. Most of these studies have been conducted in the manufacturing sector, with little attention given to the impact of clients in the service sector with the exception of Scarbrough and Kinnie (2003). Rainnie (1989) looked at small- and medium-sized enterprises and identified the dependent, dominated, isolated and innovative types and also characterized the workplace relations that were likely to be associated with each of these. McMahon (1996) noted that subcontracting reduces risks and overheads for large firms and can lead to greater stability for their own employees while supplying firms have to cope with the uncertainty leading to greater instability and more flexible working practices.

Beaumont, Hunter and Sinclair (1996) argued that customers influence the HR practices of their suppliers in two ways. Direct influence is exercised when the customer questions the suppliers about the existence and performance of various HR practices. 'The customer organization may establish an auditing instrument for its suppliers which asks a series of questions about the existence (and performance) of certain employee relations practices in the supplier organization' (1996, p. 13). These may include questions about workforce training and employee–management communications in order to be deemed a 'good supplier'. This process may be extended with the introduction of supplier development programmes where the client is seeking to have an explicit influence over how employees are managed by requiring, for example, suggestion schemes and attitude testing.

More indirectly, increased customer performance demands will often require the supplier to change their arrangements for managing HR. This influence is more common and although there may be no direct

104 *Managing Client, Employee and Customer Relations*

references to employee relations 'evidence indicates both that supplier firms use this as a basis for self-assessment with a view to upgrading performance and that the upgrading process puts a premium on employment-related issues such as training, shop floor organization and communications' (1996, pp. 13–14). Sinclair, Hunter and Beaumont (1996) discussed different types of customer–supplier relations including the demands, audit and supplier development models and concluded that 'only a minority of customer organizations has yet developed a significant concern with suppliers' HRM' (1996, p. 73). These influences have also been studied by researchers from the purchasing and supply field examining what they term as the process of vendor assessment (Lamming, 1993).

This research provides a basis for beginning to understand the influence exercised by external customers on the HR practices of their suppliers. It also contributes to the debate over whether the most effective HR practices are those which adhere to a universal model of best practice which applies in all circumstances or whether these practices need to be developed so that they achieve a close fit with the pressures in the external environment (Purcell, 1999). In order to contribute to this debate we need to know more about the particular circumstances affecting service organizations in general and commercial call centres in particular. Before this, the research methods adopted in this study will be outlined.

Research methods and setting

The research, which is part of a larger project sponsored by the Chartered Institute for Personnel and Development (CIPD),[2] was conducted between late 1999 and mid-2002 and involved the collection of data by means of semi-structured interviews with directors, senior managers and team leaders, structured interviews with CSRs and the study of secondary internal sources including two employee attitude surveys.[3] The structured interviews each lasted between 45 minutes and an hour and included around 100 questions dealing with all aspects of the management of HR, the role of line managers and employee attitudes towards their work. Some of these questions were the same as those included in the Workplace Employee Relations Survey (WERS), which allowed comparisons to be made with a nationally representative survey.[4]

Analysis of the case

The chapter now analyzes the case in detail drawing on these data. After describing the case setting it examines the direct and indirect ways in which clients seek to influence the management of HR. This is followed by a discussion of managers' actions in the case as they seek to manage relations with their clients. Particular attention is drawn to the changing interaction over time between client influence and managers' responses and initiatives. We witness a dynamic interplay between the exercise of strategic choice and the constraints on this choice.

Background to the case

Contact 24 operates two call and contact centres in Bristol and also provides a small managed service activities on two client sites.[5] It employs around 950 people in total, has an annual turnover of approximately £20 million and is part of a much larger organization. The two main call centre sites have a total of 470 seats. Historically much of Contact 24's contracts came from other parts of their parent organization, but this declined significantly during the period of the study. Most calls are inbound, although there is some outbound work and there is a facility for handling e-mails and providing customer support for client websites. Before looking at their internal organization we need to consider the external environment within which the company operates.

External environment

Outsourced call centres have a distinctive set of relationships with their clients who buy marketing and particularly contact services for a variety of reasons. In the early days of the industry much of the buying was highly reactive, for example to satisfy the need to handle a telephone response to a media campaign at a few days' notice. These relationships have evolved to the point where some clients make a strategic decision to work with their providers such as Contact 24 as an expert or partner, entrusting a large and significant portion of their customer service activity to them.

Between these extremes there are a variety of relationships. Some clients buy expertise and are more 'hands-off', either because of their mature understanding or because they do not have the resources to manage the relationship in detail. Other, larger clients will place their own staff on-site and expect, or develop, a very 'hands-on' relationship. This relationship will also change over time. Winning and losing clients, pitching, re-pitching, reviewing and renewing contracts are a constant reality for commercial call centre managers. Once awarded, new contracts take time to settle down as personal relationships become established and both parties get to know one another. The cautious client may seek to

106 *Managing Client, Employee and Customer Relations*

exercise a high level of influence to start with and gradually let this decline as the supplier builds up expertise.

Even when relationships are established there are other sources of instability. Successful clients, or clients in a panic, will introduce new projects, often at very short notice, introducing volatility into the relationship. Clients in trouble may not generate projects or will seek to take 'closer order' if they feel performance is a worry, perhaps by trying to manage costs down. The key contact person within the client may change, bringing differences of style, emphasis or priority and even the threat of losing the account. The renegotiation of a contract brings opportunities for change in contract terms or the nature of the work itself. In view of these multiple sources of instability in their commercial relationships Contact 24 has devoted a great deal of time to understanding the needs and behaviour of each of their clients.

Contact 24, like many other call centres faces a local labour market which is highly competitive and volatile. Following the recent explosion in employment in this industry there are very low levels of unemployment in the area (1.7 per cent) and over 70 other call centres operating in the city, many of which are in-house. The workforce is typical of many call centres in that it is young (just over half our interviewees were under 30) and fast moving (approximately a half had been in their job for less than a year). The internal surveys told a similar story, only 18 per cent of the respondents had more than two years' service. Some have a transient relationship with their employer, lacking a sense of career and take advantage of the reputation of the industry for employment of temporary, agency and student workers. This, together with the particular pressures of the work and the working environment, results in higher levels of attrition than those experienced by many industries.

Internal organization

The company provides call and contact centre activities for around 25 clients in a variety of industries and services. There are broadly two types of client contracts. Longer contracts with larger clients tend to be over two to three years and often include work where the aim is to build up long-term relationships with customers involving repeat purchases or a range of related products. For these contracts project teams of CSRs, up to 200 people, are set up dedicated to that client. Typically they are managed by a senior operations manager, with a customer services manager and team leaders providing the day-to-day line management. The CSRs will spend all of their working day taking calls from customers on behalf of their client. These calls will vary from operating a customer care line giving advice on the use of products to taking orders for telephone shopping and handling complaints from customers.

The second type of client has smaller and shorter contracts, perhaps lasting only a few weeks or even days. These contracts are handled in the bureau section and involve short, high-volume calls including dealing with data capture and handling brochure requests, for example in response to advertising campaigns. Around 30 people work in the bureau and typically each CSR will be taking calls for five clients at any one time.

The HR department is headed up by an HR director who is on the main board of the company. She has six staff reporting to her including a HR manager, an HR officer, two HR advisors and two HR administrators.

Following our discussion of the external environment and internal organization we now turn our attention to the direct and indirect influences of the client on call centre management.

Direct client influences

The different types of clients exercise a varying influence on the HR practices of Contact 24, so we will look first at the influence of these larger clients and then consider the smaller clients.

The client influences are particularly strong within the dedicated project teams. Here the client often wants managers and employees to identify strongly with their own brand and they will go to some lengths to ensure that the customer cannot tell they are not speaking to the client's own direct employees. Employees are encouraged to identify strongly with the client's customers and they may identify less strongly with their own employer.

Partly in order to achieve this level of identification the client may seek to influence the HR practices of Contact 24 and the managers and employees working on their account in a variety of ways. Clients exert considerable influence on the client service and operational management structure and through them they affect the CSRs working on their account.

This influence may be overt, with clients 'interviewing' Contact 24 proposed managers or, more often, affecting who stays and who leaves the account. In turn this can influence the attitudes of those, predominantly young managers, who might find themselves 'in the sun' for a year or two, securing above average pay rises or faster career progression because of their favourable relationship with the client, making internal moves more difficult. Discussions on individual client line-ups in marketing agencies and call centres often take up much time at board level and the

108 *Managing Client, Employee and Customer Relations*

effect of these tensions could be to place stress on the assessment of performance and the management of succession and careers. On the downside, there would be instances where the client would want a particular employee 'off the account' sometimes for genuine and objective reasons of suitability or performance, sometimes for subjective reasons, causing pressure on the company's aim of being perceived as a good and fair employer.

Clients also seek to have a direct influence on employees working on their account. Before November 2001 the most direct HR influence was on CSR pay which some clients negotiated as part of their contract with Contact 24. In an attempt to attract the best CSRs some clients were prepared to pay a premium over and above the standard rate paid by the company. Consequently CSRs working for different clients could be paid different basic rates (varying by between 10 per cent and 20 per cent) for doing very similar jobs. CSRs working for different clients also got incentives or gifts in kind to try to increase their loyalty to the client. Although this meant that some employees were being paid different rates of pay for doing essentially the same job depending on which client they worked for, this did not seem to have a major influence on the attitudes of our interviewees towards pay. Just under half were either very satisfied or satisfied with their pay in the second year, compared with a third for the WERS sub-sample of clerical and sales employees, and just over half were satisfied with their pay compared with the pay of others in the second year, although this had declined from two-thirds in the first year. The reasons for this are probably linked to the team-based reference point adopted by the CSRs which we discuss in greater detail below.

Clients also influence the recruitment and selection of CSRs by jointly defining with Contact 24 the skill sets needed and by becoming involved in the selection of employees especially at the start of a contract. They also fund training conducted by Contact 24 concerned with the client's products or carry out training themselves either on the Contact 24 site or their own premises. This is designed to ensure that not only do employees have the appropriate knowledge but also that they identify strongly with the brand. This is reinforced by performance management activities organized by the client which involve running competitions and awarding prizes for Contact 24 employees. Eighty per cent of respondents in the internal survey said that their team was focused on customer needs.

The consequences of these client actions can be seen in the employee attitudes towards Contact 24. Employees demonstrated low levels of loyalty and pride towards the company. In both years only around a half of employees interviewed said they felt loyal to Contact 24 compared with the WERS sub-sample of 65 per cent for clerical employees and 82 per cent for sales. Similarly, the internal survey in October 2002 found that only around a half of all employees (42 per cent of CSRs) were proud to work for Contact 24 which is below the national figures for clerical (55 per cent) and sales (82 per cent). Approximately a half of all employees in this survey and a third of CSRs said they were aware of the company vision and knew Contact 24's business objectives.

The internal management structures and work organization (apart from the bureau) are based on teams focused on the clients. So although loyalty to and identification with the organization is weak, the team identity is much stronger. The company attitude surveys found that 84 per cent of all employees (70 per cent of CSRs) said they had a clear understanding of the team's objectives. Similarly, around three-quarters of our respondents felt the sense of team working to be either strong or very strong in both years and in year two 89 per cent felt that teamworking was quite or very effective in encouraging them to improve their performance and nine out of ten felt that the team shared knowledge.

The internal structures and movement of staff are influenced as contracts are won and lost. As one senior manager said, 'We have to have a flexible structure because the business comes and goes.' The ebb and flow of staff might be at very short notice or over longer periods as contracts, or smaller projects within contracts, are awarded or renegotiated and staff are moved from one client to another. This can cause problems in matching supply and demand because CSR skills and knowledge can be very client-specific. Moreover, the client may intervene directly to ask for CSRs to be moved into or out of their project team, usually on the basis of customer feedback. One manager said, 'the main contact with the client thinks he knows how to manage people. He comes up with different ideas for motivating people and for incentives.' According to one director, 'we try to minimize this, but the client often feels, "these are my people"'.

Multiple clients

The complexity of the situation is intensified when there are a number of clients being served by the same group of employees. The impact of operational pressures is very typical in the bureau where the work is often very short term and transactional and difficult to predict and can lead to greater use of agency and part-time working.

110 *Managing Client, Employee and Customer Relations*

The influence of the client may be felt in the bureau as part of the contract pricing which is based on the number or the length of calls and, according to one manager, 'if we don't work, we don't get paid'. This tends to exaggerate the pressures felt in the dedicated teams especially for certain types of work, for example direct response to TV advertising where the demand may be short, intense and difficult to predict. Indeed, the task of matching fluctuating supply and demand for multiple clients presents managers with a formidable challenge.

Managers here are right at the boundary between their clients, the client's customers and their employees. They are seeking to balance the service levels agreed with the client, with the costs of providing that service, with the numbers of employees and the mix of skills available. The trick being to balance these demands so that they hit their service levels and their internal productivity level targets and in the words of one senior manager 'if you want service up, then productivity goes down, the trick is to keep all the balls in the air. This is the Holy Grail of the bureau.'

Parent influence versus client influence

As we have mentioned Contact 24 can obtain work through two routes: indirectly through the parent organization or directly from their own new business. In the period of study, a particular feature of the company was the changing relationship it experienced with its parent organization.

Where contracts are gained via the parent organization this adds a further consideration because the parent may have negotiated the contract and there will be a director who may deal more directly with the client. Indeed, historically Contact 24 managers may have had little contact with the client until it comes to operating the contract and they may then find that promises have been made by the parent that are difficult to keep. This had a consequent impact on the potential profit margin, productivity expectations and the number type, duration and complexity of calls. The source data, for example names and addresses of retail customers, upon which Contact 24 must rely may well be of dubious quality.

A key feature of Contact 24's strategy is to go out and find its own work directly and the sales side of the business has been successful in increasing the percentage of their 'own' work. This work may, for example, be in the evenings to use equipment that would otherwise be idle and hence can be provided at low marginal cost. However, this can produce various problems resulting from a clash between in-house and out-house demands. The in-house work given to Contact 24 may not fit their skills, for example it may be that the contract requires multilingual CSRs who have a good knowledge of a particular industry sector but Contact 24 has few of these and knows they are difficult to recruit. It may be important but relatively low-value work or may have a very low margin for the call centre part of the contract, whereas work which it gains itself may be higher value and more suited to their CSRs' skills. This might lead to demotivation among staff and an increase in labour turnover. Hence the company may come under pressure to fulfil the parent contract, but is also charged with achieving its own financial performance targets and, as we have seen, the imperatives for the client and resultant pressures will change over time. This need to balance supply and demand and to achieve their own targets can mean that the company takes on 'sub-optimal' work which is unsuited to the skills or perceptions of their CSRs, possibly resulting in increased labour turnover as good employees feel they can find more interesting work elsewhere.

Perhaps more importantly, the demands of the parent's high-profile blue chip companies may clash with the work for Contact 24's own clients which is high value and high margin. The needs of the parent's client may have preference over those of their own clients which can lead to tensions. One consequence of this is that staff may be poached internally. Moreover, if things go wrong with contracts for the parent's clients then Contact 24 tends to get the blame because they cannot always respond quickly.

Indirect client influences

In addition to the direct influences on HR practices there are indirect influences associated with the award and management of contracts. The winning and losing of contracts and changes of clients' preferences during the length of the contracts produces a dynamic and unpredictable working environment for call centre managers. There are, in effect, a whole series of contract life cycles within the organization, many of them at different points. Particular instability is associated with the early period of a contract, and this then settles down as the relationship matures only to become more uncertain when the contract is up for renewal or there are opportunities for additional work to be won. Even during relatively stable periods there are still many opportunities for the client to alter their strategy.

Contracts

The type of contract negotiated will have an indirect influence on HR practices. Perhaps the most extreme difference in the nature of the work

112 *Managing Client, Employee and Customer Relations*

awarded in commercial call centres lies between inbound service and outbound sales calls. Outbound sales contracts are associated with higher pressures and tend to attract employees who are skilled at and confident with calling customers at home and applying sales techniques to them. This work will typically have incentives linked to conversion rates, for example calls to sales, or the achievement of pre-set targets. Inbound work attracts employees who are more comfortable when responding to customer requests or in dealing with complaints. Such work tends to have fixed rates of pay but demands close adherence to performance and service-quality levels set by the client. In short, the skill sets and attitudes of these two groups of employees are often quite different and many employees are quite unwilling to move between these types of work.

Contracts vary significantly in their length between a few days to two to three years. The very short contracts of perhaps a few weeks or even days to handle the response to an advertising campaign are typically dealt with by temporary or agency staff while the longer contracts tend to be handled by the more experienced staff. Sometimes these contracts are agreed with very little notice, possibly only six days, which can create very short-term problems of recruitment, selection and training. They also vary in their pricing terms and performance targets.

In some contracts Contact 24 will agree to provide a set number of dedicated staff at a fixed fee per call centre seat. This is usually supplemented by a service-level agreement (SLA) with rewards and penalties attached to the achievement of set targets, for example, 80 per cent of calls to be answered in 20 seconds and an abandoned call level not exceeding 5 per cent. Alternatively a transaction pricing model will be used where payment is based on CSR activity, for example on the number of calls or e-mails handled, rather than the number of hours worked on the account. Key performance indicators will reflect this and are likely to include targets for calls and sales. These contract characteristics influence the types of employees selected and the training and development practices, for example employees on transaction pricing contracts need to be performance- and sales-orientated.

Performance monitoring and client contact

Performance against the SLA is often monitored daily by e-mail and, although clients vary, it is clearly important to achieve these targets. In an extreme case the client might terminate the contract if performance was unacceptable. Contact with the client is usually frequent and takes various forms. Formal meetings will be held with managers, typically on a fortnightly basis, to review progress and to make changes. In addition, the client might be physically present on the Contact 24 site where contact can be with employees at all levels including CSRs. Indeed, the client, especially the larger clients, may be very keen to influence the employees chosen to work on the telephones as we have seen. This close working relationship results in improved service to and good support from the client. As one senior manager said, 'We are in partnership with [this client]. It has its advantages because they can see the problems we face on a day-to-day basis, but it also has its drawbacks. It's very transparent, we can't hide, it's very visible.'

Changes in client strategy

Contact 24 has to respond to changes made to the strategy and tactics of the client and this can have a big impact on HR practices. For example a change of strategy might involve a move away from making outbound telephone calls to greater use of alternative channels such as a direct sales force. Thus, while there are fewer outbound sales calls there will be an increase in inbound calls dealing with recent new customers and existing customers. This can have an indirect impact on CSRs, such as a reduction in the level of commission payments. The actions of the client, and more importantly the client's customers can have an immediate effect on the number and types of calls to be handled. This presents particular problems to managers in Contact 24 as they seek to match the supply of staff and the demand from customers which can vary considerably over very short periods of time.

Some of this work is easily substitutable whereas other work is not. Typically, higher-value work is unique to that client while the lower-value work tends to be moved more easily between suppliers. More generally, the nature of the work for the client may fluctuate over time. Some of this is very seasonal and may be arranged at very short notice.

How does Contact 24 seek to manage this client influence?

Although the company finds itself facing a series of potentially strong clients it seeks to manage their influence in different ways. Even in such a client-driven organization managers exercise some control by seeking to manage the boundaries with their clients. One director said they try and resist the influence of buyers, 'The buyers can't own the employees.'

Some of these actions were already in place when the research commenced, but others emerged during the period of the research demonstrating the dynamic interplay between client actions and the company's

114 *Managing Client, Employee and Customer Relations*

reactions and initiatives. These changes tended to be associated with the renegotiation of commercial contracts and the acquisition of new business. As contracts were renewed or new clients were gained contract terms were negotiated and project teams had to be set up producing a period of volatility as the immediate context for the management of HR for the group of employees concerned was defined.

Managing the direct influence: HR strategy and policies

Changes were made to both the employment model and to HR policies with the aim of improving both employee loyalty and flexibility. In the early stages of the research Contact 24 was using a flexible employment model designed to respond to the varying demands of their clients and their customers. One senior manager said at the time, 'whatever relationships we have with our clients dictates the relationship we have with our employees'. Short-term contracts with clients used a combination of permanent and employment agency employees because often this work was transactional and few relationship-building skills were needed. Longer outsourced contracts were typically staffed by more experienced employees who understood the client's brand values and were good at relationship-building. The aim was to transfer the high-performing employment agency workers to direct, permanent employment.

For about nine months between late 2000 and mid-2001 the company subcontracted their recruitment mainly to an agency to reduce their costs. This, however, proved to be only partially successful because employees were being recruited by an agency and then employed immediately onto a client team and had little involvement with Contact 24 as their employer. The benefit of being able to release these employees quickly was outweighed by the very high attrition (reaching the equivalent of 70 per cent per annum in some cases), an unwillingness to move between teams and the lack of loyalty displayed.

Two key changes were made. First, in a move designed to reduce turnover and increase commitment, the number of agency workers has been substantially reduced (it had been as high as 35 per cent of total staff) and all new staff are now employed by Contact 24 on the company's terms and conditions of employment. Second, Contact 24 managers now recruit staff themselves rather than using the agency, allowing them to maintain a holding pool of people who can be employed at short notice and to be more selective over who is recruited. In response to their employee attitude survey they reinstated the induction programme to improve employees' identification with the company as a whole rather than just the client team. The internal attitude surveys in February and October 2002 revealed an increase in employees saying they were aware of the Contact 24 vision (41 per cent to 51 per cent) and that they had knowledge of the company's business objectives (46 per cent to 52 per cent).

These changes coincided with an attempt to improve the mobility of staff between project teams because it was recognized that the strong boundaries between them was a source of inflexibility and inefficiency. Staff specifically recruited to meet the needs of one client were found not to have the skills needed by other clients. If the contract came to an end these staff might have to be made redundant or they were reluctant to move to teams with shortages.

Changes were also made to the pay system and structure to encourage employee mobility and loyalty. As we have discussed, the standard HR policies in Contact 24 are under pressure from the demands made by clients and there is a danger that two sets of policies will emerge leading to a situation described early in the research by one manager as 'there is the Contact 24 way and the client's way'. Perhaps the most sensitive area here is pay where, as we have seen, employees effectively doing the same work could be paid up to 20 per cent more if they worked for a particular client. If left unattended, this could create problems of inconsistency and unfairness and inhibit the movement of staff because there was little incentive for employees to move from one team to another if they were going to be paid less for doing the same work.

In response to this problem Contact 24 managers decided to revise the pay structure and system in November 2001. First, a new competency-based structure was introduced to grade the jobs of all CSRs irrespective of the client they worked for. Second, each employee was to be appraised by their team leader and awarded increments based on their performance forming the basis for career progression within the call centre workforce. These moves to increase flexibility were strongly supported by changes made to the business model which has an indirect effect on HR practices.

Managing the indirect influence

Contact 24 has sought to manage the indirect influences on HR practices by making changes to both its business strategy and structure. Perhaps the most important way is as a result of the business strategy of trying to minimize the risk and uncertainty in the business by having a mix of types of contracts. Ideally, Contact 24 will have a series of stable long-term high-margin contracts dedicated to large clients which will form the basis of the call centre. In addition to this they will have shorter

116 *Managing Client, Employee and Customer Relations*

contracts which are typically more unstable and difficult to predict. Over the last few years the company has been able to reduce its dependence on these short-term contracts. Contact 24 managers deliberately seek to convert the clients that come into the bureau into more dedicated contracts. They might take on a very short, small piece of work, in the hope that they can create a good impression with the client so that they will be able to grow the business and gain new contracts. One way of doing this which emerged during the research was the practice of transferring experienced and capable employees on to new contracts and filling the gaps left in existing teams with new employees.

Perhaps the most significant way of increasing employee flexibility arose from the renegotiation of the contract with the largest client. Up until 2001 this contract had involved Contact 24 supplying a set number of dedicated staff at a fixed price per seat within the terms of the SLA. The advantage of this for Contact 24 was they had a guaranteed revenue stream while the client had their own dedicated team. The new contract in 2001 involved moving to a transaction pricing model which put the onus on good staff rostering and making productivity improvements. It also offered potentially lower costs for the client and an improved margin for Contact 24. In theory this allowed the company to use their employees on other teams to match demand because they were not tied exclusively to this client. This movement of staff was designed to smooth out the peaks and troughs across the company as a whole and to encourage staff to see themselves as Contact 24 employees and not those of the client.

Another way Contact 24 managers can exercise influence is by making sure they have a mix of inbound and outbound work. Inbound work is difficult to manage because it is unpredictable and the demand is mostly outside their control. Outbound calls are more under their control and can be staffed by employees working short evening shifts when cost-effective use can be made of equipment. According to one director, 'We get back the control which we lost to the client when we were driven by someone else.'

Contact 24 has also recently made some changes to its internal structure in order to manage better its client relations. Until January 2001 clients tended to have direct access to operational managers which meant they were effectively doing three jobs: managing the client relations, managing the employees and looking for ways to grow the business. In essence they were at the focal point of the pressures from these different sources and were difficult to replace because of the combination of skills involved. Consequently changes were made so that by the end of the research period the client relationship was managed by a series of specialist senior managers whose task was to stay in close contact with the client, to review current performance, take action as appropriate and plan for future changes. Internal operational management was handled separately by line managers with team leaders reporting to them.

The cyclical nature of contracts means that Contact 24 managers seek to develop their own expertise in managing call centres and will use this maturing relationship to try to influence clients. This may be quite difficult at the beginning of a dedicated contract where all parties are new to the business and arrangements are settling down. However, as the contract proceeds managers will develop an expertise as they gain experience. Some clients want the company to take the lead because they do not have sufficient experience themselves; as one manager said, 'Now that things are set up they value our experience, we are not being driven by them. They have always been reasonably easy clients to deal with; they say, "you're the experts".' In effect they are trying to educate the client. According to one manager:

> Service costs money. I wonder if they know what it means to raise the service level from 80–90 per cent – this is a massive increase in cost. We really need to ask our client – what do your people, your customers, actually want? It may be that the clients are asking for service levels that their customers do not want.

Contact 24 made changes to its business and employment strategy during the period studied to achieve, according to one director, 'a balancing act of keeping the client happy and doing the right things for staff'. They are trying to create a synergy between their branding in the product market and in the internal and external labour markets. Contact 24 are seeking to develop a culture which is both attractive to clients and to employees, to be 'The first choice provider and employer in the strategic customer contact marketplace.' This is in an environment where there are pressures, which, if allowed to go unchecked, would create inconsistency in HR practice and fragment the company culture. In essence, they are seeking to make the client, employee and Contact 24 requirements complement one another. A strong company culture, if it can be developed, would have advantages in the external labour market and have value when pitching for new business.

Discussion: balancing client, employee and other customer relations

The analysis has revealed that the HR practices adopted by Contact 24 are affected by both the direct and indirect influences of its clients and by the attempts made internally by managers to control these influences. The combined effect of these pressures is to create a tension between the objectives of clients and the wishes of Contact 24 managers to manage their relations with their employees. Clients are ideally looking for suppliers who are responsive and flexible, who are able to deliver the service that they are paying for reliably and on target. Their emphasis is on the project team working for them and their ability to deliver results, especially meeting the terms of their service-level agreement. Suppliers, like Contact 24, on the other hand, are looking to gain some control over their clients, to be able to predict and forecast demand and to achieve the internal targets that they have been set. They are concerned to achieve some consistency, particularly over the interpretation of their own HR policies and practices.

There are two questions which are now central to our discussion: what are the consequences of these conflicting tensions for the management of HR? Why do these tensions exist? Before we can answer the first of these questions we need to look a little more closely at the nature of the relationship that Contact 24 has with its clients.

Although attention has been drawn to the influence of clients on HR practices, the situation is complicated because there is not one, but a number of clients, and, moreover, these clients may not always want the same things and what they want to do changes. This makes the task of managing client relationships much more difficult because not only is there a tension between internal and external pressures, but there is also a potential conflict between different types of external demands. We have to recognize the importance of multiple client relationships.

The desire to serve clients by shaping HR practices to meet their needs can cause inconsistencies within the organization. Although these were most clearly seen when pay rates were linked to the client they were present more subtly in the varying ways in which employees are treated including key issues such as the relative intensity of their jobs, their level of monitoring and the pace of work. This is also shown in the perspectives adopted by different managers. HR managers will be looking to develop common policies which are applied consistently, while operational line managers, with a demanding client to keep happy, may be tempted not only to vary the formal policy but also to change the way in which these policies are implemented.

Differing demands of clients will create not only a clash with internal policies but they may also conflict with one another. Dedicated teams involve investment in recruitment, selection and training and development to create a high level of knowledge and brand awareness. Sometimes this will be paid for by the client but in other cases it will not be. Not only does Contact 24 have to bear some of these costs but it can also create inflexibility, for example when moving employees from one project to another, making it difficult to respond quickly to client demands because it may take up to two weeks or longer to fully train CSRs. The level of specialist knowledge required is such that temporary agency workers cannot be used to work on the account. The situation is not completely straightforward even when the demands of clients are very similar because there may be an acute shortage of employees who have the skills which are most sought after. Thus, CSRs who have good outbound sales skills may be moved from one account to another, perhaps to the detriment of their own development. Indeed, there may be internal disagreements between managers who are adopting solely a project-focused outlook while others are taking a company-wide perspective.

Effectively we are witnessing the combination of centrifugal forces instigated by the clients which, if allowed to go unchecked, could effectively pull the organization apart and centripetal forces which are created by Contact 24 managers who are trying to maintain the integrity of the organization and its practices. This combination of forces is not simply dependent on external clients, because in the period under examination account also has to be taken of whether the contract has come from inside another part of the organization or whether it is the result of a direct sale from outside. This may lead to a tension between managers responsible for delivering relatively low-value contracts, which are themselves part of much bigger contracts for the parent company as a whole for high-profile clients, and those looking after contracts which are dedicated to Contact 24 and are of much higher value.

Despite all these forces it has been shown that managers in Contact 24 are not simply at the mercy of external clients. They work hard to gain control and reduce uncertainty by making changes to their business and HR strategy. They seek to establish a base of long-term, high-value, high-quality contracts that give them a guaranteed income which, in theory, allows them to turn down inappropriate short-term contracts. They try to increase employee mobility by changing the pricing terms

120 *Managing Client, Employee and Customer Relations*

when renegotiating contracts and seek to develop expertise so they have interdependent rather than dependent relations with their clients. They also try to broaden the range and complexity of services offered to become an indispensable part of the client's business. The company developed and then modified a flexible employment model and changed their pay policies to mitigate some of the client influence over their employees. In essence Contact 24 is attempting to manage the tensions it faces by attracting long-term stable clients who have customers who require relational services and who are dealt with by CSRs who are well treated and managed.

The key task now is to explain the pattern of influences on the management of HR in Contact 24. In order to do this we need to look more closely at the product and labour market contexts of the company.

In the ideal situation, Contact 24 provides a high-value added-service to their clients which closely meets their needs in a cost-effective way. This is a well-defined niche and when it works it can be very profitable for both Contact 24 and for the clients who would not be able to provide this kind of service at this cost internally with this level of flexibility. Their clients are seeking to minimize the employment risk associated with the fluctuations in demand over the very short term and the uncertainties in the labour market but at the same time encouraging CSRs to provide a high-quality service and to identify with them.

As we have seen there are clear consequences of this business model for the management of HR within Contact 24. However, Contact 24 not only has to manage the client relationships, it also has to manage relationships with the retail customers. It is their CSRs who are in direct contact with the retail customers, and these relationships have to be managed successfully if the company is to satisfy its clients. Moreover, these customers are the customers of the client rather than of Contact 24. It is hardly a surprise, therefore, that the clients seek to exercise influence over the CSRs. They know that the performance and attitudes of the CSRs have a critical effect on their customers and these customers have a direct effect on the performance of the client itself, or at least a section of the client. They are looking for the CSRs to display the commitment they would expect from their own employees without actually having the risk of employing them directly. There are times, especially when dealing with complaints, that the CSRs are protecting the image of the client and, even though they do not work for them, the clients are expecting the CSRs to display a high degree of loyalty to the brand. In effect, the clients are contracting with the CSRs and the team of which they are apart, rather than with Contact 24 as a whole.

The company not only has to balance the demands of the clients and customers, it also has to pay attention to the integrity of their HR policies and the needs of their own employees. It is essential that they are able to recruit and retain the employees who have the essential mix of skill and knowledge to enable them to meet the needs of their clients and their customers. Consequently, they have to pay attention not only to the HR policies themselves, but also to how these are actually put into operation by line managers who feel the pressure of the client most intensely. In addition, they need to look at the broader issues of work design and career prospects for their employees. Moreover, all this takes place within the context of a very tight labour market where unemployment is low, attrition is high and alternative call centre employment opportunities are plentiful. Movement between firms is relatively easy because there are some generic call centre skills and the level of product knowledge required is relatively low for most jobs, perhaps requiring only a few days' training and, as we have said, a significant proportion of the call centre workforce is transient.

Managers in Contact 24 are caught between a labour market that is competitive and susceptible to competitor actions, a product market where clients are seeking to manage the employees on their behalf and a set of customers who usually have high service expectations. They know that one way to solve this problem to attract and keep clients whose work is not only high margin but also is high value added, producing interesting work for the CSRs. If they can get this right then they can develop a virtuous circle of keeping both employees and clients happy.

However, there are times when Contact 24 cannot get the balance right and it is unable to obtain the level of business required from long-term contracts with dedicated clients. Consequently, they then have to take on work that is not necessarily ideal. This may be low-skill, low-value work, outbound sales, or even higher-value work at a lower margin, perhaps dependent on a poor-quality client database. They take on this work because they have their own internal financial targets to meet or they have directly employed staff who do not have enough work to do. This can have negative consequences for employees, for example, those who have got used to a particular type of work, who identify with a client, or are simply settled within a team. The practical impact of the volatility in the marketplace for a CSR means major changes to the people they work with and who manage them, the client they work for and the skills they need to carry out the work. Some may enjoy this and stay, others will find this disruptive and unsettling and will leave as the volatility in

122 *Managing Client, Employee and Customer Relations*

the marketplace is communicated to the shop floor. Thus, the organization may lose a valuable resource because of the changing type of work they are forced to take on in order to balance the books thus weakening their chances of winning back the best work.

We have seen that managers in Contact 24 are frequently seeking to balance conflicting demands. They are not simply reconciling the varying demands of external clients and their customers against their own internal polices, but they are also, with greater difficulty, managing the conflicting demands of their own internal targets and the needs of their employees. From a different perspective CSRs find themselves at the interface of combined pressures where they have to provide a service to customers, defend and promote the interests of the client, try to hit their own targets and consider their own interests.

If we step back from the detail of the case we can identify a generic model which maps out these influences. We referred to the model developed by Frenkel *et al.* (1999) in the introduction as being one of the few that adopted an analytical approach to the pressures facing CSRs. We argue that another model is needed to identify the pressures that managers of call centres face and which influence the way they manage HR. Figure 5.1 identifies the importance of client, employee and customer relations. This model is not only two way but it is also dynamic. Although Contact 24 is influenced by and seeks to influence the three parties the importance of these will change over time. For example, at the beginning of a contract the client will exercise a strong influence, but as the relationship matures and the two parties get used to one another then Contact 24 will be able to exercise more influence. Similarly, employee influence will fluctuate depending on the state of the local labour market and the mix of skills and rewards from particular clients, projects or types of work. The demands made by customers will change depending on the nature of the product or service offered. Contact 24 managers therefore have to sensitize themselves to take account of changes in these potentially volatile influences and establish an appropriate balance in their HR policies between stability and responsiveness to these external influences.

Conclusion

We have seen that there are elements of strategic choice exercised by managers in Contact 24 but that this is constrained by the varying demands that their clients make upon them. Indeed, the company

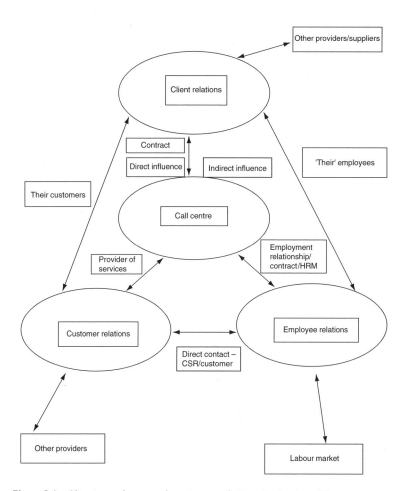

Figure 5.1 Client, employee and customer relations in Contact 24

illustrates some of the problems of achieving a 'best-fit' when the pressures in the external environment are complex and fast changing. One consequence of this approach is that managers are almost constantly trying to match the demands an external environment made up of clients who may want different things and the danger is that they will pull the organization apart when trying to respond to these pressures (Scarbrough and Kinnie, 2003). This situation has parallels with the small and medium-sized enterprize research examined earlier in this chapter where a small number of clients have a big influence over HR practices.

124 *Managing Client, Employee and Customer Relations*

However, there are two important differences in the situation discussed here compared with manufacturing industry.

First, although as in manufacturing volatility is introduced as contracts are won and lost one difference in this sector is that the services provided are intangible and perishable. Consequently the normal fluctuations associated with stages of the contract life cycle are exaggerated because the client influences can be immediate, short term and intense to solve a particular problem or react to a competitor's action. Second, the external influence is more than simply responding to the demands of a small number of clients because Contact 24 also have to satisfy the demands of the customers whom they serve on a daily basis.

This suggests it is necessary to develop an idea put forward elsewhere (Kinnie *et al.*, 1999) which argued that the HR practices of small and medium-sized manufacturing organizations are shaped by the client rather than being driven by customers in the marketplace. In the organizational context of the commercial call centre this is a false dichotomy, because HR practices in Contact 24 are strongly influenced by *both* their clients *and* their retail customers who make up the market. Moreover, strategic choice over HR practices is constrained not only by both clients and customers, but also by the internal and external labour market, the interests of employees and the need to achieve internal targets. The impact of external relations on internal relations in fact turns out to be much more important when we are looking at a service environment in which employees are in contact with customers for long periods especially when those customers are customers of the client.

Our analysis presents a much more dynamic and volatile interplay between clients, employees and customers than that found in the manufacturing sector where the influences are less immediate, where there are more buffers between the company and its markets and the company as a whole may be at one stage in the growth cycle (Boxall and Purcell, 2003). This case therefore draws attention to contexts shaping the management of HR which are quite different to those encountered by more slowly moving organizations that face mass customer markets where the influence of clients is much less or even absent. However, this fast-changing and unpredictable context is likely to be found in other parts of the service sector where commercial relationships predominate. Indeed, the situation discussed here is likely to become more widespread as customer-facing service work and subcontracting become increasingly common features of employment.

Notes

1. Commercial relations refer to the situation where one business makes a formal contract for the supply of goods or services with another business or part of that business. These businesses are referred to as clients to distinguish them from retail customers with whom their employees interact. These contracts will be re-negotiated periodically and may be extended by the award of additional contracts for particular projects. Many call centres have evolved into contact centres because they communicate with customers by a variety of media including the telephone, e-mail and websites. The emphasis in this chapter is on telephone communications hence the use of the phrase call centre.
2. This case was part of a wider study funded by the Chartered Institute for Personnel and Development looking at the links between people management and organizational performance; other members of the team were John Purcell, Sue Hutchinson, Bruce Rayton and Juani Swart. See J. Purcell *et al.* (2003).
3. Eleven directors, senior managers and team leaders were interviewed. Interviews with CSRs concentrated on four teams and were carried out on two occasions approximately a year apart, the first round with 32 CSRs in 2000 and the second with 40 CSRs (including 23 who had been interviewed on the first occasion) in 2001. The internal employee attitude surveys of all employees were carried out in February and October 2002 with response rates of around 60 per cent. The authors would like to thank the directors, managers and employees of Contact 24 for their high level of assistance when carrying out this case study, especially Laurie Jeffrey and Rachel Shimeld.
4. The WERS data quoted here refers to a sub-sample of the complete dataset covering employees working in the clerical and sales roles in the business services sector.
5. The managed service operation is of increasing importance and raises a number of important HR issues, but discussion of this has been omitted to reduce the length of the chapter.

References

Batt, R. (1999) 'Work organization, technology and performance in customer service and sales', *Industrial and Labour Relations Review*, 52(4), pp. 539–64.

Beaumont, P. B., L. C. Hunter and D. Sinclair (1996) 'Customer–supplier relations and the diffusion of employee relations changes', *Employee Relations*, 18(1), pp. 9–19.

Boxall, P. and J. Purcell (2003) *Strategy and Human Resource Management*, Basingstoke: Palgrave.

Callaghan, G. and P. Thompson (2001) 'Edwards revisited: technical control and call centres', *Economic and Industrial Democracy*, 22(1), pp. 13–37.

Fernie, S. and D. Metcalf (1998) '(Not) Hanging on the Telephone: payment systems in the new sweatshops', Discussion Paper no. 390, centre for economic performance.

Frenkel, S., M. Korczynski, K. Shire, and M. Tam, (1998) 'Beyond Bureaucracy? Work organization in Call Centres', *International Journal of Human Resource Management*, 9(6), pp. 957–79.

126 Managing Client, Employee and Customer Relations

Frenkel, S., M. Korczynski, K. Shire, and M. Tam, (1999) *On the Front Line: Organization of work in the information economy*, Ithaca, NY: Cornell University Press.

Hutchinson, S., J. Purcell, and N. Kinnie, (2000) 'Evolving high commitment management and the experience of the RAC call centre', *Human Resource Management Journal*, 10(1), pp. 63–78.

Kinnie, N., J. Purcell and S. Hutchinson (2000a) 'Fun and surveillance: the paradox of high commitment management in call centres *International Journal of Human Resource Management*, 11(5), pp. 967–85.

Kinnie, N., J. Purcell and S. Hutchinson (2000b) 'Managing the Employment Relationship in Telephone Call Centres', in K. Purcell (ed.), *Changing Boundaries in Employment*, Bristol: Bristol Academic Press, pp. 133 –59.

Kinnie, N. J., J. Purcell, S. Hutchinson, M. Terry, M. Collinson and H. Scarbrough (1999) 'Employment Relations in SMEs: market-driven or customer-shaped?', *Employee Relations*, 22(3), pp. 218–36.

Korczynski, M., K. Shire, S. Frenkel and M. Tam (1996) 'Front line work in the "new model service firm": Australian and Japanese comparisons", *Human Resource Management Journal*, 6(2), pp. 72–87.

Lamming, R. (1993) *Beyond Partnership*, Hemel Hempstead: Prentice Hall.

Lane, C. and R. Bachmann (1996) 'The Social Constitution of Trust: Supplier Relations in Britain and Germany', *Organization Studies*, 17(3), pp. 365–95.

McMahon, J. (1996) 'Employee Relations in small firms in Ireland. An exploratory study of small manufacturing firms', *Employee Relations*, 18(5), pp. 66–80.

Purcell, J. (1999) 'The Search for Best Practice and Best Fit in Human Resource Management: Chimera or cul-de-sac?', *Human Resource Management Journal*, 9(3), pp. 26–41.

Purcell, J., N. Kinnie, S. Hutchinson, B. Rayton and J. Swart (2003) *Understanding the People and Performance Link: Unlocking the black box*, London: Chartered Institute of Personnel and Development.

Rainnie, A. (1989) *Industrial Relations in Small Firms*, London: Routledge.

Rothwell, S. (1992) 'Polishing up the Supply Chain', *Personnel Management*, September, pp. 28–32.

Scarbrough, H. and N. Kinnie (2003) 'Barriers to the development of team working in UK firms', *Industrial Relations Journal*, 34(2), pp. 135–49.

Sinclair, D., L. Hunter and P. Beaumont (1996) 'Models of Customer–Supplier Relations', *Journal of General Management*, 22(2), pp. 56–75.

Scase, R. (1995) 'Employment Relations in Small Firms', in P. Edwards (ed.), *Industrial Relations in Britain*, Oxford: Blackwell.

Taylor, P. and P. Bain (1999) '"An 'assembly line in the head": work and employee relations in the call centre', *Industrial Relations Journal*, 30(2), pp. 101–17.

Part II

Characteristics and Organizational Features of Call Centre Work

6
Keeping Up Appearances: Recruitment, Skills and Normative Control in Call Centres

Paul Thompson, George Callaghan and Diane van den Broek

The call centre debate

Much of the literature on call centres focuses on work organization and surveillance. While this is valuable in its own right, issues of recruitment and socialization of labour tend to be neglected. In our case companies there is considerable evidence for the primacy accorded to the identification and shaping of social competencies as integral to interactive service work.

Little explicit emphasis has also been placed on workforce skills. However, it is possible to identify a general contrast between optimistic scenarios associated with the new service management literature and bleaker pictures of routinization painted by radical critics. The new service management literature (Schneider and Bowen, 1999) tends to emphasize general trends in service work, but the essential themes are largely consistent with the official call centre industry image of empowered, highly skilled and committed employees, delivering customized, quality service. While critical of such views, Frenkel *et al.* (1998; 1999) argue that the need to meet customer requirements in front-line service work places constraints on routinization and pressures to enhance knowledge and skills within hybrid mass customised bureaucracies.

In contrast, radical critics, noting highly scripted job tasks and closely monitored performance, draw parallels to assembly lines and information-age factories. Poynter (2000) extracts the most unambiguous conclusions about skill and the labour process. Call centres and other new forms of service work embody practices once the preserve of manual employees, routinizing and deskilling professional work: 'A form of organisation that was once the preserve of manual labour has rapidly diffused within industries

130   *Keeping Up Appearances*

that were previously associated with white collar workers and the exercise of "mental" labour' (Poynter, 2000, p. 151). Stanworth(1998), too, refers to the creation of a new, deskilled workforce that does not need qualifications and extensive training.

Actually, most critical researchers recognized from the beginning differences from classic manual and white-collar work regimes. Most significantly the labour and product of call centre work is relatively intangible. Though this intangibility is not specific to services, the emphasis is almost exclusively on the qualities such as of communication. Call centres are, therefore, a good example of interactive service sector work. In such work particular attitudes and feelings – sometimes summed up in the term emotional labour – are combined with product knowledge in order to maximize the quality and quantity of output, often measured in terms of customer satisfaction (Taylor, 1998). While call centres extend the possibilities for the Taylorization of white-collar work, the conflict between the requirements for quantity and quality are the driving force of managerial practices (Taylor and Bain, 1999).

This chapter proceeds from the view that one way of assessing these claims and the characteristic practices in the industry is by focusing on the actual processes of skill formation. Traditionally, social scientists have tended to focus largely on inputs into this process, notably labour market and training institutions, qualifications and formal skill hierarchies. This may, of course, still be pertinent in situations where call centres are operating in dense institutional frameworks that condition their labour strategies; or in company/sectoral circumstances where there is a positive association between traditional skills and new job requirements. One example is provided in Batt's case study of a US telecom's operation. The skill requirements for a customer service representative (CSR) are customer interaction skills, keyboard skills, knowledge of procedures, products services and legal regulations, technical proficiency in programming languages and databases. This reflects both the varied and complex demands of the job, and an 'institutional context' where, 'the historic HR practices of the Bell system had created a highly skilled work force with tremendous tacit knowledge of the customers, the telecommunications infrastructure, and the use of information systems' (Batt, 1999, p. 557).

However, it is not obvious how generalizable such conditions are. The traditional signifiers of skill formation are largely absent or inverted in much of the UK call centre industry. For example, a recent study in Scotland (Watson *et al.*, 2000) showed that 22 per cent of telephone sales staff possessed a degree compared to 7 per cent of clerical workers and

3 per cent of sales. In their case studies, the figure was even higher at almost 40 per cent (though this included management grades). Yet even the most generous interpretation of call centre work would find it hard to see a connection between such qualifications and the nature of work or opportunity structures.

Something different, then, is going on. Influenced in part by the experience of Japanese transplants where management sought to develop enterprise-level skills and reward systems among largely unqualified non-traditional labour on greenfield sites, there has been a general shift towards 'extra-functional' skills to cope with new organizational requirements, or as part of the growth of teamwork (Flecker and Hofbauer, 1998). As Crouch, Finegold and Satro note:

> These changes lead employers to seek in new recruits both a continuing ability to learn and what they usually call 'social skills', which might mean anything from ability to co-ordinate and secure co-operation, through ability to communicate effectively, to simple willingness to obey orders.
>
> (1999, p. 222).

Sectors using call centres have been able to develop a similar enterprise orientation, drawing on local labour markets, and attempting to fashion it in its chosen image. This parallels general trends in service work to select staff with the required attitudinal and behavioural characteristics, rather than on skill or qualification levels (Redman and Mathews, 1998; Korczynski 2002). Whereas social skills and competencies are a part of the profile of manufacturing work, in interactive services they are the main part (Thompson, Warhurst and Callaghan, 2001). Indeed, according to the industry, such qualities constitute the primary source of competitive advantage.

Given that traditional indicators are unreliable, the role of selection, recruitment, induction and training in identifying and shaping social competencies is moved to the centre of the stage. Yet, there are few critical studies in this area. This is surprising given that call centres are putting considerable emphasis on attempting to identify potential employees who are predisposed to become effective CSRs. In this context, training becomes less a function of imparting technical knowledge and skills, but more one of a broader socialization of labour. In other words it becomes a springboard for a process of normative control. In contrast to recruitment and skills, critical research has generated some focus on these issues. This is most obvious in Foucauldian-influenced studies

132   *Keeping Up Appearances*

that put emphasis on the willing incorporation of employee subjectivity into identification with brands and customers (Knights *et al.*, 1999; Alferoff and Knights, 2002). The problem with such perspectives is that they counterpoise normative controls to more traditional mechanisms of reward, sanction, bureaucratic control and surveillance. Our case studies rest on the view that call centres operate through integrated systems of technical, bureaucratic and normative controls (see Callaghan and Thompson, 2001). We would endorse Houlihan's observation that within such systems:

> Employment begins with a four to six week induction and training programme. During this time, newcomers are heavily socialised to the culture and beliefs of the organisation. Most of the time is spent on systems training, but this is interleaved very skilfully with an imparting process based on apparently informal and spontaneous storytelling which frames norms, values and coping mechanisms.
>
> (2000, p. 231)

The chapter therefore seeks to move from a discussion of the role the interrelations of skill formation, recruitment and selection, to the development and limits of normative controls through training and other mechanisms. We use call centre case studies from Scotland and Australia in order to explore these issues. The Scottish case, Telebank, is a large low-end financial services operation; while the Australian case focuses on similar operations in a large telecom firm, Servo. In both the British and Australian contexts, a similar methodology of semi-structured interviews[1] with managers and employees, plus non-participant observation of recruitment, training and work processes. Though some of these issues have been separately examined by the authors (Callaghan and Thompson 2001, 2002; Thompson and Callaghan, 2002; van den Broek 1997, 2002), the cases make useful and viable comparisons, not only because they have broadly similar labour processes and product markets, but because of both the similarity and differences with respect to employment and work practices. It should be emphasized that the retrospective bringing together of the materials from the two cases prevents a systematic case comparison. Nevertheless, the character and effectiveness of managerial strategies and normative control practices across the companies gives a useful opportunity to compare practices and strategic choices.

Recruitment, selection and skills

Given that CSRs are unlikely to last much more than 18 months in the job, employers such as Telebank and Servo devote considerable attention to recruitment, selection and training. In Telebank, for example, applicants go through a four-stage process – an initial form, a telephone interview, a role-play exercise and a formal interview. The various stages of recruitment and selection are used by both companies to try to identify different customer service skills. In the Telebank case this complex process results in the recruitment of seven employees from an initial 100 potential entrants.

While some levels of product and systems knowledge are prerequisites for the job, personality and communication skills are seen by management as the crucial differentiating qualities – because as one manager commented 'If one bank invents a new savings product and markets it tomorrow, the rest would have it on Friday' (T: Manager 5). The same manager goes on to observe that while keyboard and technical skills can be taught, 'Customer Service. That's not a skill. That's in you. It's the attitude towards customer service.' The word that crystallizes the quality managers seek is 'attitude', which must be 'positive', 'right' or 'can do':

> I firmly believe that if you have a CSR who has the right attitude and approach, so long as you've got somebody who's willing to learn, who will be receptive to their feedback and sees it as an opportunity to develop themselves, then I believe that you can get them to where they need to be.
>
> (T: Manager 2)

Similarly word cues such as 'win/win situation', 'team approach', 'loyalty' and 'empowerment' were ways in which Servo differentiated themselves from other so-called 'rigid' corporate environments during recruitment processes. For example, one customer service representative recalled a manager stating during recruitment and induction that Servo were: 'more interested in employing people who didn't come to them with a lot of old baggage from other corporate environments, so that Servo could mould them into the right sort of employee' (S: Senior Manager 1).

As with Telebank, attitude was important during Servo recruitment processes involving group exercises and role-plays. The three-stage recruitment process initially screened via telephone interviews involving broad questions related to previous work experience. Those who

134 *Keeping Up Appearances*

displayed good telephone communication skills progressed to a second interview involving group exercises, role-plays and simulations. Multi-tasking exercises required applicants sitting back to back to construct 'Lego' models that relied on verbal communication. During these exercises, communication skills, skills of persuasion, corporate and team commitment were closely observed and assessed by managerial staff (S: CSRs 1, 3; Senior Manager 3; Team Leader 10). Candidates who performed well in these activities then attended a final interview where technical exercises might be set, including tests that assess typing speed and ability.

Within the general view of management that 'we recruit attitude', specific emphasis is placed upon positivity, energy and enthusiasm:

> To fit into the category you need to be first of all, very, very enthusiastic. You need to really want to do it, because it's a tough six-weeks training. You need to be positive, the whole company is geared towards a positive attitude, again a can-do approach, not 'I've never done that before, but yes, let's give it a bash, let's try it.'
>
> (T: Manager 4)

The other characteristic that emerged was sense of humour. This is not simply a quality of the autonomous, individual personality. CSRs have to know when to deploy this humour and must decide when it is appropriate to engage in banter: 'It depends on the customers, the more experience they [the CSR] have the best they can judge the type of customer they've got on-line.'

This is an example of how it is not enough to simply possess 'person-ality'; CSRs must know how to communicate it. More broadly, commu-nication competencies include verbal tone, pitch, fluency and energy and enthusiasm. These constitute a cluster of technical and emotional competencies ranging from body language to language itself:

> If I'm not hearing energy and enthusiasm, what I'm looking for is energy drop. Energy drop is where you've got someone who's started a sentence, sounded quite bright, and then it drops off. And also looking for sentence shape, are they melodic, are they using good pitch, or are they monotonous, have they got the one tone they always speak at. Are they too musical, do they give a little squeak at the end of the sentence?
>
> (T: Manager 7)

Servo management reiterated a desire for such attributes. One senior manager felt that:

> One of the underlying things in this organization is the youthfulness and the high energy levels. There are no clocks in the place ... no one signs in, no one signs off, and people just work until the job is done.
>
> (S: Senior Manager 2)

The focus on enthusiasm and call quality was measured through key performance indicators at Servo. Central factors determining the quality of a call were disaggregated into three areas including how the call was opened, the manner in which the body of call was performed and call close factors. The basic call requirements included assessment of phone manner, attempt to build rapport and courtesy to customers (S: internal company document).

A number of commentators, but particularly Belt (2002), have noted the congruence between some of the above social competencies and gender characteristics. At Telebank, female and male Telebank managers resisted any attempt to link skills and gender characteristics. They pointed to the growing percentage of men in the centre and argued that, 'The job itself – the guys are just as happy doing it as the girls are.' If pressed, managers tended to use labour market rather than labour process rationales; notably that the company goal of flexibility through a workforce that is at least 50 per cent part-time would most likely be met through predominantly female recruitment. A minority accepted a traditional association between women and social skills, but believed that the recruitment net would also pick up suitable men:'Very, very much so, but then we would hope to pick that up at interviews, male and female'(T: Manager 10). However, such sensitivity to gender links is partly disingenuous. Recruitment information sent out to applicants states that 'running a house and raising children requires many of these skills we are looking for'.

Labour market rationales were also evident at Servo. Within some sections of the organization there seemed an obvious preference for gay men, as they were considered more flexible than workers who had children. Indeed one team leader described his section as the 'Pink Zone' and the annual Christmas party developed quite a reputation within the gay Sydney set. For example, a leading Australian newspaper reported that the Servo Christmas party had 'become quite the event on the Sydney social scene and is considered the third most popular event

136 *Keeping Up Appearances*

on the city's gay calendar after the Mardi Gras and the Sleeze Ball' (S: Team Leader 8; Lacy, 1999).

The awareness of Servo management of the significance of the relation between group identity and potential individual and team performance indicates a broader and more explicit focus on the cultural dimension of recruitment. This surfaced most clearly in a preference for staff who appeared antithetical to unionism. At Servo, an elaborate interview process was designed to identify young, enthusiastic and committed recruits; however, there was also an explicit exclusion of staff who had come from corporate backgrounds where trade unionism was strong and on occasions an explicit discrimination of those who had been active union members. Here 'flexibility', the 'right attitude' and 'cultural baggage' became euphemisms for a managerial preference for employees who showed little interest or history of trade union membership.

The director of human resources stated that Servo had 'specific selection criteria to make sure we get the staff who are culturally a good fit'. Part of that 'fit' reflected in management's need to identify those who 'come with the right mindset to start with'. Wishing to avoid employees with 'cultural baggage', Servo explicitly stated that they were not interested in employing staff from strongly unionized firms preferring those from (non-union) organizations like IBM and American Express (S: Managers 1, 4).

The following incident dispels any ambiguity about what sort of 'baggage' Servo was wishing to avoid. After a recruitment officer has sent a job offer to a successful recruit, her supervisor enquired whether she had 'read that he had been a union member for many years', because 'you know that it is our policy not to employ union members'. The supervisor demanded that the recruitment officer withdraw the offer and when she refused to follow through with the request, the supervisor withdrew the offer to the applicant himself. According to the officer, 'that was the way it worked all the way along ... the companies [Servo] most despised were the public service ... If you worked for a union you were definitely "no go"'(S: CSR 13).

Induction procedures reinforced the concentration on corporate culture and culminated in a workshop known as the 'Servo Challenge' which all employees were required to attend. Corporate literature states that the objectives of the Challenge were to 'create a common understanding and "ownership" of the Servo vision and values' (Servo corporate literature). The Challenge had considerable populist appeal to staff. One CSR stated that as a result of recruitment and induction, she felt that Servo staff were well treated and had more involvement in managerial issues than she had experienced at other workplaces. Another CSR felt that to

Paul Thompson, George Callaghan and Diane van den Broek 137

work for Servo was 'an extreme privilege and only a select few would receive such an opportunity'(S: CSRs 7, 3, 1).

Tensions and contracts

The focus on social competencies and cultural characteristics in different ways in the two companies was not without tension and challenge. One of the problems faced by call centre management is to balance the search for positive personalities with communicating a message about the tough nature of the job. During the role-play at Telebank, for example, the applicant is placed in a separate room and asked to play the part of a travel agent. The door of this room is fitted with a bell so the interviewers, sitting in an adjoining room, can hear if the applicant tries to run away. The pressure is such that this has happened. The interviewers later went on to acknowledge, as they did at the end of every session, that the job is boring and repetitive. Interestingly, then, at the end of a recruitment process that emphasizes the importance of a warm personality, people are told their job will be mundane and routine.

This tension is further revealed in the contrast between managerial and employee responses to the question, 'what kind of skills do you think are necessary to do this job?' Interviews with CSRs at Telebank did reveal some continuity with management on perceptions of skill requirements. In particular, there is common ground that social rather than technical competencies and knowledge are primary. But the emphasis was often different. CSRs were much more likely to associate job requirements with surviving stressful and repetitive work – and therefore the 'skills' of patience, tolerance, level-headedness, sense of humour, listening, flexibility and emotional self-management – rather than applying a particular set of personality characteristics to the enthusiastic pursuit of customer service:

You've got be very tolerant, I think. You have to be able to take a deep breath, the customer is always right, kind of thing. But it's very repetitive. I've been here for six months now and it's very mundane – just waiting for the next beep!

(T: CSR 8)

Patience with the customer ... It's patience to let them go through it at their own pace. Sometimes they ask, will you give me a statement, and you wonder if it's a balance or a statement to be sent out ... But

138   *Keeping Up Appearances*

you can't make out that they're in the wrong, that they're stupid. It's patience and knowing where to direct it.

(T: CSR 13)

However, the difference between management and employees may be less than it appears. The following quote makes clear that management are fully aware of the characteristics of the labour process at the low end of the financial services market:

At the end of the day, a call centre job is boring, it's call after call, day after day, week after week, month after month. There is very little variety. Now for someone to be able to cope with that, the challenge there is, each customer is different and therefore you have to treat each customer differently, that's where the challenge comes. You have to be tenacious and you've got to have energy, and that energy has got to last if you're a full-timer say from 9–5pm at the same constant level of energy. You have a passionate belief in customer service and all that entails.

(T: Manager 6)

Similarly a tension frequently emerged between Servo requirements for cultural conformity and employee identity concerns. For example, while an important aspect of the Challenge was to communicate Servo's corporate identity to employees, other employees viewed the Challenge as corporate hype designed to unduly influence new recruits. One participant recalled the experience as:

Two days of propaganda Servo-style as they were introduced to the Servo culture, Servo vision and watched a video of Servo CEO on a huge screen welcoming us to the team, while the Servo theme song 'One Team One Goal' was played in the background.

(S: CSR 1)

Another CSR believed the induction process was:

a mass brainwashing session where new employees are blinded by the hype that is Servo. Servo was portrayed as a non-conflict company where nobody had differences with each other and all problems could be resolved through discussion. Employees were filled with extravagant hype and expectations of their future with the company.

(S: CSR 7)

Paul Thompson, George Callaghan and Diane van den Broek 139

As indicated above, both firms tried to shape attitudes and enhance social competencies, but the recruitment and selection process was undoubtedly used to screen-in those predisposed to display the desired attitudes and behaviours.

Socialization and training: technical and normative controls

Once employed, in both companies trainees are taught about the technical equipment and given some information on basic products and systems. The focal point is to ensure competency in navigating around systems and the procedural knowledge necessary to deal with queries. The main emphasis, however, is on communication skills. During this time trainees are taught how to vary their voice and manage conversations to ensure every caller gets the same level of customer service. Trainees are told they need not only master specific techniques (such as controlling the conversation) but also must learn how to manage themselves; customers should not be able to tell if CSRs are unhappy. Together these begin to give trainees an awareness and influence over the regulation and management of feelings.

At Telebank such an orientation is manifested in training geared to managing a conversation (techniques of conversational control) and managing yourself (control over one's energy and enthusiasm). A 'conversation cycle' is used to teach trainees to 'build rapport' with the customer. While 'rapport' evokes images of empathy, the actual focus is on specific techniques of managing the information flow through question prompts and appropriate answers:

If someone says I want to order some money, I'm going to Australia to see my daughter, they should reply 'Oh, wonderful.' They then need to retain that information so at the end of the call they say, 'Have a really good time.'

(T: Manager 7)

Some employees are understandably puzzled at the balance of priorities in training;

When I first came here I'd never heard of the conversation cycle in my life. I think I would rather have more training with the systems than concentrate on how we are supposed to have a conversation with a person.

(T: CSR 2)

140   *Keeping Up Appearances*

The other procedure is known as the eight elements of conversation, including using the first person, stating intention and giving attention. Together with techniques developed in 'rapport sessions', such as varying voice pitch and tone, these are used as tools to guide interactions and maintain an emotional distance.

So it would appear that one of the of the most important call centre skills is the ability to manage yourself and therefore your emotions. We shall return to this more conceptually later, but such an orientation is only implicit in recruitment and training processes. At Telebank, while managers frequently referred to the need for CSRs to 'change themselves', they proved highly resistant to the notion that employees may be 'acting', whether superficially or deep down. Instead, during recruitment and training management the proxy of 'people skills' seemed to be used for emotional labour. The evidence looked for is in what can be seen on the surface, such as body language. Once in training the focus shifts away from characteristics of personality and moves to developing techniques that allow workers to apply their personality in different work situations. Evidence of non-compliance or poor performance, such as 'energy drop', are treated as technical issues rather than the genuine constraints in delivering manageable emotions in circumstances where, 'We know the job is boring and you don't know whether the next call is going to be Mr Angry or Mr Nice' (T: Manager 1).

The training period is also used to institutionalize workers into required social and organizational frameworks. At Telebank, this was focused on the 19 'core standards of behaviour'. These standards are bureaucratic norms that emphasize specified behaviour and are consistent with socialization based on normative control. They are continually reinforced in training and are printed on laminated cards as well as pasted on walls and doors. However, this co-exists with the elaborate apparatus of surveillance and technical controls typical of call centres. Telebank monitors calls through the 'Research Department' and by team leaders, with the subsequent statistics graded as a basis for feedback and discipline. For example, out of every 10,000 calls the target is that only three should produce complaints. Not surprisingly, adverse reaction to 'the stats' was a familiar feature of CSR interviews.

Of equal significance, technical and normative controls do not necessarily work harmoniously. Training to develop empathy and rapport requires time and discretion, qualities that are heavily constrained by the nature and extent of surveillance. Employees noted contrasts with expectations at recruitment interview and in training:

Paul Thompson, George Callaghan and Diane van den Broek   141

I thought that each customer was supposed to have individual needs, so you've got to give them time. But it's 'we need to bring those down, let's look at bringing your stats in line with everybody else's'. It's on top of you all the time... Basically, at the moment I feel like a machine. The personal touches have gone and they need to bring them back. But then you've always got the stats at the back of your mind.

(T: CSR 12)

Most Servo CSRs interviewed did not appear overly concerned about the level of surveillance, but rather more concerned about the work intensification and managerial emphasis on productivity targets. Pressure to perform stemmed in part from the fact that CSR's statistics influence payment structures and promotional prospects within the firm. One recently promoted CSR, believed that the two team leaders and manager who interviewed him were looking primarily for productivity achievements (S: CSR 3).

Although collective action rarely occurred at Servo, the issue of increased workloads and managerial pressure did prompt collective responses. One group of Servo employees openly voiced their resistance to the introduction of 'call forcing' by confronting management and signing a petition registering their opposition to work intensification and excessive monitoring. The petition stated that:

As there has been no quality circle or our voices heard regarding this matter, we just thought that you should know what we think. The... queue is 50 per cent outbound and 50 per cent inbound – the problem lies with the fact that we are understaffed, not the period of time it takes us to answer the phone.

(S: CSR 1; internal company correspondence)

CSRs' perception that the introduction of statistics was encouraging a 'worse service' is reinforced by broader research. One Australian study of Telstra call centres revealed that while 98 per cent of customer service representatives thought customer service was important, 72 per cent did not believe that management had a high regard for service quality and 66 per cent thought they were inadequately rewarded for customer service. (Deery and Iverson, 1998, pp. 12–13). Of course, for management the ideal situation is a labour process that produces a high quantity of consistent quality units of customer service. But the central paradox of much call centre work means this ideal situation is rarely achieved. A labour process whose architecture is based on the foundations

142 *Keeping Up Appearances*

of high volume and low cost is always going to find it difficult to provide consistently high-quality customer service. They are also going to find it hard to sustain employee morale.

This does not, of course, stop management trying. Servo put considerable effort into social and recreational gatherings that were also designed to ameliorate the intense nature of call centre working. Open and direct managerial communication was not confined within the walls of the organization as social and recreational gatherings were organized both during and after office hours. Regular outings were scheduled and 'events' were organized periodically throughout the year. During these events management discussed company profitability and distributed achievement awards such as plaques, gift vouchers, certificates and movie tickets. The events generally had a theme and were usually hosted by particular departments (S: Manager 7; CSR 3).

For management 'it's a lot of fun and it's also very business-related...reps love it, they're right into it' (S: Manager 4). Many employees reiterated this support. One CSR stated that 'they did make people feel like they were doing an important job. That was the good side of the company, making people feel valued' (S: CSR 11). However, feeling valued appeared to be mandatory as there was no lack of managerial pressure to attend such meetings. Indeed, many CSRs were actively coerced into attending as management viewed non-attendance as a refusal to be a 'team player' (S: CSRs 11, 3). Such coercion reflected in this management e-mail sent to employees in one department stating that while the gatherings:

> are not compulsory, all staff should be encouraged to attend, and it will be noted if they do not attend...I require the name and reason for every staff member including Team Leaders who do not attend these sessions.
>
> (S: internal company e-mail)

The customer service representative responded to the e-mail by stating:

> I would be more than happy to attend...but have now got second thoughts when it is stated that all who do not attend will be noted. The message seems to be 'attend or else'. Perhaps positive influencing such as 'I would encourage all to attend, as it should be informative and interesting' would have a greater effect than shadowy threats. I feel it is better to bring my opinion to your attention than to join in on the unsettled murmuring of the department.
>
> (S: internal company e-mail)

Other incentives designed to bolster morale involved individual and team prizes. Employees might win $500 for guessing the correct day of Servo's 500,000th new customer, mystery trips were offered to employees who attracted customers to the firm and team bonuses were awarded to high-output teams. On occasions employees' families and friends also visited the workplace to get an idea of where they work and what they do. Visitors could view themselves on satellite television, or even play with 'Ace T Freckle' the clown (S: internal company magazine).

The emphasis on teams as a form of socialization and as a means of offsetting the negative aspects of an individualized division of labour is common in most call centres. At Servo it was an explicit part of recruitment criteria and efforts were made to link team output to performance-related pay structures. Peer pressure to increase output was, as one manager put it, where the 'team dynamics kicked in'. She observed that within some teams members might draw attention to CSRs who were under-performing, by saying 'come on, you're letting the side down or your having too much sick leave' (S: Centre Manager, 4). At Telebank, the purpose of teams was pitched at a more general level:

> At busy times it can be quite isolated, although normally someone wouldn't spend two hours on the phone without having a break. The team thing comes in like breaks, lunchtime, social events outside work, theme days. For instance, on Friday we had Halloween and you will find if you've been here on Friday, that every team has some sort of decoration for Halloween. And if you go to people 'who did all this', oh, so and so did this, and so they work as a team.
>
> (T: Manager 2)

The limited nature of team operations at Telebank is illustrated by the fact that, unlike Servo, management saw no need for team meetings of any kind. Not surprisingly, the privilege of being able to paint their own area and receive small gifts for particular performance outcomes received a mixed response:

> Morale is a big thing in here, they try to build morale. We actually have quite low morale in our team at the moment ... You'll see they've decorated, a lot of bright coloured walls, this is all psychology. Once you've been here a long time it's basically bollocks. You come in and do your job. You don't really feel part of a team. In a sense it's a big team, but you're in 12 segments.
>
> (T: CSR 17)

144 *Keeping Up Appearances*

Limits to normative control

Our own and other case studies have established that, contrary to popular and some academic images of electronic surveillance, panoptic power and perfect control, call centre employees have developed a repertoire of informal and formal means of contesting the technical control aspects of managerial regimes (Houlihan, 2000; Bain and Taylor, 2000; Callaghan and Thompson, 2001; van Den Broek, 2002). What can also be observed is evidence of a degree of employee distance from, disenchantment with and resistance to normative controls.

This was particularly evident at Servo given the prominence and intensity of such controls. For example, the fact that training workshops were designed to instil corporate values, rather than provide technical training, led some to feel 'there was no real common ground to discuss problems related to the job'. Others described Servo's induction programme, the Challenge, as 'a cult that wasn't natural in a Western corporate environment', or a 'religious aura where there was no room for dissent' (S: CSRs 11, 1). The cynicism felt by some CSR was tempered by their recognition that attitude and performance, displayed during the Challenge, influenced future prospects within the organization. One CSR who questioned a performance appraisal that she received several months after attending the Challenge was informed by management that the reason for a low appraisal was that she did not take the workshop seriously enough. During the meeting over her appraisal, she rebutted this criticism by stating that:

> There was a real distinction between recognizing the capabilities of corporate culture and recognizing that corporate culture can be about solving problems. But it's not about social construction . . . I don't think I was hostile to sections of the Challenge that were about working and achieving X, I was hostile to the silliness.
>
> (S: CSR 11)

Interviews revealed that elements of normative and cultural control manifested in the managerial recruitment of staff that 'culturally fit' with corporate values. This was designed to promote individualism and enthusiasm and to develop important tacit skills required of the job. However, many CSR were aware of this and were 'in no doubt that attitude was the most important thing they were looking for'. As such in many cases, CSRs merely acted out required behaviour such as enthusiasm and allegiance to team and company goals during recruitment and induction (S: CSRs 2, 4).

Whilst in the job CSRs also sought to ameliorate the repetition and regain a degree of control by maximizing job and increasing customer satisfaction. As already indicated, Servo CSRs lamented their inability to deliver high-quality customer service levels with many feeling that increased focus on statistics was encouraging an unsatisfactory level of service. However, while there is considerable evidence that CSRs became frustrated by their inability to deliver quality customer service, concern for customer satisfaction should not be (mis)represented as employees self-disciplining themselves (van den Broek, forthcoming). On other occasions, CSRs might just as easily control the pace of their work by 'flicking' calls to other departments or just hanging up on customers.

Similarly social and recreational events organized inside and outside the firm were intended to focus on commitment and productivity output, however such responses were not always forthcoming. Therefore various aspects of normative and cultural control were passively or actively resisted. While CSRs are aware of the need to vary their face, the actual responses are themselves extremely varied, with little evidence of deep acting. Many put minimal emotional effort into the work:

> My way of handling it is coming in and saying to myself 'I do my shift from two to ten, it's not a career, it's a job. I answer the phone and that's it.' By not looking for anything more than that, that's my way of handling it. When I first came in, I thought it was maybe just me, but speaking to other people it's the same.
>
> (T: CSR 8)

> There is one part of your brain that does go into repetitive mode just so you can deal with the repetition over and over again.
>
> (T: CSR 4)

This 'satisficing' strategy is linked to the types of 'endurance' skills identified earlier as primary by CSRs. Others wish to determine the emotional effort bargain on their own terms, for example, displaying emotional labour as a 'gift' to customers even when that means calls go on longer than management would like; 'We have our regulars that call...And they'll call once or twice in the night and sit and talk for a wee while, they just want a bit of company. I just feel you can't cut

146 *Keeping Up Appearances*

them off' (T: CSR 11). Others relieve the pressure by simple forms of misbehaviour such making fun of the customer, 'They can't see us so we can actually take the mickey out of them while they're trying to speak to us' (T: CSR 1).

Such responses echo Bolton's (2000) development of Hochschild's conceptual framework through a fuller exploration of the way workers manage their own emotions. She argues that workers do not simply provide passive emotional labour but are active and skilled emotion managers, with the possibility of conflict with managerial objectives. While some managers are reluctant to talk openly about the needfor workers to act, CSRs readily discuss emotional management and the need to act: 'I work until seven o'clock at night, and it's the last thing you want to do, be bubbly on the phone, you can't be bothered. So there is a bit of pretence behind it sometimes' (T: CSR 9). The emotional effort bargain thus constitutes a hidden and contested dimension of skill formation. Nor does it necessarily stop at the workplace gate:

> It takes about an hour to totally unwind, not thinking about this place at all. I find I'm saying the phrases they want us to say in here, at home, because it's become part of my vocabulary. Oh, I can do that for you! All these positive phrases.
>
> (T: CSR 19)

In many cases, the emotional effort bargain and the relentless stress associated with call centre work was not sustainable, as CSRs temporarily or permanently exited from the firm. This is confirmed in studies that focus more specifically on turnover and absenteeism, such as the Australian investigations of Deery and Iverson (1998). The Australian call centre industry is renowned for high employee burnout (average 18 months), turnover (average 22 per cent) and various rates of absenteeism (ACA Research, 1998; 1999, p. 57; 2001). At Telebank turnover was more than 20 per cent and many managers believed that this was a necessary 'sacrificial HR strategy', as Wallace, Eagleson and Waldersee (2000) call it, despite the investment in recruiting and training each new employee.

Discussion and conclusions

The apparent paradox of much call centre work is why do employers invest so heavily in systematic selection, training and socialization

Paul Thompson, George Callaghan and Diane van den Broek 147

processes for routinized, heavily scripted and monitored work with a limited career structure and high likelihood of burnout and exit? Taylorism, technical control and high surveillance are characteristic features of call centres, yet as Deery and Kinnie observe, 'Tightly specified work regimes are not sufficient to secure quality service delivery. Consequently, most organisations have sought to instil values of good customer service in their staff by way of cultural or normative control' (2002, p. 5). Quality, here, is an ambiguous term that certainly differs from the industry self-perception of committed employees delivering the type of services that customers value. Instead it should be conceived as both a codeword for consistency with managerial objectives of high-volume, standardized service, and as a contested terrain between the participants in that interaction: managers, employees and customers.

In that light, the recruitment and selection process is used to try and identify those, who through experience or predisposition, have the social competencies functional to service interactions; 'Basically they're looking for the potential to mould' (T: CSR 13). This constitutes a form of ex-ante control that addresses aspects of the indeterminacy of labour (Hales, 1999, p. 7; Callaghan and Thompson, 2002, p. 251). Training and subsequent normative control practices are then used to make those competencies appropriate to the particular workflow and management strategy. Through recruitment, induction mechanisms and the development of skills and social competencies, socialization and normative controls both Telebank and Servo sought to identify and modify the behaviour and attitudes of their employees. Part of the rationale for developing these mechanisms was to engender a sense of shared identity and sociability, contributing to enhanced commitment and 'discretionary effort'. The two companies differed somewhat in both the objectives and mechanisms geared towards shaping call centre labour. Servo had a more explicit cultural agenda, more defined targets such as countering potential union influence and a more sophisticated attempt to integrate normative controls into a broader performance management framework. However, despite a more developed high-commitment strategy to engender the internalization of corporate values, these initiatives only met with partial success. The differences with Telebank are ultimately fairly small along a spectrum of call centre practices and those differences can be explained by reference to corporate culture and strategy rather than the national institutional settings in which the two companies operated. Though the British and Australian settings manifest quite distinctive features with respect to industrial relations and employment systems, there was limited impact in these instances. Indeed, it is

148 *Keeping Up Appearances*

characteristic of the call centre industry globally, even in countries with denser institutional frameworks such as Germany, that call centres are devised and operated in ways that allow some distance from those potential impacts compared, for example, to traditional banking operations (Shire, Holtgrewe and Kerst, 2002).

Whatever the differences in intent and outcome across the two companies, we would resist the use of the term deskilling in a call centre context. This is partly because it underestimates the extent to which interactive service work is distinct from rather than a debased version of previous white-collar occupations such as those in banking; and it fails to recognize that such social competencies and emotional labour do not fit neatly into the classic manual/mental divide. As Becker (2000) argues, the skills of the CSR are of a basic human character that is ubiquitous in everyday life. Neither they nor unit leaders require any significant formal knowledge or technical skills. However, his case study research demonstrated that those who stay and move upwards in the limited hierarchy are a repository of tacit knowledge and need to develop judgement and problem solving. In other words the skills of unit leaders and supervisors are predicated on the planned routinization of the CSR role. In call centres such as Telebank and Servo, low-complexity work and flat structures mean that the most generous interpretation is that they are developing or enhancing a set of generic, transferable social skills that makes them more employable in other call centres or service settings. It is true that some firms, including Telebank, are introducing vocational qualifications in customer care, these do no more than formally certify the practice of existing social competencies within a low-skill ecosystem.

While we would argue that this analysis is typical of high-volume, standardized call centre operations we accept that the constitution of skills and competencies is not uniform in the industry, let alone in service work more generally. In their US case studies, it is argued by Batt (2000) and Batt and Moynihan (2002) that work organization and HR practices reflect product market segmentation between high-value (professional-service model) and low-value (mass-production) customers. It is accepted that the norm is mass production, but Batt and Moynihan explore the potential for a hybrid mass customization model similar to high-involvement and performance practices in manufacturing. Such contrasts are observable elsewhere. Watson *et al.* (2000) compare two Scottish cases in which 'M' is embedded in a market segment of the financial services industry that allows some of its CSRs to acquire formal knowledge, qualifications and mobility within the company;

and 'T', which is predominantly an outsourced centre supplying services to a variety of clients. Like Telebank and Servo, the transferable, generic skill pathway is more characteristic. We might also add that labour markets can influence choices and outcomes. A 'sacrificial' or revolving door policy is only possible when a continual and appropriate labour supply is readily available.

Recognition of diversity is always necessary, but there is a limitation to the market segmentation argument. Identifying investment in skill, plus high involvement and commitment, with servicing high-value customers (see Batt and Moynihan, 2002, p. 15), neglects two factors. First, as we have argued, there is qualitatively higher investment in call centre recruitment, selection and training than in conventional Taylorized settings. Second, the characteristic low-value call centre operation can itself be considered a hybrid, dubbed by Houlihan 'low discretion, high commitment'. In her four case studies, a variety of HR practices and normative control measures were used to generate commitment and mediate the tensions arising from the organization and control of the labour process. Ultimately the latter outweighed the former, 'The common theme to these cases was low discretion, routinised customer service' (2002, p. 82). There is, then a double strategic choice, between models constrained by product and labour market conditions, and within the constraints of the dominant mass-market, socio-technical system. Furthermore, in most circumstances the latter set of choices may be more typical and more significant than the feasibility of a 'mass customization' model.

Reference to the term socio-technical system normally refers to attempts by management and other actors in the employment relationship to construct mutually supportive and jointly optimized relations between the technical and social dimensions of work systems. Within the dominant pattern of call centre practice management have indeed created a closely aligned set of arrangements, but that integration results in perverse and negative outcomes for employees and to some extent the organizations that employ them. Management at Telebank and Servo are aware of the limits and counterproductive effects arising from the socio-technical system and like managers elsewhere in the industry, are continually assessing the existing technical division of labour and the potential for adjusting the balance of practices. Yet, as a Telebank manager reported, 'The main dilemma facing call centres at the moment is the increase in call volumes. Call volumes have gone up 22 per cent this year and they went up 18 per cent last year.' The likelihood is that the outcomes will

150 *Keeping Up Appearances*

be different ways of managing rather substantially resolving the tensions in the call centre labour process.

Note

1. Source material drawn from the Telebank interviews is signified by T and from Servo, S, before any quote/reference.

References

ACA Research (1998) 'The 1998 Call Centre Agent Study: Call Centre Hang-ups', ACA Research Pty Ltd, Sydney, July.

ACA Research (1999) 'The Australian Call Centre Industry Study' ACA Research Pty Ltd, April, Sydney.

ACA Research (2001) 'The 2001 Australia and New Zealand Call Centre Industry Benchmark Study', ACA Research Pty Ltd, Sydney.

Alferoff, C. and D. Knights (2002) 'Quality Time and the "Beautiful Call",' in U. Holtgrewe, C. Kerst and K. Shire (eds), *Re-organising Service Work: Call Centres in Germany and Britain*, Aldershot: Ashgate.

Bain, P. and P. Taylor (2000) 'Entrapped by the "electronic panopticon"?: Worker resistance in the call centre', *New Technology, Work and Employment*, 15(1), pp. 2–18.

Batt, R. (1999) 'Work organization, technology and performance in customer service and sales', *Industrial and Labour Relations Review*, 52(4), pp. 539–64.

Batt, R. (2000) 'Strategic segmentation and front-line services: matching customers, employees and human resource systems', *International Journal of Human Resource Management*, 11(3), pp. 540–61.

Batt, R. and L. Moynihan (2002) 'The viability of alternative call centre production models', *Human Resource Management Journal*, 12(4), pp. 14–34.

Becker, M. C. (2000) 'The Constitution of Competence in a Call Centre: An Empirical Contribution of a Theory of Competences', unpublished paper, Judge Institute of Management, Cambridge University.

Belt, V. (2002) 'Capitalising on Femininity: Gender and the Utilisation of Social Skills in Telephone Call Centres', in U. Holtgrewe, C. Kerst and K. Shire (eds), *Re-organising Service Work: Call Centres in Germany and Britain*, Aldershot: Ashgate.

Bolton, S. (2000) 'Emotions Here, Emotions There, Emotional Organisations Everywhere', *Critical Perspectives on Accounting*, 11(2), pp. 155–71.

Callaghan, G. and P. Thompson (2001) 'Edwards revisited: technical control and call centres', *Economic and Industrial Democracy*, 22(1), pp. 13–37.

Callaghan, G. and P. Thompson (2002) '"We Recruit Attitude": the selection and shaping of routine call centre labour', *Journal of Management Studies*, 39(2), pp. 233–54 .

Crouch, C., D. Finegold and M. Sako (1999) *Are Skills the Answer? The Political Economy of Skill Creation in Advanced Industrial Countries*, Oxford: Oxford University Press.

Deery, S. and R. Iverson (1998) 'An Examination of the Causes of Absenteeism at Telstra', University of Melbourne.

Deery, S. and N. Kinnie (2002) 'Call centres and beyond: a thematic evaluation', *Human Resource Management Journal*, 12(4), pp. 3–13.

Flecker, J. and J. Hofbauer (1998) 'Capitalising on Subjectivity: The "New Model Worker" and the Importance of Being Useful', in P. Thompson and C. Warhurst (eds), *Workplaces of the Future*, London: Macmillan.

Frenkel, S., M. Korczynski, K. Shire and M. Tam (1998) 'Beyond Bureaucracy? Work organization in call centres', *International Journal of Human Resource Management*, 9(6), pp. 957–79.

Frenkel, S., M. Korczynski, K. Shire and M. Tam (1999) *On the Front Line: organization of work in the information economy*, Ithaca, NY: Cornell University Press.

Hales, C. (1999). 'Embellishing Empowerment: Ideologies of Management, Managerial Ideologies and the Rhetoric and Reality of Empowerment Programmes', paper for the 18th International Labour Process Conference, March, Royal Holloway.

Hochschild, A. (1983) *The Managed Heart: Commercialization of Human Feeling*, Berkeley: University of Californian Press.

Houlihan, M. (2000) 'Eyes Wide Shut? Querying the Depth of Call Centre Learning', *Journal of European Industrial Training*, 23(2/4), pp. 228–40.

Houlihan, M. (2002) 'Tensions and Variations in Call Centre Management Strategies', *Human Resource Management Journal*, 12(4), pp. 67–85.

Knights, D., F. Noble, H. Willmott and T. Vurdubakis (1999) 'Constituting the CSR: consumption, production and the labour process in call centres', paper to the 17th International Labour Process Conference, School of Management, March, Royal Holloway, University of London.

Korczynski, M. (2002) *Human Resource Management and Service Work: The Fragile Social Order*, Basingstoke: Palgrave.

Lacy, C . (1999) 'Rear Window', *Australian Financial Review*, 15 February.

Poynter, G. (2000) '"Thank You for Calling": The Ideology of Work in the Service Economy', *Soundings*, 14, Spring, pp. 151–60.

Redman, T. and B. P. Mathews (1998) 'Service Quality and Human Resource Management: A Review and Research Agenda', *Personnel Review*, 27(1), pp. 57–77.

Schneider, B. and D. E. Bowen (1999) 'Understanding Customer Delight and Outrage', *Sloan Management Review*, 41(1), pp. 35–45.

Shire, K., U. Holtgrewe and C. Kerst (2002) 'Re-organising customer service work: an introduction', in U. Holtgrewe, C. Kerst and K. Shire (eds), *Re-organising Service Work: Call Centres in Germany and Britain*, Aldershot: Ashgate.

Stanworth, C. (1998) 'Telework and the Information Age', *New Technology, Work and Employment*, 13(1), pp. 51–62.

Taylor, S. (1998) 'Emotional labour and the new workplace', in P. Thompson and C. Warhurst (eds), *Workplaces of the Future*, London: Macmillan, pp. 84–103.

Taylor, P. and P. Bain (1999) '"An assembly line in the head": work and employee relations in the call centre', *Industrial Relations Journal*, 30(2), pp. 101–17.

Thompson, P. and G. Callaghan (2002) 'Skill Formation in Call Centres', in U. Holtgrewe, C. Kerst and K. Shire (eds), *Re-organising Service Work: Call Centres in Germany and Britain*, Aldershot: Ashgate.

Thompson, P., C. Warhurst and G. Callaghan (2001) 'Ignorant theory and knowledgeable workers: interrogating the connections between knowledge, skills and services', *Journal of Management Studies*, 38(7), pp. 923–42.

van den Broek, D. (1997) 'Human Resource Management, Cultural Control and Union Avoidance: An Australian Case Study', *Journal of Industrial Relations*, 3(3), pp. 332–48.

van den Broek, D. (2002) 'Monitoring and Surveillance in Call Centres: Some Responses from Australian Workers', *Labour and Industry*, 12(3), pp. 43–58.

152 Keeping Up Appearances

van den Broek, D. (forthcoming) '"We Have the Values": Customers, Control and Corporate Ideology in Call Centre Operations', *New Technology, Work and Employment*.

Wallace, C. M., G. Eagelson and R. Waldersee (2000) 'The Sacrificial HR Strategy in Call Centres', *International Journal of Service Industry Management*, 11(2), pp. 174–84.

Watson, A., D. Bunzel, C. J. Lockyer and D. Scholarios (2000) 'Changing Constructions of Career, Commitment and Identity: The Call Centre Experience', a paper to the 15th Annual Employment Research Unit Conference: 'Work Futures', September Cardiff University.

7
Professionals at Work: A Study of Autonomy and Skill Utilization in Nurse Call Centres in England and Canada

Caroline Collin-Jacques

Introduction

The aim of this chapter is to examine the experience of professional labour in call centres within a cross-national framework. More particularly, it focuses on the work organization of nurses employed in call centre settings to provide public healthcare services by telephone. The experience of England (NHS Direct) and Quebec (Health-Info CLSC) are examined in a comparative analysis.

Notwithstanding the fact that call centres have spread from the private to the public sector and to more dedicated helplines staffed by occupational groups with strong identities, the phenomenon of professionals and technical staffs in call centres has been neglected by both British and American academics. Indeed, the academic literature on call centre work has remained focused on private-transaction-based call centres in the same loci of industries (for example, finance, telecommunications and retails), and employing routine white-collar workers (Frenkel *et al.*, 1998; 1999; Taylor and Bain, 1999; Batt, 2000; Kinnie, Purcell and Hutchinson, 2000; Callaghan and Thompson, 2001; Bain *et al.*, 2002; Taylor *et al.*, 2002). That is to say, while call centres have been a workplace unit of analysis for the assessment of new technology in office work, no empirical evidence has explored the work organization of call centres through the lens of an occupation and more

154 Professionals at Work

dedicated helpline call centres. Crucially, there is an equally credible conceptual rationale to study call centres that employ a highly qualified workforce with more status and authority than a standardized clerical occupation. Frenkel *et al.* (1999) advocated that models of work varied according to different occupational bases. Similarly, Smith (1997) suggested that an occupational group with a consciousness of work practices could likely shape ways of organizing.

Furthermore, despite the fact that call centre work has an increasingly global presence, all the studies have restricted their focus in one national setting, with the exception of Frenkel *et al.* (1998). However, their international focus was not comparative. Likewise, the recent edited book by Holtgrewe, Kerst and Shire (2002), *Re-organising Service Work: Call Centres in Germany and Britain*, drew mainly on German and British contributors, but the analysis was largely non-comparative. Therefore the literature on call centres has generally ignored the question that work can be nation-specific. This is rather surprising given significant cross-national organizational comparisons demonstrating the influence of nations and institutions upon work organization and variations across borders (Maurice, Sellier and Silvestre, 1986; Lane, 1989; Maurice and Sorge, 2000).

The aim of the research is to contribute to a greater understanding of the experience of call centre work through the lens of a strong occupational group and national context. In other words, occupation and nation are important filters for assessing the work organization of call centres. With a clear lack of empirical evidence drawing from academic research on professional call centres, it is difficult to know if all call centre work operates in the same way for all categories of labour – for expert or skilled occupations as well as routine ones. I address the debate by examining the experience of tele-health centres staffed by nurse advisors and located in two national territories. What is the labour process of nurse call centres in Quebec and England? To what extent have nurses been able to shape their call centre activities? Although it seems, likely that call centre work for professional nurses is organized differently from that of routine white-collar workers, there is no empirical evidence to confirm this assumption. Some time ago, Thompson correctly observed, 'as the starting points of occupations are different, experiences and consequences will vary correspondingly' (quoted in Webster, 1990, p. 84). This also raises the question of possible variations between Quebecois and English nurse advisors working in a call centre setting, as well as national work features which could emerge between Quebec and England.

Research methodology

The core objective of this research is to examine the experience of a different call centre workforce: one that is highly qualified and one that possesses a consciousness of work practices. Nursing is different from routine customer service work. Nurses form a credential-based occupation, in which they share distinctive qualifications, skills and knowledge gained through education and registration. With qualifications increasingly defined in an academic corpus and with a strong consciousness of work practices it is possible that nurses could seek to infuse their knowledge into the labour process. This could be done, for example, by defining work techniques and practices, and by determining the time spent on telephone consultations. The second objective of this research is to examine the call centre work within a cross-national framework. Nurse call centres have developed similarly in several countries, including, Canada (MSSS, 1994), the UK (DoH, 1997), and the USA (Quilter Wheeler and Windt, 1993).

Canada and the UK were seen as the most appropriate sites for comparative purposes as both have developed similar tax-funded national health systems (Hart, 1994, pp. 117–18; Rathwell, 1994, p. 7). However, the focus had to be restrained to Quebec and England. In Canada, not all provinces have initiated a round-the-clock nurse-led telephone service. What pertains to a Canadian province in the field of healthcare is circumscribed within this provincial context.[1] In the UK, Scotland has followed England in the development of nurse call centres, but has chosen to remain separate and differentiated itself with a distinct name, NHS 24. Findings related to England therefore cannot be generalized to the UK nationwide.

With this focus on two societal contexts, a case-study approach was adopted. Two sites in England and two in Quebec were selected, with a concern for comparability between the four settings. The sites were matched as far as possible in terms of call centre environment, size and similar clinical assessment support software. Data were collected at the macro, organizational and micro-levels. Direct access was granted in each site, and organizational and micro-level data were collected intensively over a three-week period. Site observations and semi-structured interviews were conducted with general managers, nurse leaders, team leaders, supervisors, nurse advisors, medical directors and call centre managers. Macro-level data on nursing education, healthcare division of labour and national health system were collected from documentary secondary sources.

156 *Professionals at Work*

In this chapter, areas of cross-national commonalities and intra-national variances of nurse call centres are not examined. Rather, the wider causality of cross-national differences and the national dimension is explained. Indeed, the labour process of a telephone consultation is nation-specific and the societal construction of doctors, nurses and state determined the degree of influence of nurses over their work methods. Moreover, national factors have influenced the response towards an American-dominant way of organizing tele-health nursing, which acted to reinforce or undermine a nurse-led and nurse controlled practice.

Background to telephone-based healthcare services in Quebec and England

Both the Quebecois and British state government have developed similar '24/7' telephone-based healthcare services. In Quebec, the state-sponsored nurse-led telephone consultation service has covered the whole province since 1995, and is known as Health-Info CLSC (*Info-Santé CLSC*) (MSSS, 1999). However, the first experience of nurses delivering health services over the phone developed locally in 1984 in the administrative region of Quebec, and the service was named Health-Info (Doré, 2000). In England, NHS Direct, the '24/7' telephone-based health service, has been available nationally since the end of the year 2000 (National Audit Office, 2002).

Despite Health-Info CLSC and NHS Direct having emerged at different historical points in time and in different national settings separated by the Atlantic, the nature of the service they provide and their mission are very much alike (MSSS, 1994; DoH, 1997). First, these services provide a rapid and practical answer over the phone to health queries of physical or psychological concerns 24 hours a day and seven days a week. Individuals experiencing a health symptom or in need of information about local healthcare providers, particular diseases and illnesses can communicate with Health-Info CLSC/NHS Direct to get an answer to their health queries and be directly referred to an appropriate healthcare resource. Second, both services' mission is to improve access and accessibility of citizens to advice and information about health, illness and the public healthcare system so that they can better care for themselves and their families.

The labour process of a telephone consultation in Quebecois nurse call centres (Health-Info CLSC)

In Quebec, the practice of tele-nursing is superimposed on the nursing process methodology. The latter is a scientific nursing discourse taught in educational institutions (Trottier, 1982) and is set in motion in several nurse settings (Hénault and Malo, 1999). The practice of nursing over the phone is therefore a continuity of pre-existing lines and embedded in a nursing methodology central to the education of Quebecois nurses. This could well explain the short training (between five and six days) received by nurses when they begin to work for Health-Info CLSC (fieldwork). They are expected to have standardized nursing skills and knowledge, and a sound clinical judgement acquired outside the organization in their training and in previous clinical experience (Leprohon and Hénault, 1998, p. 12; fieldwork). A minimum of three years of work experience with a diversified clientele is required (Leprohon and Hénault, 1998, p. 12). In fact, in the two sites I studied, access to organizational documentation demonstrated that 99 per cent (Health-Info CLSC A) and 80 per cent (Health-Info CLSC B) had more than five years of diversified experience.

The nursing process is a systematic methodology of four steps: assessment, planning, implementation and evaluation (Witz, 1994, p. 30). On the one hand, this approach is problem-solving-focused allowing nurses to provide healthcare based on their capacity for clinical judgement and informed by their experience and clinical knowledge. In Quebecois nurse call centres, the labour process of a telephone consultation service reflects the four steps of this methodology and translates into assessment, planning/intervention and evaluation. Equally, the labour process of a telephone consultation is supported by a computerized infrastructure.

The computerized infrastructure

The primary screen of the computerized knowledge infrastructure is a 'call record card' (*fiche d'appel*) based on the four-step nursing methodology, and has a 'form-filling' metaphor. It enables nurses to formalize and document their telephone consultation in a computerized format, thereby augmenting the quality of the service and protecting nurses against potential complaints. The 'call record card' was first designed in a paper format and later integrated into the software application. Other elements that were incorporated into this computerized knowledge infrastructure were the nursing protocols, the resource directory and the 'caller identification and registration card'. These are hyperlinks and pop-ups accessed from the primary screen. All these elements of the labour process were first designed on paper format.

158   *Professionals at Work*

When the Health-Info programme of the region of Quebec developed in 1984, unprecedented developments of micro-electronics and semi-conductors in terms of price, power, reliability and capability had yet to emerge. In the early 1980s, the use of desk-top computers in offices was still in its infant stage, with expensive costs related to it. Consequently, in the early years of a nurse-led telephone consultation service, the labour process did not rely on technology such as computers and software. At the beginning of the 1990s, the regional nurse call centre in charge of adapting and maintaining the contents of the nursing protocols presented a plan of computerization prepared by nurses to the Ministry of Health and Social Services. In turn, the Ministry mandated a health-care computing management society, SOGIQUE, to computerize the Health-Info programme following the project plan designed by nurses. Since 1997, nurse advisors have been working with the computerized version. The introduction of computers has not dramatically changed the job content and methodology of the labour process, which has remained centred on the nursing process. Rather than the computer software creating new office procedures, the computerized infrastructure has been invented in response to specific needs and a labour process already socially shaped.

Assessment, planning/intervention and evaluation steps

Beyond welcoming and greeting the client, the first step of the labour process of a telephone consultation is to make an assessment of the health situation of an individual. The assessment consists of collecting, investigating and reformulating relevant data on the health situation of a client. Nurse advisors have complete flexibility and autonomy to direct the conversation and talk back and forth to gain valuable information on the person's health situation. The pattern of questioning is not standardized either in the form of prompts or explicit questions. Nurses have to rely on their theoretical knowledge and clinical expertise to ask questions that allow clients to describe their health situation. The nurse advisor decides what to ask and when to ask it, allowing the natural process of analysis to take place. The process of assessment is highly interdependent between nurses and clients. While the nurse advisor possesses the theoretical knowledge, the individual provides the contextual knowledge. The assessment step is based on highly contingent knowledge and nurse advisors organize and document the data collected on the computerized 'call record card'. They are firmly in control of the machine. Once they obtain a clear picture of the issues involved nurses use their clinical judgement to identify the health problem that might require intervention. The planning/intervention step is supported by the use of scientific nursing protocols. These are written scientific guidelines to support nurses in the provision of healthcare. The interactive link on the primary care screen enables nurse advisors to navigate easily within the scientific nursing protocols database, which has over 400 protocols. The content of the protocols are reviewed and developed by a Scientific Nursing Forum composed of experts in nursing care from diverse milieu,[2] and excluding doctors and government representatives. The principal *raison d' être* of the nursing protocols is to maintain high-quality standards, safety and consistency of advice and information for clients whatever part of the province they are phoning from. Yet, strict adherence to rules in the nursing protocols is not compulsory. The protocols must allow nurse advisors to make a patient-centred intervention, which is central to the nursing process methodology. Referring to interviews conducted with the lead nurses of the two sites, nurse advisors are expected to make a judicious use of the nursing protocols in the context of the individual and using their clinical expertise:

> The clinical judgement is what enables nurse advisors to use the nursing protocols. Some elements of the assessment won't be consistent with the nursing protocols and nurses have to use their clinical judgement... Nurses are dependent on their expertise and the judicious utilization of the nursing protocols.
> Lead nurse, Health-Info CLSC A, the author's free translation

> The protocols come to support nurses in their nursing intervention. People perceive the work of nurse advisors wrongly, saying that the nurse is forced to make rigid use of the nursing protocols to provide a telephone response. This is incorrect. Nurses need to rely in their clinical judgement to use the protocols in the context of the individual.
> Lead nurse, Health-Info CLSC B, the author's free translation

Nurse advisors are able to function with autonomy and exercise their clinical judgement to find a 'fit' between the nursing guideline and the health situation of the individual. The protocols are never used in a mechanical way and nurse advisors are allowed and expected to make use of their expertise and address the solution holistically. As long as their clinical judgement is within the ground of safety and formalized

160 *Professionals at Work*

into the computerized 'call record card', nurse advisors have authority to override the nursing protocols. This authority is not challenged. Experience and clinical judgement are central and the machine has a secondary role, acting as an electronic extension of nurses' knowledge.

Nurse advisors know that the protocols generalize a situation while each case is unique, making their expertise and clinical judgement necessary. They can, however, obtain help if necessary. Nurses have access to a documentation centre, with reference books and other related health articles, and encyclopaedia they can consult. More importantly, they can ask advice and share knowledge with a nurse supervisor or a colleague whose expertise in a specialist area is recognized among peers. Commenting on their level of autonomy, nurse advisors from both sites stated:

> We have a lot of autonomy. I don't depend on the doctor, I am independent and I depend on my clinical judgement to enable the individual to deal with the problem...we have to go with our expertise in combination with the protocols and we are not blamed if we do not use a protocol, as long as we have a clinical judgement well documented to prove us right.
> Nurse advisor, Health-Info CLSC A, the author's free translation

> I am autonomous. We have the protocols, but we have to customize our intervention to provide relevant information, education and advice relevant to the context. We can't read everything... sometimes the protocols do not assist us to empower the client. We have to use our expertise and clinical judgement.
> Nurse advisor, Health-Info CLSC B, the author's free translation

After the nurse advisor has instructed the client on what to do, the final phase is to evaluate the client's understanding of this information and his/her satisfaction with the course of action that has been proposed. As with the previous steps, this part of the nursing methodology over the phone must be documented through the computerized 'call record card'.

The labour process of a telephone consultation in English nurse call centres (NHS Direct)

In contrast to the work methods of tele-nursing in Quebec, in England there has not been a transfer of the nursing process methodology in the 'phone-side' environment. The telephone consultation methodology is embedded into the clinical decision support system's own logic of assessment, which is independent of nursing knowledge. Indeed, there is a general ambiguity about the methodology or the structure of the assessment embedded in the software. 'The assessment model is CAS [Clinical Assessment System]. But if you're talking in terms of a model of nursing, I don't know what model the system is based on' (Senior nurse supervisor, NHS Direct C).

The NHS Clinical Assessment System (CAS) – previously called Axa Assistance – was originally designed by an American physician and is a yes/no decision tree based on rigid algorithms. Central to this physician-designed triage system is the medical model of care, which is fragmented and adopts a symptom-based approach instead of a holistic approach to care. This facilitates the use of a mass model whereby callers can be treated according to a standardized menu.

The telephone nursing practice in NHS Direct is subjected to CAS. Nurse advisors must have a minimum of five years' post-qualification experience. (National Audit Office, 2002, p. 15). To assist nurses to take on their new roles they undergo a fairly lengthy period of training: five and six weeks in NHS Direct D and C (fieldwork). While the content varies from one site to another it normally involves training in the CAS software and clinical nursing knowledge and a period of 'nursery desking' or 'buddying' in which the new nurses listen to live calls before taking supervised calls.

The assessment process

CAS plays a central role in the tele-nursing process. During the assessment stage of a call the system takes the consultation down a predetermined route. It poses a series of automated questions in logical sequence. It effectively tells nurse advisors what to say and when to say it. The questions take two forms: either leading questions requiring a simple 'Yes', 'No' or 'Uncertain', or a list of symptoms to which the patient must respond. Although there is a 'Free Text' box to add further notes related to the questions, nurse advisors have little discretion to lead the assessment process. Tele-nurses cannot bypass the questions. Once in the decision tree, they are required to follow it through to the end even in situations where it is obvious that the line of enquiry is inappropriate. Moreover, the questions generalize a situation without considering factors such as gender and age, sometimes putting nurse advisors in rather embarrassing situations. As one nurse commented, 'some questions you wanna die – Have you been raped?' A second nurse explained

162 *Professionals at Work*

her story when a mother called for her one-year old baby who had a nose bleed. One question that came up was: do you take cocaine?

CAS reflects the third principle of Taylorism, which is direct control by management of each step of the labour process and its mode of execution (Braverman, 1974, p. 113). This principle suggests that the execution of work should be planned out and determined by management. When Taylorism first emerged, these directives were communicated in a top-down manner on written instruction cards. In the case of English tele-nurses, the assessment process has been mathematically pre-planned and rigid scientific algorithms embedded in CAS determine in a precise manner its mode of execution. Written instruction cards are obsolete and replaced by automatically prompted written questions that are imposed on nurse advisors in conducting an assessment. As in classic Taylorism, these standardized questions specify in complete details what nurse advisors should ask and when to ask it.

The rigidity of the software interferes with the inherent clinical reasoning and questioning of tele-nurses. This became clear during the fieldwork undertaken at NHS Direct D, where the CAS software had just replaced a previous clinical decision support system (TAS). TAS was a British guideline-based software built on a cognitive model that allowed more flexibility and did not impose a predetermined pathway and did not arrive at a final decision (The Plain Software Company Limited, 1999; Sanders, 1999). The comments made by tele-nurses of NHS Direct D during the semi-structured interviews revealed marked differences in their attitudes to the two systems. Most believed that the CAS software overly directed the assessment process and left them with little flexibility:

> They [algorithms] are very new. I didn't like them at first. They are so different. With the new algorithms, you can't see the whole picture. I don't like this. And with the previous system, you could flick back and forward quite easily ... equally with the old system you could override at any moment. With CAS, you have clear-cut questions and you go down through a predetermined pathway. It's more diffi-cult to see a picture.
>
> Nurse advisor, NHS Direct D

> TAS [previous software] allowed you a lot of autonomy to practice. CAS narrows down the process. It tells you what to ask ... it takes away this autonomy. It does not allow thinking any more. It's assess-ing one symptom only. I can't work like that.
>
> Nurse advisor, NHS Direct D

With TAS, it was a picture-building exercise. You had to open boxes, categories: ears, baby crying...and it would say what questions to ask. As we were talking, we were building a picture. You would then have a summary of what was urgent and less urgent and you would make a clinical judgement on where to send the patient. CAS takes you straight to a line somewhere.

Nurse advisor, NHS Direct D

This provides evidence of the fragmentation of knowledge and its separation into 'parcels' or 'bits' which are co-ordinated through the system's algorithm-based logic. This too is classical Taylorism: 'the dissociation of the labour process from the skills of the workers' (Braverman, 1974, p. 113). The necessary knowledge used to complete a 'whole' task or product is fragmented and then co-ordinated by rules and laws determined by management. 'The managers...assume the burden of gathering together all of the traditional knowledge which in the past has been possessed by the workmen and then of classifying, tabulating, and reducing this knowledge to rules, laws and formulae' (Taylor, quoted in Braverman, 1974, p. 112). Following this 'scientific management' principle, workers are deprived of the need to employ their intellect or judgement in performing a whole task or product, increasing the speed of the labour process by repetition of a simple and fragmented job. Moreover, in this 'world' of calculated and tabulated co-ordination of work, it becomes increasingly more complex for workers to understand the process in which they function. In the case of English nurse advisors, CAS fragmented the assessment process by prompting one question at a time, which were then co-ordinated by the software's own calculated set of rules, laws and formulae. These 'logics' embedded in CAS overrode rather than supported nurses' clinical knowledge with nurse advisors being locked within its constraints. For tele-nurses it became more difficult to understand the labour process of a health assessment. They found it difficult to see the 'whole picture' of an assessment. The software led them in a straight line of questioning and had the effect of 'narrowing down' their clinical reasoning.

The intervention process

Not only does CAS direct the assessment of a health situation, it also contains a process for determining an appropriate intervention. The clinical decision support software can produce an 'automated' disposition

164 Professionals at Work

which ranks from A&E, GP, Pharmacy or Home-Care. However, CAS is not a complete 'machine takeover'. Nurses do have the opportunity to override the system.

This of course is quite consistent with the growing professionalism of nursing and the consolidation of their position in the area of healthcare (Hicks, 1998). There has been a growing desire to make greater use of their expertise and clinical judgement in the context of the patient (Beardshaw and Robinson, 1990; Salvadge, 1992; Witz, 1994). Crucially, since 1992 nurses have been required to be accountable for the care they deliver. Indeed, the new code of practice (UKCC, 1992) provides a basis for independent, professional judgement where principles for practice replace certificates for tasks and a rule-focused approach (Williams, 2000, p. 30).

The knock-on effects of these changes in nursing have been noted in clinical settings (for example, Williams, 2000, pp. 70–4). In NHS Direct nurse advisors can use their expertise and clinical decision-making if they feel that the final 'automated' outcome is inappropriate in the context of the individual. If, in the course of the conversation with the patient, the nurse detects some factor that warrants a higher or lower level of care than given by the software's own logic, she can override the disposition as long as the clinical decision is safe and documented. Overriding is the act of not following the solution or disposition (999, A&E, GP, Pharmacy and Home-Care) prompted by the clinical decision support software.

All nurse advisors interviewed felt that they were using their knowledge, skills and clinical judgement when they were downgrading or upgrading the referral instruction of the software:

> You need a nursing background to upgrade or downgrade.
>
> Nurse advisor, NHS Direct D

> You need your clinical judgement when it says Home-Care and I think it's more serious.
>
> Nurse advisor, NHS Direct C

> You can override the system, but you have to write down why you override it. It makes it user-specific.
>
> Nurse advisor, NHS Direct D

The software used by nurse advisors does not completely eliminate the conceptual element of the work. The nurse has to exercise choice over the appropriate course of action to take. However, the extent to which nurse advisors are encouraged or restricted by management in using their clinical expertise to oppose the standardization logic of the software varied across sites. Moreover, while nurse advisors felt autonomous in overriding the software, this process is tightly monitored. The technical fabric of the software monitors any deviations from the automatically populated disposition. In this sense the system provides facilities to extend monitoring to the clinical practice of nurse advisors. CAS generates detailed feedback on individual nurse performance in terms of the range of dispositions they have used, the frequency at which they have overridden the automatically prompted outcome, and the number of calls taken.

The software makes the work of nurse advisors highly visible allowing for better job analysis and greater knowledge and control by management and doctors. This corresponds to the Taylorist principle of 'the separation of conception from execution' (Braverman, 1974, p. 114). This refers to the systematic study of work by management to strengthen its power over the labour process. With CAS, traditional time and motion studies, which involved monitoring and direct surveillance, are embedded in the technical fabric of the system. It allows monitoring of nurses' work in terms of quantity (for example, number of calls taken and average call length) and individual performance of nurse advisors in terms of the disposition they use and the frequency with which they override the system. These are powerful tools by which management can improve 'either methodological efficiency or the working pace desired by capital' (Braverman, 1974, pp. 113–14).

National context and dominant industrial practices

The remaining section of this chapter provides an explanation of the different work methods of telephone nursing found in Quebec and England. While the work methodology of telephone nursing in Quebec has developed within existing lines of the nursing practice, in England it has been influenced by US technological software. At first sight, it seems surprising that Quebecois nurses have shaped their tele-nursing practice locally, without evident influence of other dominant practices from their American neighbours, and that English nurses use a US-developed software on which to base their telephone consultation. Furthermore, in the case of England, one of three initial software providers in pilot sites was a product developed and commercialized in Britain. Why have Quebecois nurses been able to shape their work

166 *Professionals at Work*

methods of the 'phone-side' practice without influence from dominant practices developed in other countries? Likewise, why have British nurses not been able to shape their work methods of tele-nursing? Why this diffusion and preference of an American clinical decision support software over a British one? The national context is held crucial in explaining the role of nurses in shaping their practices over the phone.

The national context of Quebecois nurse call centres and 'neutral' diffusion of a dominant industrial practice from the USA

The first experience of a '24/7' telephone-based healthcare service in the province of Quebec developed in 1984 in the administrative region of Quebec, and the service was named Health-Info (*Info-Santé*). Contrary to expectations, the service became permanent and spread to other regions. As the service expanded, nurses organized and formalized their nursing practice over the phone. Initially developed in 1984, Quebec was an 'early mover' in the provision of nurse-led telephone consultation services. At this time, no other Canadian provinces had introduced 24-hour tele-health centres; the Northwest of the USA witnessed the development of their first 24-hour nurse service the same year (Quilter Wheeler and Windt, 1993, p. 4). As an early mover into the industry of tele-nursing there were, as yet, no external models that had been tested or established. This left Quebecois nurses with more room for experimentation and growth nationally. Indeed, nurses have developed their 'phone-side' practice based on their knowledge and copying within existing national nursing practices.

When it became the intention of the Quebecois government to develop a provincial-wide '24/7' telephone-based healthcare (MSSS, 1994), nurses had already developed the expertise in providing telephone consultation services in some regions of the province. More importantly, under this state-ownership of the service, nurses and their professional association kept authority and control over the development and improvement, as well as the evaluation of the quality of the nursing practice over the phone. One could argue that the central role played by nurses in the decision-making power structure of Health-Info CLSC is due to the national specificity of origins; with past local experience of nurses in delivering a telephone consultation service, they have constituted themselves as the main players within tele-nursing as it moved from a local to a province-wide system. But how did nurses and their professional association maintain their authority given the state-ownership of the service and why did doctors not challenge their autonomy? The explanation is found in the socially constructed role of state, nurses and doctors.

The Ministry of Health and Social Services did not specify that the state-sponsored '24/7' telephone-based healthcare would be the Health-Info programme, which was already in use in several regions of Quebec and available to 58 per cent of the population (MSSS, 1999, p. 3). It simply mandated the Regional Board[3] to oversee the implementation of this 'new' service and to allocate funding for the CLSCs[4], which in turn were responsible for running '24/7' telephone-based healthcare. These three levels of decisions respected the decentralized role that Quebec's Ministry of Health and Social Services has historically developed for itself. The key principle underlying this decentralization is that achieving results was not a tool for technocrats (O'Neil, 1992, p. 296). Therefore, it fell to the CLSCs to operationalize the service. This decentralized healthcare system of Quebec has generated the opportunity for health professionals to extend their practice in a new clinical milieu and organize the provision of the telephone service within the CLSCs. The healthcare division of labour has determined which health professional group would operationalize the '24/7' telephone-based healthcare services.

Over the years, supported by governmental legislation, nurses have socially constructed themselves as the professional healthcare group capable of assessing the health needs of people, educating and informing, and possessing the ability to help and encourage people to take charge of their health considering their social milieu. These are their core tasks and they are legally recognized in the Nursing Act (1973). The independent role of nurses corresponded exactly to the functions of the '24/7' telephone service set out in the frame of reference (MSSS, 1994), which were to assess the health needs of people, providing them health information and self-care advice to allow them to take control for their health. Moreover, since 1973 the Code of Professions (see, for example, Chagnon, 1992) legally recognized the nursing occupation as a profession and provided it with a legal duty to evaluate and supervise the quality and practices of nursing in the healthcare establishments, including tele-nursing. This meant that no other professional healthcare group, such as doctors, could supervise and assess nurses' work over the phone.

In 1995, when the service became available on a national basis and fully integrated to the CLSCs, all notions of how work was organized remained under control of Quebecois nurses. By this time their American neighbours had developed an expertise in the tele-health industry.

168 Professionals at Work

Robust algorithm-based systems supported US nurses in their work, and allowed little chance of error and reduced the risk of adverse outcomes. This became a dominant practice in the American industry of telephone nursing (Sabin, 1998). However, this dominant technological practice did not diffuse to Quebec. Yet again, the national context is important. More particularly, the national language prevented this transfer from the USA to Quebec.

Following the Charter of the French Language (1977), Quebec's official language is French. It is the language of law, education and communications. Crucially, its purpose is to make French the language of business and the workplace. This had important implications for the transfer of an anglophone dominant clinical decision support software. Under the Charter of the French Language and to conform to the linguistic legislation, all Anglo-American clinical decision support software would have required a francization programme. When the Health-Info programme became state-sponsored, the service had been developed using the French language, respecting the official language of the workplace, and the computerization that came later was done in French. It is difficult to explain why American software did not diffuse to Quebec but the national linguistic legislation should not be neglected as an element that has filtered the diffusion of these practices.

The national context of English nurse call centres and diffusion of a dominant industrial practice from the USA

British nurses have been more dissociated from the development of their tele-nursing practice than their Quebecois counterparts. In England, authority for strategic and operational decisions is concentrated at the top via the NHS Direct Central Project Team within the Department of Health. This is consistent with the centralized role the British government has historically played in the delivery of public services (Handy, 1993, p. 267). Despite more recent involvement of management at operational level, the centralized structure is still forceful and the role of the British state in delivering public services has been characterized as the 'surveillance state' (Clarke and Newman, 1997, in Calveley and Shelly, 2002) and the 'evaluative state' (Walsh, 1996, in Calveley and Shelly, 2002). With a strong emphasis on results, targets and achieving major cost efficiencies there has been little room for health professionals to define the clinical practice in a 'phone-side' environment.

The medical profession however was also involved in decision-making processes. This mirrored the societal effect of the social settlement between British nurses and doctors in the healthcare division of labour. British nurses have not yet gained their operational autonomy over their day-to-day work (Witz, 1994). There is continuing evidence of doctors' control over the nursing labour process (Williams, 2000). Moreover, UK GPs have had a taken-for-granted central position in the primary healthcare sector (Williams *et al.*, 1993; Ashburner and Birch, 1999; Williams, 2000). The recent implementation of Primary Care Groups (PCGs) for assessing the needs of local people and developing and implementing primary care services has remained GP-dominated (Ashburner and Birch, 1999).

England was a relatively 'late mover' in the industry of tele-nursing. NHS Direct was a state-sponsored project announced in late 1997. During the end of the 1980s and early 90s, the USA had developed the industry of telephone nursing and the practice of nursing triage based on algorithmic systems had become the most structured approach and dominant way in the US tele-nursing industry (Sabin, 1998). The market was competitive and several algorithm-based software providers existed. Consequently, the NHS Direct Central Project Team was exposed to established or dominant industry's recipes. With the first wave of development of NHS Direct, two out of three software systems were American-designed (Sanders, 1999; Munro *et al.*, 2000). The other one was British (Munro *et al.*, 2000). The first few users of the US software were trained in Colorado and Chicago (Shamash, 1998, p. 22). The Central Project Team and some general managers of the pilot sites went to the USA to get a better understanding of the tele-nursing industry (Confidential, 1999). Prescriptive formula put technical knowledge and 'expertise' in the hands of management and civil servants, who otherwise had little experience in the development of telephone nursing practices. The common English language of the UK and the USA also encouraged the exchange of 'best practices'.

The software system that was chosen for NHS Direct had a number of important characteristics. First, the algorithm-based yes/no decision tree ensured high consistency of the nursing triage. It was an assessment tool with standardized questions to make a precise, safe and 'risk-free' evaluation of a symptom. Second, the technological fabric embedded in the system generated detailed reports on standardized and measurable goals in terms of level of triage and variability of nurse advisors, facilitating comparability and standardization of the nursing triage across sites. Third, the system permitted calls to be routed to the

170 *Professionals at Work*

most appropriate staff (that is health information advisors or nurse advisors) and from (expensive) clinical staff to (less expensive) non-clinical staff such as information assistants. Fourth, the software system was able to reduce the average call time from 12 minutes to 6.1 minutes (Donnelly, 2000, p. 5).

Conclusions

The work experience of Quebecois and British nurse call centres was found to be quite different. In Quebec, nurses filtered the development of tele-nursing through their own nursing practices. They made extensive use of their abstract knowledge and clinical judgement to assess the health needs of their clients. There was no automation of nurse-led telephone consultations. Computerization came later and respected the work methods that were already socially created. The introduction of computers did not dramatically change the job content of nurse advisors nor reduced their high level of work autonomy. In England, nurse advisors were subordinated to an American-designed algorithm-based software. From an analysis of the nurse-machine interface the evidence suggested that this system was akin to classic Taylorism.

From a cross-national perspective it can be seen that the labour process of tele-nursing was quite different in Quebec and England. The extent to which nurses were able to shape their nursing practice over the phone was also different in each national context. These variations were shaped by societal factors, by national factors such as whether the service was an 'early' or 'late' mover and by national language. Although Quebecois and English nurses constituted a credential-based occupation, possessing distinct knowledge and skills, they were socialized differently within the healthcare system. More precisely, the societal construction of nurses, doctors and the state helped determine the extent to which the nursing occupation had legitimate authority to develop their practices over the phone. These findings support the societal effects approach in which it is recognized that the social construction of actors impact on an organization's hierarchy and co-ordination of work (Maurice, Sellier and Silvestre, 1986; Maurice, 2000). On the other hand, national factors such as historical development and language have also influenced the extent to which nursing practices have been exposed to American influence in the tele-health industry. This in turn has acted to reinforce or undermine a nurse-led and nurse-controlled practice.

Through the lens of nurse call centres in two national settings, this research has therefore lent support to the move towards an integrated understanding and explanation of the nature of call centre work staffed by professional labour. It would therefore be sensible for further research in the call centres sector not only to look beyond the limited range of occupations and industries so far studied, but also to frame this research in such a way to capture these rich contextual features.

Notes

1. Although the ten provinces share the same basic principles of the national healthcare system (Medicare), a province is left free to administer, design and organize its health system. There are therefore considerable variations between the healthcare system of one province to another one.
2. University, the professional association of nurses of the province of Quebec (*Organization des infirmières et infirmiers du Québec* [OIIQ]), public health and Health-Info CLSC.
3. The regional boards are integrated to the Ministry of Health and Social Services. All health and social work facilities are geographically grouped under one of the 18 regional boards of Quebec's healthcare system. The boards, whose members are mostly citizens, have legal responsibilities to ensure regional planning, implementation, co-ordination and funding of the health services according to the needs of the population of the specific territory, and those elaborated by the MHSS.
4. Networks of healthcare organizations throughout the province of Quebec since the 1970s to act as the first point of access to primary care services. By law, the CLSCs are mandated to provide first-line health, social and community care to the population of their geographical territory. Today, there exist 147 CLSCs spread out in the 18 administrative regions of Quebec's healthcare system.

References

Ashburner, L. and K. Birch (1999) 'Professional Control Issues Between Medicine and Nursing in Primary Care', in A. L. Mark and S. Dopson (eds), *Organizational Behaviour in Health Care: The Research Agenda*, London: Macmillan.

Bain, P., A. Watson, G. Mulvey, P. Taylor and G. Gall (2002) 'Taylorism, Targets and the Pursuit of Quantity and Quality by Call Centre Management', *New Technology, Work and Employment*, 17(3).

Batt, R. (2000) 'Strategic segmentation in front-line services: matching customers, employees and human resource systems', *International Journal of Human Resources Management*, 11(3), pp. 540–61.

Beardshaw, V. and R. Robinson (1990) *New for Old? Prospects for Nursing in the 1990s*, London: King's Fund Institute.

Braverman, H. (1974) *Labor and Monopoly Capital: The Degradation of Work in the Twentieth Century*, New York: Monthly Review Press.

Callaghan, G. and P. Thompson (2001) 'Edwards revisited: technical control and call centres', *Economic and Industrial Democracy*, 22(1), pp. 13–37.

172 *Professionals at Work*

Calveley, M. and S. Shelley (2002) 'Does Sector Make a Difference? A Comparative Study of "Managerialism" in Secondary and Higher Education', paper presented at the 20th Annual International Labour Process Conference, 2–4 April, Glasgow, Strathclyde Business School.

Chagnon, M. (1992) 'Continuous Improvement of Nursing Practice: Experience in Quebec', *Quality Assurance in Health Care*, 4(3), pp. 179–86.

Confidential (1999) Interview conducted by C. Smith with a general manager of a NHS Direct site.

DoH (1997) *The New NHS: Modern, Dependable*, London: Department of Health.

DoH (2000a) *Department of Health Response to the Independent Review of GP Out-of-hours Services in England Report: Raising Standards for Patients. New Partnerships in Out-of-Hours Care*, London: Department of Health.

DoH (2000b) *The NHS Plan: A Plan for Investment, A Plan for a Reform*, London: Department of Health.

DoH (2000c) *New National NHS Direct Computer System to Benefit Patients*, London: Department of Health.

Donnelly, L. (2000) 'The Bastard Let us Down: NHS Direct bidder', *Health Service Journal*, 110(5722), p. 5.

Doré, C. (2000) 'Info-Santé CLSC, un Succès qui s'Exporte', *Le Réseau Informatique*, 12(3).

Frenkel, S., M. Korczynski, K. Shire and M. Tam (1998) 'Beyond Bureaucracy? Work organization in call centres', *International Journal of Human Resource Management*, 9(6), pp. 957–79.

Frenkel, S., M. Korczynski, K. Shire and M. Tam (1999) *On the Front Line: Organization of work in the information economy*, Ithaca, NY: Cornell University Press.

Greenword, L. (2000) 'IT Looks Like Trouble', *Health Service Journal*, 14 September, pp. 13–14.

Handy, C. (1993) *Understanding Organizations*, London: Penguin.

Hart, G. (1994) 'The NHS: Founding Principles and the Reforms', in K. Lee (ed.), *Health Care Systems in Canada and the United Kingdom: Can they Deliver?*, Keele: Ryburn Publishing.

Hénault, M. and D. Malo (1999) *L'Exercice Infirmier en Santé Communautaire: Les Services de Santé Courants et Info-Santé*, Montreal: Ordre des Infirmières et Infirmiers du Québec.

Hicks, C. (1998) 'Barriers to Evidence-Based Care in Nursing: Historical Legacies and Conflicting Cultures', *Health Services Management Research*, 11(3), pp. 137–47.

Holtgrewe, U., C. Kerst and K. Shire (2002) *Re-organising Service Work: Call Centres in Germany and Britain*, Aldershot: Ashgate.

Kinnie, N., J. Purcell and S. Hutchinson (2000) 'Fun and surveillance: the paradox of high commitment management in call centres', *International Journal of Human Resource Management*, 11(5), pp. 967–85.

Lane, C. (1989) *Management and Labour in Europe: The Industrial Enterprise in Germany, Britain and France*, Aldershot: Elgar.

Leprohon, J. and M. Hénault (1998) *Lignes Directrices pour l'Exercice Infirmier à Info-Santé*, Montreal: OIIQ.

Maurice, M. (2000) 'The Paradoxes of Societal Analysis: A Review of the Past and Prospects for the Future', in M. Maurice and A. Sorge (eds), *Embedding Organizations*, Amsterdam: John Benjamins.

Maurice, M., F. Sellier and J.-J. Silvestre (1986) *The Social Foundations of Industrial Power: A Comparison of France and Germany*, Cambridge, MA: The MIT Press.

MSSS (1994) *Service Téléphonique: Accessibilité Continue 24/7*, Quebec: MSSS.

MSSS (1999) *Évaluation Provinciale des Services Info-Santé CLSC: Rapport Final 1994–1999*, Quebec: MSSS.

Munro, J., J. Nicholl, A. O'Cathain and E. Knowles (2000) *Evaluation of NHS Direct First Waves Sites: Second Interim Report to the Department of Health*, Sheffield: University of Sheffield, Medical Care Research Unit.

National Audit Office (2002) *NHS Direct in England*, London: HMSO.

O'Neil, M. (1992) 'Community Participation in Quebec's Health System: A Strategy to Curtail Community Empowerment', *International Journal of Health Services*, 22(2), pp. 287–301.

Quilter Wheeler, S. and J. H. Windt (1993) *Telephone Triage: Theory, Practice and Protocol Development*, New York: Delmar Publishers Inc.

Rathwell, T. (1994) 'Health Care in Canada: a System in Turmoil', *Health Policy*, 27(1), pp. 5–17.

Sabin, M. (1998) 'Telephone Triage Improves Demand Management Effectiveness', *Health Financial Management*, 52(8), pp. 49–51.

Salvadge, J. (1992) 'The New Nursing: Empowering Patients or Empowering Nurses?', in J. Robinson, A. Grey and R. Elkan (eds), *Policy Issues in Nursing*, Buckingham: Open University Press.

Sanders, T. (1999) 'Two Vie for NHS Direct', *Health Service Journal*, 109(5646), p. 3.

Shamash, J. (1998) 'Between the lines', *Nursing Standard*, 12(28), pp. 22–3.

Smith, C. (1997) 'Labour Process', in A. Sorge and M. Warner (eds), *International Encyclopaedia of Business & Management: The Handbook of Organizational Behaviour*, London: International Thompson Business Press.

Taylor P. and Bain, P. (1999) '"An assembly line in the head": work and employee relations in the call centre', *Industrial Relations Journal*, 30(2), pp. 101–17.

Taylor, P., G. Mulvey, J. Hyman and P. Bain (2002) 'Work Organization, Control and the Experience of Work in Call Centres', *Work, Employment and Society*, 16(1), pp. 133–50.

The Charter of the French Language (1977; 1993) Available at: *www.olf.gouv.qc.ca/english/charter/index.html#t2olf*, accessed 16 December 2002.

The Plain Software Company Limited (1999) *The Natural Triage Solution for NHS Direct. Designed to Augment Nursing Judgement not Imitate it*, Bracknell: Agilent Technologies.

Trottier, L.-H. (1982) 'Evolution of the nursing profession in Quebec from 1920 to 1980', MSc dissertation submitted to Faculty of Nursing Sciences, University of Montreal.

UKCC (United Kingdom Central Council for Nursing, Midwifery and Health Visiting) (1992), *The Scope of Professional Conduct*, London: UKCC.

Webster, J. (1990) *Office Automation: The Labour Process and Women's Work in Britain*, Hemel Hempstead: Harvester Wheatsheaf.

Williams, A. (2000) *Nursing, Medicine and Primary Care*, Buckingham: Open University Press.

Williams, S. J., M. Calnan, S. L. Cant and J. Coyle (1993) 'All Change in the NHS? Implications of the NHS Reforms for Primary Care Prevention', *Sociology of Health and Illness*, 15(1), pp. 43–67.

Witz, A. (1994) 'The Challenge of Nursing', in J. Gabe, D. Kelleher and G. Williams (eds), *Challenging Medicine*, London: Routledge.

8
A Female Ghetto? Women's Careers in Telephone Call Centres*

Vicki Belt

Introduction

The rapid growth of telephone call centres has attracted a considerable amount of attention in the business, media and academic communities in several advanced industrial economies over the last decade. During this period, call centres have become an important new source of employment in many countries, particularly for women. Recent studies have estimated that female employees make up around 70 per cent of the call centre workforce in a number of different national and local labour market contexts (see Richardson and Marshall, 1996; IDS, 1997; Mitial, 1998; Bain and Taylor, 1999; Buchanan and Koch-Schulte, 1999; Breathnach, 2000; CWU, 2000). However, in spite of this, academic researchers have to date not examined the role and position of women in this growing 'industry'. The objective of this chapter is to explore one dimension of this issue, namely the nature of the career prospects open to women within call centres.

Questions about careers have been largely overlooked so far in call centre literature. Researchers have tended to focus instead upon the management techniques and forms of work organization used in call centres, with particular interest in the role of new technologies in the labour process. However, in the few cases where the issue of careers *has* been mentioned, call centres have been criticized for being largely 'career*less*' (see, for example, Taylor and Bain, 1999; Stanworth, 2000). Concerns have been expressed about the high rates of labour turnover

---

*This chapter originally appeared in the *Human Resource Management Journal*, 12(4), pp. 51–66.

present in the industry (see TUC, 2001), and employers have been accused of providing large numbers of part-time, low-skilled, highly repetitive, pressurized and 'dead-end' jobs. Further, the fact that many call centres are concentrated in old industrial areas with higher than average levels of unemployment (IDS, 2000; Bristow, Munday and Gripaios, 2000) has led some to argue that employers are playing a part in the production of geographical inequalities in terms of career opportunities (Stanworth, 2000; Stanford, 1999). This picture is worrying for those concerned with gender inequality in the workplace. On the basis of current evidence, it appears that significant numbers of women are currently entering into an area of employment that offers them very little in the way of career prospects. In fact, it would appear that call centres share many similarities in this regard with other older female-dominated workplaces and occupations. Women working in typing pools within large organizations in the past, for example, were similarly mainly dedicated to one highly repetitive work activity, with promotion prospects restricted to movement to a role as a senior typist or supervisor (Webster, 1990). In addition, secretaries have also been described as 'organizational isolates', segregated from the career structure of the broader organization in which they work (OECD, 1998). Call centre work seems to bear many of the old hallmarks of these traditional female employment 'ghettos', defined as places occupied mainly by women, offering low-skilled, low-status, undemanding jobs which employees find it extremely difficult to move on from (OECD, 1998).

Although this argument looks persuasive, it has not yet been the subject of detailed academic research. There are also indications that call centres may actually be at the forefront of recent processes of organizational change associated with opening up new possibilities for women to move into positions of higher status, rewards and responsibility. These include for example the decline of traditional organizational hierarchies and the 'linear' managerial career (see Halford, Savage and Witz, 1997; Wajcman, 1998), as well as a shift in emphasis towards what have been termed more 'feminine' 'empathetic and co-operative styles of management' (McDowell, 1997, p. 11; see also Kanter, 1977; Rosener, 1990; Scase and Goffee, 1993; Tomlinson, Brockbank and Traves, 1997; Maddock, 1999; Rutherford, 2001). It is possible, therefore, that women working in call centres may in fact enjoy *more* opportunities to move into positions of responsibility than they do in many other work environments. These issues are worthy of further investigation and discussion, and are the focus of this chapter.

176 *A Female Ghetto? Women's Careers in Telephone Call Centres*

Research methodology

This chapter draws on research evidence collected by the author between 1998 and 2000 as a part of a larger study on women's work and careers in call centres (see Belt, 2002). This research consisted of a number of different elements, including interviews with call centre industry representatives as well as analysis of documentary evidence in the form of specialist call centre literature. However, the main part of the fieldwork (and the part that is given most attention in this chapter) consisted of case studies of 11 different call centre organizations based in the United Kingdom and Ireland.[1] Each of these case studies involved semi-structured interviews with call centre operators or 'agents', team leaders and managers as well as non-participant observation of work processes and the collection of personnel data. The organizations were located in four contrasting industry sectors, namely retail financial services, mail order, information technology and the 'third-party' or outsourced sector.

In total, 85 interviews were carried out in the case study workplaces, varying in length from 45 minutes to two and a half hours. The interviewees were mainly female, although some male managers were also interviewed where necessary (in those organizations in which the call centre manager or human resources manager was male). The vast majority of interviews were conducted on a one-to-one basis, but on two occasions two team leaders were interviewed together, and on one other occasion two managers were interviewed at the same time. Overall, 27 of the interviewees were employed in managerial roles, a further 28 were team leaders, and 33 were agents. In addition to the one-to-one interviews, seven group interviews were undertaken with female agents, each lasting for approximately one and a half hours and involving between six and eight participants. A mixture of part-time and full-time, temporary and permanent, sales and customer service staff, as well employees of different ages were interviewed.

In two of the call centres I selected the agents and team leaders interviewed myself using a list of employees supplied to me in advance. However, in the remaining organizations, the managers selected the interviewees. This was not ideal as it raises obvious questions about managers 'hand-picking' staff. However, taking this approach was unavoidable given that most managers stated that it would be extremely problematic for me to choose participants myself, largely because of intricacies of the shift systems in place within the call centres, and the unpredictability of the workflow. Importantly, there was little evidence when it came to the analysis of the research findings of any marked differences in terms of the responses of those interviewees that were chosen at random and those that were selected by the managers. Indeed, the interviews were generally characterized by a considerable degree of similarity. All of the interviews were carried out within the workplace in private offices, and in the case of the agents and team leaders, were conducted in the absence of managers. The interviews were generally 'conversational' in style. The general aim was to gather in-depth information from female call centre employees about their experiences of working in this rapidly growing, feminized industry. As a consequence, the interviews explored a broad range of subjects, but around a third of the time in each interview was dedicated to discussing the issue of career development. From the outset my aim was to pay attention to the actual views of women workers themselves. In other words, I was centrally concerned with capturing women's *own* attitudes, beliefs and understandings about their careers. Many academic studies on work and workplaces (particularly those coming from within the labour process tradition) have in the past been criticized for neglecting the particular experiences of women workers (see Thompson, 1983; Webster, 1996; McDowell, 1999). My research was specifically designed to uncover the 'hidden voices' of women call centre workers, and I have endeavoured to reflect this in the discussion of the findings that follows.

Gender and career paths in call centres

Deciding not to develop a call centre career

Appearing to lend support to the 'ghetto' thesis, my research findings indicated that a large proportion of call centre employees (both male and female) do not ever move off the 'bottom rung' of the career ladder within their organizations. These employees fall into two very different groups. The first group consists of workers that have made a decision to remain in agent-level positions and are not actively seeking promotion. The view amongst managers and industry representatives was that this group was made up overwhelmingly of *female* employees, a large proportion of whom were said to have caring commitments, with many working on a part-time basis.

Although this group made up a small part of the workforce in the information technology and outsourced call centres, by contrast, in the mail order and financial services sectors they formed a significant presence in numerical terms. In both of the mail order call centres for example, there was a substantial 'core' of long-serving female employees who had been working in agent roles for over ten years, estimated to make up between 30 and 50 per cent of the workforce. Most of these women were over 40 years of age. Notably, in both sectors, managers looked upon the presence of this group very positively, with one male manager referring to them as constituting the 'bedrock' of his organization. Another manager similarly explained that older women and women with childcare commitments in particular provided valuable 'stability' to the workforce because they were 'not interested' in developing a career, and were 'happy' to remain in agent roles:

> Our best staff are not the so-called high-flyers, in fact you could argue that our best staff are the ones in the middle ground because they are happy to stay with [a job as an agent]. Women with kids are the ones that will do that, but a high-flyer will go and get a job somewhere else.
>
> Male call centre manager, financial services call centre

In fact, managers across all sectors openly stated that they would ideally like to recruit more women returning to work after a break from employment to bring up children for the same reasons. At least four organizations were making deliberate attempts to target this group during recruitment processes. It also appears that these trends are widespread in the call centre industry in general. One of the industry representatives interviewed (a male management consultant) referred to the development of what he termed a substantial 'female underclass' within the call centre industry, which he claimed consisted mainly of women (and especially *working-class* women) with childcare commitments, remaining solidly at the bottom of career ladders.

The findings show, therefore, that call centre employers are capitalizing on gender divisions by actively recruiting women that they perceive will not be interested in promotion. It is important to note too that many of the female agents interviewed supported the assumptions held by managers about the lack of career orientation amongst older women and women with children. Several interviewees clearly stated that they had no interest in moving out of their roles as agents because their domestic situation meant that it was essential that they had a job that they could 'leave behind' or 'switch off' from when they went home. Some of the older women interviewed also stated that they felt that they were not confident enough to take on the extra responsibilities required for promotion, nor ambitious or 'career-minded' enough to do so.

In this context, for example, the following female agent (aged 45 years) stated that:

> I think for promotion here you need to have ambition, you need to have drive and a willingness to go for targets and that. At my stage of life it would not be something I'd like to do.
>
> Female agent, information technology call centre

Here, the research findings appear to parallel the observations made by Catherine Hakim (1996) about the existence of a significant group of women in the labour market who prioritize their domestic lives rather than their workplace careers. According to Hakim, this group tend to choose jobs for their 'convenience factors' and 'social interest' and as such tend to be concentrated in low-status, undemanding work. Hakim's work thus emphasizes the importance of women's own individual tastes and preferences in explaining gender divisions in the labour market, suggesting that women themselves in fact play a role in the creation of female employment ghettos. In the specific context of call centre work, my research findings show that some women clearly *are* making choices *not* to move up career ladders, and it could be argued that they are effectively ghettoizing themselves. However, as Walby has influentially argued, it is vitally important to recognize that for women decisions about careers are not freely made, rather made in response to social constraints, and that 'Women make choices, but not under the conditions of their own making' (1997, p. 25).

In addition to those (mainly female) employees that had made decisions to remain in agent roles, it is also possible to identify a second group of employees that never make it onto the first rung of the call centre career ladder for very different reasons. This group consists of those individuals that decide to leave their organizations entirely before moving beyond agent level. Although none of the case study organizations was able to provide statistical evidence on this issue, given the high rates of annual labour turnover reported in the industry as a whole, this group of employees is likely to be sizeable. One recent report for example claimed that although many call centre employers publicly admit to turnover rates of between 20 and 30 per cent (compared to a national average of 20 per cent), they privately admit rates of double that (TUC, 2001, p. 5). It was widely acknowledged during the interviews, by managers and agents alike, that a large proportion of agents left the case study call centres after only a year or two, largely because of the repetitive and pressurized nature of the

180 *A Female Ghetto? Women's Careers in Telephone Call Centres*

work. The remarks made by the interviewee below was typical in this respect:

> Normally they [the agents] will only stay for about a year or a year-and-a-half, because, you know, 'burnout' occurs. It's very difficult to do that kind of job for five or ten years.
>
> Female team leader, information technology call centre

Rates of staff turnover were particularly high in the outsourced organizations, and here agents were reported to remain in their posts for even shorter periods of time. In this context, the following agent explained that:

> The average call centre agent spends six months to a year on the phones, and then you either move up or move on. The standard length of time people stay is, I would say – male and female – two to three months, maybe six months . . . It's not a job that you can do for the rest of your life.
>
> Female agent, outsourced call centre

Young, middle-class, well-educated and single people of both sexes (particularly university graduates) were generally perceived to be the most likely to move out of call centre work quickly. Many respondents related this to the fact that this group tends to have higher expectations in terms of work and careers:

> The younger people are coming through with a degree of ambition. Some of the older ones are quite content to sit here for four or five hours a day and go home at the end of it, but there are a lot of young people coming through who want a good deal more than that.
>
> Female team leader, mail order call centre

Indeed, many of the younger and more highly educated women interviewed expressed frustration about what they perceived as the lack of opportunities for promotion in their organizations. Although organizational structures vary between call centres, it is nevertheless true to say that organizations tend, on the whole, to be typified by relatively flat hierarchies. This is illustrated in Figure 8.1.

As the diagram shows, call centres tend to have few layers in their organizational structures, with large numbers of employees at the base of the organization working in agent positions and performing the

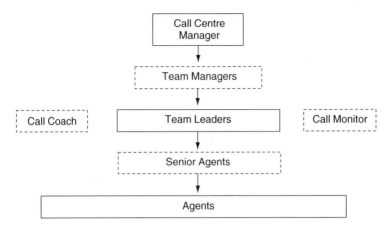

Figure 8.1 An ideal-typical call centre organizational hierarchy
Note: The solid lines are used to indicate the very flat hierarchy that typified call centres in the early to mid-1990s. The broken lines are used around those roles that have emerged more recently in many call centres, adding new layers to organizational structures.

same or similar tasks, with few management positions. As call centres are usually run as specialized offices distinct (and sometimes geographically separated) from other areas of the business, they also tend to house few other job roles or functions, allowing little opportunity for lateral career movement. All of the case study organizations had similar flat structures in place (information on the numbers of team leader and managerial positions in each centre is included in Table 8.1 below). Furthermore, the interviews revealed that in each of the call centres, employees were, on the whole, expected to move up the career structure in strict hierarchical order, starting off as an agent, moving up to team leader level, and then into a management role. Rungs on this promotional ladder were rarely missed out. This created a situation in which large numbers of employees were effectively 'queuing' for a limited number of job vacancies. In relation to this, agents frequently spoke about the high degree of competition for promotion that existed in their call centres, as the following interviewee explained:

> I think once you get on the ladder it can probably go quite quickly. It's just getting on the first rung of the ladder, which is quite competitive because you've got 600 agents and about 50 senior agents and only 40 team leaders.
>
> Female agent, financial services call centre

Table 8.1 Percentage of females in supervisory and management positions in the case study call centres

Centre number	Total number of employees*	Percentage of workforce female	Team leaders		Managers**	
			Total number	Percentage female	Total number	Percentage female
Financial services call centres						
Centre 1	1,037	80%	103	71%	15	80%
Centre 2	429	76%	40	73%	9	33%
Centre 3	1,060	70%	60	80%	17	53%
Centre 4	434	79%	45	73%	18	44%
Mail order call centres						
Centre 5	1,781	89%	95	75%	51	67%
Centre 6	810	86%	48	98%	16	88%
Outsourced call centres						
Centre 7	250	65%	64	55%	60	60%
Centre 8	630	62%	76	47%	45	36%
Centre 9	105	68%	10	80%	5	80%
Information technology call centres						
Centre 10	400	59%	30	67%	18	50%
Centre 11	1,200	46%	70	57%	45	44%

Source: Data provided by case study companies.
Notes: *Figure includes all call centre-related staff on-site; **Figure includes all employees with the word 'manager' in their job title.

In all of the call centres, managers accepted that this situation led many of the more career-minded employees to look for employment elsewhere.

Women and promotion in the case study call centres

Although many employees do not move beyond agent level, others of course do go on to achieve promotion within call centres. I now turn to discuss the extent to which women workers had done this in the case study call centres.

Call centre employees follow two main career paths. The first (and most commonly taken) path taken involves individuals moving up the hierarchy *within* the call centre itself, either from agent into team leader and then into managerial positions, or sideways into other functions located on-site such as training or IT. The second path involves movement *outside* of the call centre, but elsewhere within the parent company. It was noted by a number of the managers interviewed that men were particularly likely to follow this second route, and view call centre jobs as a 'foot in the door' to the wider organization. This was especially pronounced in the information technology call centres, where it was frequently stated that many men had ambitions to move into more technical roles outside of the call centre. By contrast, it was reported that women interested in building careers were more likely to follow career paths *inside* the call centre, moving into team leader and managerial roles.

There was evidence that across all of the sectors considerable numbers of women were developing careers within call centres by moving up internal career ladders. Table 8.1 below shows the percentage of women in team leader and management positions in the case study call centres.

As regards movement to team leader level, the table shows that in all but one of the call centres, women made up the majority of team leaders. They were particularly well represented at this level in the financial services and mail order call centres. Across all sectors, the general view was that if agents interested in promotion were prepared to stay in the call centre and wait for an opportunity to arise, the vast majority would eventually achieve this. Those agents that did move into team leader positions were said to spend around two years in agent roles before doing so. However, it was also the case that in some cases, the women interviewed had been promoted to team leader roles very rapidly. This was especially so in the outsourced call centres, where one team leader for example had been promoted to her position after working as an

184   *A Female Ghetto? Women's Careers in Telephone Call Centres*

agent for a period of only three months. Such rapid promotions are related to the rate of growth of the call centre industry, and the high levels of labour turnover found in some workplaces. This situation is creating opportunities for promotion that do not tend to exist in more mature industries and organizations.

As has been reported in other industries (see, for example, Tomlinson, Brockbank and Traves, 1997), there was considerable variation between the case study organizations in terms of the representation of women in the managerial roles. However, in general women were less well represented at this level than they were at team leader level. This was especially pronounced in the financial services sector. However, the interviews conducted with industry representatives revealed a perception that the under-representation of women at management level is widespread in the call centre industry as a whole. One industry representative commented, for example, that 'all too often I go into call centres where it is virtually all women on the phone and a man is in charge'.

Nevertheless, women made up 50 per cent or more of all of the managers in most of the case study organizations, and in five of the call centres, the overall call centre manager was female (interestingly, *none* of these call centres were based in the financial services sector). These statistics compare very favourably with women's presence at management level in many other industries and organizations, even those within other female-dominated areas of the service sector (see Cockburn, 1991; Green and Cassell, 1996; McDowell, 1997; Tomlinson, Brockbank and Traves, 1997; Rutherford, 2001). In fact, the 'visibility' of women in management positions in call centres in general compared with other workplaces was frequently remarked upon during the interviews.

Call centres: female-friendly working environments?

> Call centres are environments where there are a lot of women. It's more a woman's environment than a man's.
>
> > Female agent, financial services call centre

Statements like the one cited above were frequently made during the interviews by managers and agents alike. Indeed, an unanticipated outcome of this research was that many women seemed to regard call centres as 'female-friendly' working environments where prospects for promotion were concerned.

A key reason for this was related to the systems of promotion used in the call centres. In spite of the under-representation of women in management roles, there was a widespread belief amongst interviewees that promotional decisions in the organizations were based strongly upon individual performance, ability and hard work. The following kind of remark was commonplace here: 'the managers are quite open. If you are a good hard worker you will get on, there's no discrimination from higher up', Female team leader, information technology call centre. Many managers were keen to emphasize that they had made efforts to design 'fair' and 'unbiased' promotion procedures. Most of the organizations used assessment centres involving activities such as role-playing, group exercises, written tests and interviews in order to identify people suitable for promotion into team leader and managerial roles. Most interviewees felt that this approach to promotion contributed to the creation of an atmosphere of gender equality, and contrasted this to other work environments they had experienced. Women working in the financial services call centres had the most to say in this regard:

> I don't think in this place it's an advantage if you are a man or a woman, it doesn't really matter...Years ago in banks it might have been difficult for women, but a lot more women get promoted here than men.
>
> Female agent, financial services call centre

Several women commented on the 'openness' with regard to access to promotion in their organizations, and stated that this greatly reduced the scope for any 'favouritism' or discrimination against women:

> I wouldn't say that my promotions have been easy, but the *access* to them has been easy...it is easier here in terms of the process than elsewhere. Women have got more of a battle in other environments to prove to people that they *do* know what they are talking about.
>
> Female call centre manager, mail order call centre

These findings resonate strongly with the findings of recent research pointing to the emergence of a new, competitive work culture that places emphasis solidly upon 'ability' and 'performance' (see, for example, Halford, Savage and Witz, 1997). There was a general view amongst the interviewees that it was possible for ambitious individuals of any sex to move up the career hierarchy as long as they were prepared to work hard and were determined to 'prove themselves'. Many respondents stated that this strong emphasis upon individual performance and ability meant that in addition to gender, other factors such as age and social class, which can disadvantage people in career terms in other work environments were not relevant to promotion decisions in call centres. Connected with this, the case study call centres were also praised by many women for their emphasis on the possession of skills and competencies appropriate to the work itself rather than upon formal qualifications. This focus on skills and competencies was seen to benefit women in particular because the emphasis was placed largely on social and interpersonal abilities, which women were generally perceived to possess in abundance.

Dead-end jobs? the career prospects of women team leaders and managers

As we have seen, there was evidence of a strong belief amongst interviewees that call centres provide positive contexts in which women are able to build careers. I shall now move on to discuss the career prospects of those women who *do* move up the call centre hierarchy into roles as team leaders and managers.

Team leader careers

We have already seen that women were well represented in team leader roles in the case study organizations. There was a general perception amongst all interviewees that team leaders performed an invaluable role in the call centre environment, and that the job required a range of skills in managing, supporting and motivating employees. These sorts of views are also frequently expressed in industry literature. Most interviewees at team leader level commented that they felt that they would not have the opportunity to move into such a position of responsibility in other work environments. One respondent for example stated that:

> Well, the team I'm managing at the moment is £60 million a year business, and that's just the one team I'm managing. If I was to be made [team] manager I would probably be managing a £300 million business. There's not many companies that you're allowed to do that – a young girl of 28 or 29 or whatever – you just don't get that opportunity in many places.
>
> Female team leader, information technology call centre

In spite of such positive remarks, however, it became clear that women faced a number of obstacles to career progression *beyond* the level of team leader. The first of these was due to the flat organizational structures, which limited the number of managerial roles available (for more detail see Table 8.1 above). This situation meant that most team leaders interested in further promotion would have to look *outside* of the call centre for promotional opportunities. One manager thus remarked:

> We have the flat structure and I'll say to people very often 'Who's job do you want next, my job?' and they say 'No, I can't get your job'. For most agents the next step is the team leader...then after maybe two years as a team leader they would have to look at opportunities elsewhere within the bank. There isn't always the career path for them, without a doubt.
>
> Male call centre manager, financial services call centre

As one manager explained, those that are not prepared to move beyond the call centre for career opportunities will severely limit their development potential:

> They have to be really ambitious and mobile and [be able to] work anywhere in the organization. If they choose not to be mobile then they restrict their own progression. There are limits to how far they can go in the branch because at the end of the day, we are only a branch.
>
> Male call centre manager, financial services call centre

In all but three of the case study call centres, movement into a position outside the call centre, but elsewhere within the organization would involve geographical relocation due to the physical distance between the call centres and other business units. Importantly, several authors have observed that women tend to be disadvantaged by this situation on the grounds that they are 'often less mobile [than men], as family priorities make them unwilling to take a position meaning longer work days, more travel or moving geographically to a new site of employment' (Alvesson and Billing, 1997, p. 140). Further, studies of 'dual earner' households have shown that women are more likely than men to have the location of their employment determined by their partners (Green, Hogarth and Shackleton, 1999).

Many of the women interviewed seemed resigned to the fact that there was simply nowhere for them to move in career terms after the level of team leader. One interviewee admitted:

188 *A Female Ghetto? Women's Careers in Telephone Call Centres*

Well, at the moment here it is a very flat structure. There's agents, team leaders, managers. I would love to progress in a call centre because I'm totally at ease with it and I love the job. I love the type of work it is, but with the structure the way it is at the moment...I don't see it happening. I don't see me sitting in [the call centre manager's] desk in five years' time.

Female team leader, financial services call centre

In addition, there was evidence that as well as a general lack of available managerial positions, traditional attitudes and stereotypes about women's abilities also acted to limit their career prospects. Some team leaders felt that they were perceived by their managers as either not interested in promotion, or as unsuited to managerial roles. Similar perceptions have been found in many other studies of women in management (see Green and Cassell, 1996). In this context, the following team leader clearly felt that she had been 'labelled' as a team leader rather than as a potential manager, and that her prospects for promotion were as a consequence limited:

Q: So do you see yourself working your way up to be a call centre manager?

It's difficult because to do that I'd probably have to move on. I've got entrenched now in what I'm doing here...Perhaps I'm wrong, but I think I'm perceived as a supervisor and I'm not likely to get any further here and the opportunities will come up, but I don't think that they will be offered to me...lately all of the management positions have been filled from the outside.

Female team leader, outsourced call centre

This team leader also highlights a further obstacle to promotion, namely the fact that in most of the call centres, *external* candidates were frequently recruited for managerial roles. It was stated that managers were often recruited externally because call centres were competitive and fast-changing environments, and as such it was important to get 'new ideas and insights' from outside of the organization. Connected with this, there was also evidence that women team leaders in the case study call centres were simply not being *prepared* for promotion into managerial positions. All but four of the call centres provided little or no introductory management training for team leaders. Most organizations seemed to rely upon team leaders picking up their skills on the job in the course of their everyday duties. Team leaders frequently talked of 'being dropped in at the deep end' and of having to 'just get on with the job'. One team leader described her induction training as follows:

> It was more on-the-job type of stuff... I was passed around the team leaders that were here at that stage and they showed me the different [computer] systems... but with regard to managing people it was more or less kind of learn as you go along.
>
> Female team leader, financial services call centre

This was the case in spite of the fact that virtually all of the team leaders interviewed had little previous management experience, and were responsible for overseeing up to 30 members of staff. This situation obviously creates serious barriers for those wishing to progress their careers to management level. This is especially so given that a considerable 'role gap' exists between team leaders and managers within call centres, and the responsibilities and day-to-day tasks carried out by each are very different (Hoskins, 1998). Higher-level managerial employees in particular are generally involved in financial management and strategic planning, whereas team leaders and line managers focus overwhelmingly on day-to-day staffing and people management issues. Call centre managers will spend some time with senior management teams, but team leaders rarely, if ever, do this. These differences in roles and levels of responsibility were reflected in the basic salaries received by senior managers and team leaders in the case study call centres, which differed by around £20, 000 to £30, 000 per annum. In this context, appropriate managerial training is vital if team leaders are ever to progress into management roles.

A further barrier which female team leaders faced in moving up the career hierarchy in call centres is one common to many women in the labour force: the challenge of combining family life with a managerial career. It has been widely observed that success in the modern managerial career depends upon a particular relationship between home and work that advantages the lone individual with no family commitments (Halford, Savage and Witz, 1997). It is well known that women's career paths tend to be disrupted as a consequence of their domestic and childcare responsibilities. Many women with young families stressed that they simply could not see how they could juggle the demands of a career in call centre management with their caring responsibilities.

In the case study call centres part-time employees in particular felt 'held back' in terms of career progression. Many had not seriously

190   *A Female Ghetto? Women's Careers in Telephone Call Centres*

considered a career in a call centre because they assumed that it simply wasn't an option for them due to the input required from managers in terms of working hours. Indeed, none of the call centres employed managers on a part-time basis, effectively excluding a significant section of employees from even considering this option. In addition, there was very little in the way of assistance with childcare for those women with dependent children wanting to increase their working hours, which was not regarded as a business priority. Such attitudes are widespread in the call centre industry as a whole. In a recent a report by the trade union Unison for example, it was stated that in call centres 'managers often see equality issues as a luxury or "add on" to the business, which they cannot afford (and often don't even think about)' (Unison, 1998, p. 37).

Women in call centre management

A range of barriers existed, therefore, which meant that the majority of women did not tend to move beyond team leader level in the case study call centres. However, it is also important to note that there were *some* women in managerial positions. So who were these women, and what kinds of career opportunities were open to them?

There was a general belief amongst agents and team leaders that the women managers in their organizations were 'not typical' and were particularly 'dedicated' to their work. This perception was also held by the female managers themselves. Crucially, only three of the 21 women in managerial roles interviewed had dependent children, and just over half were single. Most worked long hours, and, as Coyle (1995) found in her case study of a telephone banking call centre, there was a strong belief amongst these women that if they did not do this they would severely limit their career opportunities. The women felt that the commitment to the organization that the job required meant that it would be extremely difficult to combine a managerial career with caring for a family:

> If you are working to an operational level like I am, I don't know how people do it [combine a career with having a family]. I think it must be terribly, terribly difficult, because the hours are erratic. My operation works 12 hours and I'm responsible for it all the way through the 12 hours ... I'm single so I don't have a problem with it, I just work it around the social life, that kind of thing. But if I knew I had to pick up a baby from the nursery or something like that I'd really have to be very hard on the time management thing.
>
> Female team manager, outsourced call centre

The female call centre managers interviewed presented themselves as ambitious women who had consciously capitalized on the opportunities that had come their way as a result of the expansion of the call centre industry. One manager for example, who had moved between call centre management jobs four times over a period of eight years, explained that she had: 'got an incredibly comprehensive range of skills in the call centre environment, just really through sticking with it, taking anything that came my way and picking up on opportunities' (Female call centre manager, outsourced call centre).

Most women managers had worked their way up the job hierarchy from positions as call centre agents, and had moved between call centres in order to climb up the career ladder. Several commentators have observed that managerial careers are now becoming less confined to a single or limited number of organizations, and instead now cross 'multiple employer boundaries' (Arthur, Inkson and Pringle, 1999), with people making more frequent moves between employers. It has been argued that in the process of doing this, individuals purposefully develop a range of personal and technical skills that can be transferred into other environments and choose to pursue *occupational* rather than organizational careers (Scase and Goffee, 1993). Other authors have noted that alongside this diversification, managers are also increasingly expected to 'manage their own careers' by collecting a 'portfolio' of skills, qualifications and experiences, moving within and between organizations more frequently in order to progress. This new 'mobile' managerial career is likely to involve increased geographical as well as organizational movement, sometimes on an international scale (Hardill, Green and Duddleston, 1997; Arnold, 1997; Wajcman, 1998). Such trends were clearly apparent in the career histories of many of the women interviewed, with most tending to regard themselves as making careers within the call centre industry rather than in a particular sector or organization.

There was a belief amongst some of the women managers that the feminization of the call centre industry was an important factor in their career success. This is because there was 'not as much competition from men for promotion' as found in other work environments. One female manager stated, for example, that she felt that women were enjoying success in call centres because they happened to be 'in the right place at the right time' and because of a 'lack of foresight by men' regarding the expansion of the industry. Indeed, at present the opportunities for call centre managers appear to be considerable. Call centre industry magazines report a good deal of movement at management level between call

192   A Female Ghetto? Women's Careers in Telephone Call Centres

centres, and a considerable amount of 'head-hunting' activity. A number of interviewees also noted that as call centre managers with experience are increasingly in demand, salaries are also rising. One interviewee stated:

> Salary levels now for team leaders and supervisors and call centre managers – particularly call centre managers – are in the stratosphere at the moment, and I mean a call centre manager with a year's experience can earn £40, 000. That's phenomenal, because there's just no experience there. That's the thing – there are opportunities if you move up the scale.
>
> Female call centre manager, outsourced call centre

Although the presence of a group of ambitious and successful women in management positions in the call centre industry was an unexpectedly positive finding to emerge from this study, the research also raises some concerns. A number of authors have recently observed that although there is evidence of an increase in the numbers of women in management positions in Britain (see Scase and Goffee, 1993; Tomlinson, Brockbank and Traves, 1997; Wajcman, 1998; Rutherford, 2001) there are also indications that *new* forms of gender inequality are developing. Coyle (1995) for example has argued that women have tended largely to move into 'middle management' jobs that carry only limited levels of authority and responsibility, and into roles that are 'expertise-based' rather than 'power-based'. She argues that these roles do little to bring women into the 'power and decision making structures of organizations' (Coyle, 1995, p. 98). My research indicates that call centre managers may well fall into this category. The managers interviewed explained that they felt that they were regarded as 'experts' in their particular field of call centre management, but were somewhat 'cut-off' from the other senior managers their parent organizations. One manager thus explained:

> Because I've moved quite a number of times, I've been deemed as somebody – there's an expert, we've bought her in to do the job, and it doesn't matter whether you are a man or a woman, but the issue has been that I'm not, I'm probably not going to be there in the long term, so as a result of that I've not been brought into fold. But then again, that's something that's also been my choice as well.
>
> Female call centre manager, outsourced call centre

Further, there were some indications that call centre managers not only feel somewhat distanced from the power centres of their organizations, but that their roles are actually *devalued* and misunderstood by senior managers. One respondent from an industry association mirrored the views of many managers when she stated that she thought that 'operating a call centre is a hugely complex task which is not understood properly by those in other areas of the business'.

This situation, of course, raises questions about the extent to which call centre managers are able to move outside of the call centre and into management positions elsewhere. Although this is an issue that affects all call centre managers, male or female, it is perhaps of particular significance for *women* managers. As I have already explained, many the women managers interviewed had worked their way up from the bottom of organizational structures. They tended on the whole to have had little previous experience of management in other contexts. It is unclear to what extent these women would be able to move to management roles elsewhere in the company. One team leader thus noted:

> I've always thought that it is relatively easy for someone to get to my position; you've got to have the ability, you've got to be recognized and you've got to make a name for yourself and it doesn't matter if you are female or male in that respect, and we are predominately a female workforce. I think once you get past my level you sort of lose the plot a little bit, because there are big differences in the numbers of females and males in managerial positions [at the Head Office], and there aren't that many differences here.
>
> Female team leader, financial services call centre

Conclusion

This chapter has examined the extent and nature of the career prospects available to women in call centres. In particular, it has attempted to shed light on the experienced realities of work and careers in these new organizations from the perspective of women workers themselves. I am aware that I have only begun to scrape the surface of these complex debates.

Several authors have recently observed that it is important to acknowledge that as a group, women are heterogeneous and diverse. As such they hold different values, aspirations and attitudes about their careers (Halford, Savage and Witz, 1997). In particular, several writers have observed that overall the structure of women's employment is tending to *polarize* (see Crompton, 1997). Wajcman for example has claimed that: 'one of the paradoxical outcomes of increased female workforce participation is a growing divergence within the female labour force, especially between women in low paid part-time or casual work and those in continuous full-time occupations' (1998, p. 32).

Hakim (1996) has also pointed to the emergence of two different groups of women with very different levels of work commitment. The first group of are 'career women', who, as the name suggests, are committed to paid work and give priority to their employment careers. The second group are by contrast uncommitted to the labour market, instead preferring to give priority to their domestic lives. If they work at all, these 'homemakers' choose to work on a part-time basis, and are concentrated in low-grade work. Although like many other commentators I would place more emphasis than Hakim on the *constraints* on the career choices open to many of the women she labels as 'homemakers', these divisions between women are reflected in my research findings.

The research indicates that large numbers of women do not move off the 'bottom rung' of the call centre career ladder, choosing *not* to develop call centre careers. Many of these women are employed on a part-time basis, and they often have dependent children. There was clear evidence in the case study call centres that employers were actively seeking to recruit such women. This is because they were seen to provide a sense of 'stability' in a working environment typically characterized by high levels of labour turnover and restricted opportunities for promotion. This finding clearly adds support to the job ghetto thesis. Whilst some women remain in agent roles, other employees (notably younger, middle-class and highly educated), frustrated by the lack of opportunities for upwards career mobility, tend to leave the work to seek jobs elsewhere.

It is important, however, not to characterize call centres as entirely 'careerless'. Considerable numbers of women *were* developing careers in the case study call centres, working in team leader and management positions. Nevertheless, the typical career structure for those women who do develop call centre careers tends to be very short, and there is evidence of a 'glass ceiling' in operation. Although reaching a managerial position is theoretically a career goal for all call centre employees, the evidence indicates that in practice career progression for most women halts at team leader level. This is due to a combination of factors, including the general lack of management opportunities available, and the absence of appropriate management training for team leaders as well as the associated 'role-gap' between team leaders and managers.

A minority of women were, however, were actively building management careers, taking advantage of the unanticipated growth of the industry. However, the research showed that, as in other contexts, call centre managers are required to work long hours, demonstrate high levels of commitment to their organizations and be geographically mobile in order to progress in career terms. It is unsurprising therefore, that very few of the women managers interviewed had children. These findings lend support to Wajcman's (1998) claim that women managers still have to 'manage like a man' in many respects in order to succeed in their careers. Finally, and perhaps most importantly it is also unclear from this research to what extent women managers are able to move *beyond* the call centre and closer to the power centres of businesses. This issue is likely to become particularly important over the coming years as technological development threatens the long-term sustainability of call centres, and as such it would be a fruitful area for future research.

Note

1. It should be noted that six of the case studies were initially undertaken as a part of a research project involving myself and other researchers funded by the European Commission (see Belt *et al.*, 1999).

References

Alvesson, M. and Y. D. Billing (1997) *Understanding Gender and Organizations*, London: Sage.

Arnold, J. (1997) *Managing Careers into the 21st Century*, London: Paul Chapman.

Arthur, M. B., K. Inkson and J. K. Pringle (1999) *The New Careers: Individual Action and Economic Change*, London: Sage.

Bain, P. and P. Taylor (1999) 'Employee relations, worker attitudes and trade union representation in call centres', paper presented at the 17th Annual Labour Process conference, 29–31 March, Royal Holloway College, University of London.

Belt, V. (2002) 'Women's Work and Restructuring in the Service Economy: The Case of Telephone Call Centres', unpublished doctoral thesis, University of Newcastle upon Tyne.

Belt, V., R. Richardson, J. Webster, K. Tijdens and M. Van Klaveren (1999) 'Work opportunities for women in the information society: call centre teleworking', final report for the Information Society Project Office (DGIII and DGXIII), European Commission, Brussels.

Breathnach, P. (2000) 'Globalisation, information technology and the emergence of niche transnational cities: the growth of the call centre sector in Dublin', *Geoforum*, 31, pp. 477–85.

Bristow, G., M. Munday and P. Gripaios (2000) 'Call centre growth and location: corporate strategy and the spatial division of labour', *Environment and Planning A*, 32(3), pp. 519–38.

196 *A Female Ghetto? Women's Careers in Telephone Call Centres*

Buchanan, R. and S. Koch-Schulte (1999) 'Gender on the line: technology, restructuring and the reorganization of work in the call centre industry', report to Status of Women Canada, August.

Cockburn, C. (1991) *In the Way of Women: Men's Resistance to Sex Equality in Organizations*, Basingstoke: Macmillan.

Coyle, A. (1995) 'Women and organizational change', Research Discussion Series No. 14, Manchester: Equal Opportunities Commission.

Crompton, R. (1997) *Women and Work in Modern Britain*, Oxford: Oxford University Press.

CWU (2000) 'A multinational research to create a social observation table of call centres: Ireland, WP1: Inventory', at http://www.toscallcentres.net/deliverables/WP1/WP1_Ireland.PDF

Green, A., T. Hogarth and R. Shackleton (1999) *Long Distance Living: Dual Location Households*, Institute for Employment Research, Bristol: The Policy Press.

Green, E. and C. Cassell (1996) 'Women managers, gendered cultural processes and organizational change', *Gender, Work and Organization*, 3(3), pp. 168–78.

Hakim, C. (1996) *Key Issues in Women's Work: Female Heterogeneity and the Polarisation of Women's Employment*, London: Athlone Press.

Halford, S., M. Savage and A. Witz (1997) *Gender, Careers and Organizations: Current Developments in Banking, Nursing and Local Government*, Basingstoke: Macmillan.

Hardill, I., A. Green and A. Duddleston (1997) 'The blurring of boundaries between "work" and "home": perspectives from case studies in the East Midlands', *Area*, 29, pp. 335–43.

Hoskins, G. (1998) 'How practical is flat?' *Call Centre Focus*, September, pp. 6–8.

Income Data Services (IDS) (2000) *Pay and Conditions in Call Centres*, London: Incomes Data Services.

Kanter, R. M. (1977) *Men and Women of the Corporation*, New York: Basic Books.

Maddock, S. (1999) *Challenging Women: Gender, Culture and Organization*, London: Sage.

McDowell, L. (1997) *Capital Culture: Gender at Work in the City*, Oxford: Blackwell.

McDowell, L. (1999) *Gender, Identity and Place: Understanding Feminist Geographies*, Cambridge: Blackwell.

Mitial (1998) *European Location Study: Call Centres in the UK, Republic of Ireland, Belgium and the Netherlands*, Wrexham: Mitial.

Organization for Economic Co-operation and Development (OECD) (1998) *The Future of Female-Dominated Occupations*, Paris: OECD.

Richardson, R. and J. N. Marshall (1996) 'The growth of telephone call centres in peripheral areas of Britain: Evidence from Tyne and Wear', *Area*, 28(3), pp. 308–17.

Rosener, J. B. (1990) 'Ways women lead', *Harvard Business Review*, November–December, pp. 119–25.

Rutherford, S. (2001) 'Any difference? An analysis of gender and divisional management styles in a large airline', *Gender, Work and Organization*, 8(3), pp. 326–45.

Scase, R. and R. Goffee (1993) *Reluctant Managers: Their Work and Lifestyles*, London: Routledge.

Stanford, P. (1999) 'The numbers game', *Independent Magazine*, 2 January, pp. 14–16.

Stanworth, C. (2000) 'Women and work in the information age', *Gender, Work and Organization*, 7(1), pp. 20–32.

Taylor, P. and P. Bain (1999) '"An assembly line in the head": work and employee relations in the call centre', *Industrial Relations Journal*, 30(2), pp. 101–17.

Thompson, P. (1983) *The Nature of Work*, 2nd edition, London: Macmillan.

Tomlinson, F., A. Brockbank and J. Traves (1997) 'The "feminisation" of management? Issues of "sameness" and "difference" in the roles and experiences of female and male retail managers', *Gender, Work and Organization*, 4(4), pp. 218–29.

Trades Union Congress (TUC) (2001) 'It's your call: Call centre workers' campaign', February, Trades Union Congress, London.

Unison (1998) *On-line Advice: A Negotiator's Guide to Good Employment Practice in Call Centres*, London: Unison.

Wajcman, J. (1998) *Managing Like a Man: Women and Men in Corporate Management*, Cambridge: Polity Press.

Walby, S. (1997) *Gender Transformations*, London, Routledge.

Webster, J. (1990) *Office Automation: The Labour Process and Women's Work in Britain*, Hemel Hempstead: Harvester Wheatsheaf.

Webster, J. (1996) *Shaping Women's Work: Gender, Employment and Information Technology*, London: Longman.

Part III

Effects of Call Centre Work on Employees

9

The Effect of Customer Service Encounters on Job Satisfaction and Emotional Exhaustion

Stephen Deery, Roderick Iverson and Janet Walsh

Introduction

An important feature of front-line service work is the participation of the customer in the production process. As a service recipient, the customer helps shape the way in which the work is performed through their specific needs and expectations. It is the customer whose requirements must be satisfied and whose orders must be met (Fuller and Smith, 1996). In some cases the customer can act as a co-producer while in other situations they can be enlisted by the organization jointly to supervise workers and help manage the labour process. This triangular relationship between the customer, the employee and management distinguishes interactive service work from industrial production where customers are external to the labour process and the dynamics of management control are more firmly located within the boundaries of the worker–management dyad (Lopez, 1996).

Front-line service workers are normally required to structure their interactions with customers or clients in such a way that will produce a desired emotional state in the service recipient. In telephone service work this has been characterized as 'smiling down the telephone' (Belt, Richardson and Webster, 1999). Organizations will usually specify how employees are to act with customers in their rules of employment. The critical task for these workers according to Wharton (1996, p. 92) 'is to display publicly an emotion that they may not necessarily feel privately'. Quite often there may be a disconnection between the emotions that an employee might feel towards a customer and what they are expected to display. The use of conversational rules, however, is designed to manage this disjuncture and ensure that front-line service

202   The Effect of Customer Service Encounters

workers adhere to the public presentation of emotions that comply with the norms or standards of the organization. Nevertheless, the form and character of these rules may vary according to the specifications of the customer. In the case of a directory enquiry, for example, the organization may be less concerned with the level of rapport between the service provider and the service recipient than with the speed and efficiency of the interaction. Consequently, the conversational rules will seek to narrow the scope for provider–customer interchange and minimize employee discretion in the delivery of the service. On the other hand, interactions involving mortgage or loan arrangements may require a greater understanding of the customer's requirements and circumstances with particular emphasis on tailoring the product to the service recipient's needs. Too much monitoring and supervision of the staff member's emotions or methods of self-presentation and the organization will spoil the service relationship and jeopardize the success of the transaction.

It has been suggested that variations in the nature of the customer–service worker interaction will lead to variations in the modes used to regulate the labour process. According to this view the human resource management (HRM) systems that are introduced to structure and manage the workplace will be shaped by the services offered by the firm. Batt (2000, p. 542) believes that 'the customer–worker interface is a significant factor in defining the organization of work and human resource practices'. Gutek (1995) has gone even further and argued that interactive service jobs are the by-product of the design of the encounter system with the customer. She claims that the work systems and employment arrangements will be built around the criteria that are used to measure what the organization seeks to optimize. A firm that seeks to maximize operational efficiency could therefore be expected to utilize a different work model and employ different HRM policies from one that was aiming to optimize customer service quality.

The purpose of this chapter is to explore the effect of different types of transaction encounters on the nature of work in two telephone call centres. The study examines how the two call centres structure their work arrangements and how this affects both the job satisfaction of workers and their levels of emotional exhaustion. The chapter first discusses the literature relating to customers and service work before setting out its research propositions. It then outlines the nature of the work in the two different centres and provides information on the research setting, the sample and measures used in the study. Finally, it details the empirical findings and discusses the meaning of the results.

Service interactions and work relationships

Encounters between interactive service workers and customers can take a number of different forms. Where, for example, customers require a standardized and homogeneous service and where employees need little individualized knowledge of the customer to deliver that service the encounter is likely to be short and simple. In these circumstances management practices will focus on maximizing efficiency and throughput (Purcell and Kinnie, 2000). The role of the employee will relate principally to the process of service delivery. The HRM practices will tend to emphasize monitoring and measurement and the training will concentrate on a knowledge of the process and the style of delivery. The aim is to achieve high throughput and low unit costs. Monitoring is applied to reduce variability in service delivery, constrain the time spent on each customer and reduce downtime by minimizing the opportunity for the employee to create space for themselves between calls. This is analogous to the processes used for the mass production of manufactured goods. Batt (2002) suggests that high-involvement employment practices such as skill enhancement and worker autonomy will normally be viewed by management as too costly to implement and generally incapable of creating a competitive advantage.

In contrast to this form of service provision there will be other types of customers whose requirements are more complex and whose particular needs demand more specialized servicing. Under these conditions it could be expected that employees would be equipped with greater skills and granted wider discretion to deal with service recipients in a more individualized and customized way. Unpredictable customer service interactions require spontaneity and flexibility from workers (Macdonald and Sirianni, 1996). They cannot be met by standardized processes and tightly scripted conversational rules. Where customer requirements are incapable of being predetermined or pre-programmed it is inappropriate to force employees to follow instructions. They must be able to interpret information, use their judgement and take responsibility for meeting the specific needs of the customer. In these circumstances organizations are forced to grant wider discretion to front-line workers to vary their interactions in response to the uncertainties and irregularities of the work. As Fuller and Smith (1996, p. 76) note:

> Quality service requires that workers rely on inner arsenals of affective and interpersonal skills, capabilities which cannot be successfully codified, standardized or dissected into discrete components and set

204 *The Effect of Customer Service Encounters*

forth in a company handbook. Indeed, to the extent that managers succeed in perfecting bureaucratic control over quality-service labor, they may extinguish exactly those sparks of worker self-direction and spontaneity that they are becoming ever more dependent upon.

It could be expected that this would have implications for HRM policies and practices. As Leidner (1996, p. 35) remarked 'Organizations that depend on the decision-making of employees are likely to pay more attention to their hearts and minds.' Indeed, it has been argued that call centres that place an emphasis on customized relationships are more likely to employ high-involvement work systems (Batt, 2000; Kinnie, Purcell and Hutchinson, 2000). This would include an emphasis on open communications, devolved decision-making, participation in teams and the extensive use of training.

There are limitations, however, to a simple and direct relationship between the type and scope of services rendered and the form and design of the work system chosen to effect those transactions. On the one hand, organizations that seek to apply an engineering model to service provision may find that the standardization of processes will seriously undermine the quality of the interactions with customers (Herzenberg, Alic and Wial, 1998). It may result in employee disenchantment and high levels of exit behaviour as well as the loss of customers. Moreover, attempts to deliver service according to a predetermined design and to routinize service recipients' behaviour may not always be possible because of the difficulties of removing all uncertainty from customer–employee interactions. On the other hand, in higher-value-added markets there may be a strong reluctance to embrace service quality in favour of call throughput and cost efficiencies (Kinnie, Purcell and Hutchinson, 2000). Evidence suggests a strong desire in most call centres to achieve low customer-waiting times and to minimize call handling and wrap-up time as well as providing high-quality service. Korczynski (2002) suggests that this tension between the two competing logics of cost-efficiency and customer service is often resolved by the idiosyncratic preferences of individual call centre managers. This argument receives support from Fernie's (this volume) study. Such decisions, however, may also be affected by head office employment policies on such matters as recruitment, selection and pay. Lastly, the choice of work systems will also be influenced by the organization's history, traditions and management style. Baron, Burton and Hannan (1996), for instance, have identified a strong path dependency in the development of employment arrangements in which the philosophies and 'organizational blueprint' of the founders of firms have been found to shape HRM policies and practices. Local labour market conditions and trade unions can also help affect employment arrangements and work systems in call centres. Despite this there is some evidence to indicate that there is a relationship between the work systems used in call centres and the nature of the customer service interaction. In the telecommunications sector, Batt (2000) found a match between the characteristics of customers and those of the workforce. In the case of low-value customers who were supplied with a simple uniform service (as in a directory enquiry) there was widespread use of technology as a control device and employees were granted little discretion over their work. They were made subject to a highly scripted text when interacting with customers. On the other hand, high-value business customers with more complex requirements were serviced by employees with greater training, more extensive skills and wider discretion over their choice of work methods. There was very limited application of standardized processes and procedures. Korczynski (2002, p. 131) has also reported that greater customer variability appears to be associated with less structured jobs, fewer standardized procedures and a wider scope of tasks. Holman (this volume) showed that employees who were required to demonstrate greater product knowledge and problem-solving skills with customers were more likely to exert greater control over the timing of their work and the manner and form of their interaction with customers. They also experienced lower levels of monitoring.

Work systems and worker well-being

The type of work system that is constructed and developed to serve the customer will have an effect on job satisfaction and worker well-being. Where services are provided by way of an engineering or mass-production model (Herzenberg, Alic and Wial, 1998) it could be expected that the lack of discretion and autonomy as well as the extensive use of electronic monitoring would result in job dissatisfaction and stress. By way of contrast, where the work regime was based on the principle of customized service there would be wider opportunities for the use of interpretative skills and less conformance to predetermined work schedules and consequently a greater likelihood of higher levels of job satisfaction and lower levels of stress.

In his study of call centres in the banking industry, Holman (this volume) examined the impact of job design characteristics and HRM practices on job satisfaction. He found that intrinsic job satisfaction – satisfaction with features of the job that relate to the nature and quality of the work itself – was higher for employees who had greater control

206 *The Effect of Customer Service Encounters*

over the timing and methods of their work, were engaged in a wide variety of tasks and who had more extensive opportunities to solve customer-related problems. Furthermore, job satisfaction amongst call centre workers was associated with less intrusive and punitive monitoring and with more supportive team leaders. In addition, significantly higher job satisfaction was reported amongst employees who possessed and utilized more extensive levels of product knowledge. These results are broadly consistent with those found in other work settings. Greater skill variety and autonomy combined with supportive, open and communicative first-line managers have long been seen as important antecedents of job satisfaction (see Hackman and Oldham, 1980). Research also suggests that job satisfaction is greater where employees enjoy interacting with their peers or members of their work group, where they have greater freedom to make decisions about their job tasks, where they do not experience high workload demands and where they have opportunities for promotion (Spector, 1997).

Job satisfaction is also related to psychological well-being. Individuals who do not enjoy their jobs are more likely to feel anxious and experience stress. In the context of interactive service work they are also more likely to become emotionally exhausted, a core component of job burnout (Lee and Ashforth, 1990). A range of other factors has been associated with emotional exhaustion. Amongst the most important of these are high workloads, role overload, work pressure and role conflict (Cordes and Dougherty, 1993). High workload, in particular, has consistently been linked to emotional exhaustion in a number of studies (see Jackson, Schwab and Schuler, 1986). Furthermore, where individuals feel that they lack the training and skills to deal satisfactorily with the requirements of their job they are more likely to experience emotional exhaustion (Maslach and Pines, 1977). The availability of resources in an organization to help individuals cope with the work demands can also affect the incidence of emotional exhaustion (Lee and Ashforth, 1996). Organizational resources, such as supervisory and co-worker support, as well as opportunities for job enhancement can act as important buffers to stress (Cordes and Dougherty, 1993).

Studies of emotional exhaustion in telephone call centres have noted a range of similar factors. Saxton, Phillips and Blakeney (1991) not only identified the importance of job satisfaction as a predictor of emotional exhaustion among airline reservation agents but also found that role ambiguity and high workloads were associated with greater stress. Deery, Iverson and Walsh's (2002) research also pointed to the relevance of high workloads and repetitive work as sources of emotional exhaustion.

Where management emphasized tightly scripted conversational rules and focused on the throughput rather than the servicing of customers, employees were also more prone to feelings of fatigue and burnout. Furthermore, where the work was highly routinized and staff lacked a variety of tasks and activities, higher levels of emotional exhaustion were reported. The support and help of team leaders with job-related problems, however, acted as a buffer to stress and was associated with lower rates of burnout. On the basis of this literature we would seek to test the following propositions:

1. Job satisfaction will be lower in a work environment that is designed to maximize customer throughput than in one that seeks to emphasize service quality.
2. Employees will experience higher levels of emotional exhaustion where they are less satisfied with their jobs and have higher workloads.

The research study

The study was conducted amongst call centre staff in two companies in Australia. The first company, Flightco, is an airline that supplies both international and domestic services. It operates a network of call centres from which customer service representatives (CSRs) are required to respond to enquiries and take bookings for flights, provide assistance with holiday packages and make arrangements for car hire, process hotel reservations and sell travel insurance to customers. Telco, the second company in the study, is a telecommunications provider that sells, installs and maintains telephones for residential and business customers. It operates a number of call centres that take customer enquiries about accounts, bills and charges, arrange telephone installations, reconnections and disconnections and assist with complaints about service problems and difficulties.

At Flightco employees are required to service customers across a range of market segments: from business customers to budget travellers. In some situations customers' needs are quite narrow and specific while in others they are broad and vague. The service provider in some cases may need to supply no more than flight schedules to a customer while in other cases they may need to help plan an entire holiday itinerary. In some situations customers are very well informed and demand little specialized information from the service provider while in other cases they are poorly prepared and it is necessary for the service provider to obtain a detailed understanding of the traveller's personal preferences and choices

208 *The Effect of Customer Service Encounters*

in order to provide suitably customized arrangements. Service interactions may last as little as a minute or as long as an hour.

The criteria used for recruitment focus on oral communication and voice quality, customer service skills, initiative and flexibility, and tolerance for stress. The company seeks to attract staff with a sound knowledge of world geography (it services 26 destinations worldwide) and individuals who have travelled widely. Many of those recruited hold tertiary qualifications. Initial training lasts eight to ten weeks and focuses on technical and computer skills, organizational products and services, and customer service and sales skills. Regular reviews of performance are made at two-monthly intervals until staff are considered fully proficient (normally at around six to eight months). The service providers are appraised in terms of both their operational efficiency and their organizational effectiveness. The centres at which they work are required to answer 80 per cent of calls within 20 seconds of the call being logged. As individuals they are also assessed in terms of a set of other service standards that include courteousness and friendliness to customers, level of product knowledge, ability to recognize and anticipate customer needs and conversion of calls into sales. The employees are regularly monitored and provided with feedback on the service quality of their calls. In turn customer satisfaction data are gathered twice-yearly for each call centre. Flightco has emphasized in its service standards to call centre staff that:

> Customers want quality...they have selected an airline that will make them feel secure, special and valued. Every time you satisfy our customers you increase their loyalty to [Flightco]...When customers have not received the level of service they expected, make it your responsibility to recover. Own the problem – and you will own the satisfaction of fixing it. Understanding our customers and their expectations – and understanding how to meet those expectations – is the key to enhancing our position as one of the world's best airlines.

Telco utilizes a different approach to the servicing of its customers and to the management of its staff. Not unlike Batt's (1999, p. 545) description of Bell in the United States, the company practises a 'mass production approach to service delivery'. The requirements of the customer and the nature of the tasks undertaken by the service providers, however, are not necessarily simple or routine. New employees must undergo a ten-week full-time training programme and the company provides additional support for a period of up to six months before full competency is thought to be achieved. The work involves a range of activities principally pertaining to customer enquiries and complaints about such matters as the installation of telephone equipment, alleged inaccuracies or errors relating to residential accounts, telephone disconnections and the timing of bills and rescheduling of payments. The staff must also respond to enquiries about new services and products that have just entered the market. Not only does the service provider have to possess good technical skills to retrieve and process customer information, they must also keep abreast of a rapidly changing portfolio of products and services and deal sensitively and empathetically with customers who may be angry, frustrated or confused. The work can often involve unpleasant exchanges with service recipients and abusive and rude calls.

Despite the variety of work that must be handled and the range of skills that must be utilized by the staff Telco has sought to standardize the way it dispenses its service in order to deliver it as quickly, efficiently and cheaply as possible. Employees are monitored on the number of calls taken, the duration of each call and the wrap-up time per call. In addition, their non-availability for customer service (downtime) is also calculated. Employees are expected to follow a tight script in their conversations with customers that includes a fixed format for the introduction and closure of the interaction. They are required to follow a documented and pre-planned work schedule that has five discrete tasks. These are designated as: greet and build rapport with the customer; fact find; provide solutions; close conversation; and follow (or wrap) up. Employees are expected to complete these work tasks in 600 seconds. Although they are closely monitored and measured in terms of these time-based (operational efficiency) standards employees are not assessed in terms of the quality of service they provide customers. In this sense issues pertaining to organizational effectiveness are given less visible and obvious weighting than is the case at Flightco.

Methods

Sample

An attitudinal survey containing a common body of items was administered to customer service representatives in both organizations. In Flightco the survey was distributed to 406 employees. It yielded 319 completed questionnaires which represented a 79 per cent response rate. In Telco the questionnaire was sent to 562 employees. This resulted in 480 completed questionnaires and an overall response rate of 85 per cent. It can be seen from Table 9.1 that the majority of call

210 *The Effect of Customer Service Encounters*

Table 9.1 Work attitudes and demographic characteristics

Variable	Flightco (n = 319) Mean (1–5 scale)	Telco (n = 480) Mean (1–5 scale)	Significance
Attitudinal outcomes			
Job satisfaction	3.40	3.11	.000
Emotional exhaustion	2.78	3.64	.000
Job design			
High workload	3.42	4.05	.000
Autonomy	3.08	2.18	.000
Skill use	3.50	2.94	.000
Work environment			
Co-worker support	3.80	3.89	.149
Supervisory support	3.90	3.41	.000
Respect	2.65	2.47	.024
Social interaction	3.41	3.14	.001
Pressure on wrap-up time	2.92	3.51	.000
Promotional opportunities	2.80	2.43	.000
Training	3.89	3.08	.000
Distributive justice	2.91	2.69	.000
Demographics			
Age (years)	33.91	37.30	.000
Female (%)	0.77	0.69	.014
Education (years)	12.63	11.75	.000
Tenure (years)	4.66	7.42	.000
Full time (%)	0.75	0.85	.000

centre staff in both organizations were female (Flightco 77 per cent; Telco 69 per cent) and worked full-time (Flightco 75 per cent; Telco 85 per cent). In both companies, educational levels were high (Flightco 12.63 years; Telco 11.75 years). The average age of respondents in Flightco was 33.91 years and in Telco 37.3 years, while tenure rates were 4.66 years in Flightco and 7.41 years in Telco.

Measures

With the exception of the demographic variables all items were measured on a five-point Likert scale (one = strongly disagree; five = strongly agree). Job satisfaction was assessed by four items (for example 'I find real enjoyment in my job') from the Price and Mueller (1981) scale and measured the overall degree to which an individual liked his/her job ($\alpha = 0.83$). Emotional exhaustion measured employees' feelings of being 'burnt out' or 'used up' at the end of the workday. It was assessed through a five-item scale taken from Wharton (1993) and included questions such as 'I feel emotionally drained from my work' and 'I feel burnt out from my work' ($\alpha = 0.91$). High workload measured employee perceptions of the pace of their work. It was assessed through a three-item scale and included items such as 'My job requires me to work very fast' and 'My job leaves me with very little time to get everything done' (Caplan *et al.*, 1975) ($\alpha = 0.68$). Autonomy was measured by a single item 'I have little or no influence over the things that affect me on the job' (Tetrick and LaRocco, 1987). The variable Skill use was assessed by the item 'I am encouraged to utilize my skills and abilities' (Caplanet *et al.*, 1975). Co-worker support was measured by the item 'My co-workers are willing to listen to my job-related problems' while Supervisory support was operationalized through three items including 'My supervisor can be relied on when things get difficult at work' (modified from House, 1981) ($\alpha = 0.89$). Respect evaluated the extent to which employees felt valued and respected for the work they performed. It was measured by the item: 'Management treats employees with respect' (formulated by the researchers). Social interaction was assessed through the item 'I am satisfied with the amount of social interaction at my centre'. Pressure on wrap-up time measured the degree to which employees felt unfairly pressured to reduce wrap-up time. It was operationalized by the item 'I feel unduly pressured by management to minimize my wrap-up time' (formulated by the researchers). Promotional opportunities measured the extent to which opportunities were available to employees for promotion and personal development and utilized a four-item scale from Price and Mueller (1986) ($\alpha = 0.81$). Training was measured by the item 'I have sufficient training to deal with the requirements of my job'. Distributive justice refers to the degree to which an organization treats employees fairly. The scale contained four items including 'I am recognized fairly for the amount of effort that I put in' and was adapted from Price and Mueller (1981) ($\alpha = 0.77$). The demographic variables were single items and were measured in the following way: age (in years), female (female = 1, male = 0), tenure (years) and full-time (full-time = 1, part-time = 0).

Results

Table 9.1 provides data on the work attitudes and demographic characteristics of the call centre respondents in the two different organizations. Based on the mean difference tests a clear pattern of results can be identified. Customer service representatives at Flightco were significantly

212   *The Effect of Customer Service Encounters*

more satisfied with their jobs (M=3.40) than those at Telco (M=3.11) and found their work considerably less emotionally exhausting (Flightco M=2.78; Telco M=3.64). In terms of those factors relating to the design of the job the data reveal that Flightco employees viewed their workloads as less onerous in terms of the speed at which they were required to work. Although both groups of employees believed that they had to work 'very hard' those at Telco reported significantly higher workloads (Flightco M=3.42; Telco M=4.05). Furthermore, Flightco employees appeared to have significantly more autonomy (Flightco M=3.08; Telco M=2.18) and received more encouragement to utilize their skills and abilities (Flighto M=3.50; Telco M=2.94). The wider work environment also appeared to be more congenial. Flightco employees reported significantly higher levels of supervisory support (Flightco M=3.90; Telco M=3.41) and social interaction (Flightco M=3.41; Telco M=3.14) in their workplace. Moreover, Flightco employees felt more respected and valued for the work they performed (M=2.65) than did Telco employees (M=2.47). They also considered that they were under less pressure from management to minimize their wrap-up time (Flightco M=2.92; Telco M=3.51) and were more satisfied with their opportunities for promotion (Flightco M=2.80; Telco M=2.43) and how well they were trained and equipped to deal with the requirements of their job (Flightco M=3.89; Telco M=3.08). Finally, Flightco employees reported significantly higher levels of distributive justice (M=2.91) than those at Telco (M=2.69) signalling that they saw their organization as delivering fairer and more equitable outcomes. Turning to the demographic characteristics of the two organizations it can be seen that staff at Flightco were significantly younger and better educated. They were also more likely to be female, to work part-time and have lower tenure than respondents at Telco.

The correlation matrix in Table 9.2 presents information on the inter-correlations between all the variables using the population samples from both Flightco and Telco. This enables us to understand how aspects of the job design and the work environment of the call centres were related to job satisfaction and emotional exhaustion. It can be observed that job satisfaction amongst all the CSRs was positively related to pro-motional opportunities (r=.51); skill use (r=.37); distributive justice (r=.35); supervisory support (r=.30); social interaction (r=.27); autonomy (r=.21) and training (r=.21). As expected it showed a negative association with emotional exhaustion (r=−.49). Job satisfaction in the call centres was also negatively related to management pressures to reduce wrap-up time (r=−.34) and to perceptions of high workloads (r=−.17). It should also be noted that call centre staff with lower tenure tended to have

Table 9.2 Correlation matrix[ab]

	Mean	SD	1	2	3	4	5	6	7	8	9	10	11	12	13	14	15	16	17	18	19
1. Flightco	.40	.49	–																		
2. Job satisfaction	3.23	.87	.16																		
3. Emotional exhaustion	3.30	1.03	–.41	–.49																	
4. High workload	3.80	.78	–.40	–.17	.55																
5. Autonomy	2.54	1.23	.36	.21	–.32	–.26															
6. Skill use	3.16	1.10	.25	.37	–.34	–.19	.22														
7. Co-worker support	3.86	.83	–.05	.09	–.03	.02	.02	.10													
8. Supervisory support	3.63	.96	.25	.30	–.36	–.18	.20	.32	.18												
9. Respect	2.55	1.08	.08	.14	–.10	–.12	.08	.16	.10	.11											
10. Social interaction	3.25	1.08	.12	.27	–.29	–.14	.12	.23	.18	.25	.13										
11. Pressure on wrap-up time	3.27	1.07	–.27	–.34	.40	.33	–.24	–.27	–.10	–.30	–.14	–.27									
12. Promotional opportunities	2.57	.89	.20	.51	–.47	–.23	.32	.48	.18	.32	.12	.34	–.35								
13. Training	3.40	1.15	.34	.21	–.37	–.29	.25	.28	.10	.24	.11	.14	–.26	.24							
14. Distributive justice	2.78	.85	.13	.35	–.39	–.24	.22	.44	.16	.36	.18	.28	–.33	.49	.26						
15. Age	35.96	13.15	–.13	.02	.12	.13	–.07	–.08	–.04	–.07	.06	–.05	.08	–.10	–.20	–.02	–				
16. Female	.72	.45	.09	.02	.00	–.01	.08	.03	.11	.02	.00	–.04	–.04	.07	–.02	.03	–.06	–			
17. Education	12.09	1.81	.24	.10	–.20	–.16	.11	.04	.00	.06	.04	.02	–.17	.08	.16	.04	–.16	–.01	–		
18. Tenure	6.33	6.45	–.21	–.14	.26	.11	–.16	–.08	–.07	–.07	.01	–.09	.12	–.22	–.16	–.06	.41	–.16	–.25	–	
19. Full-time	.81	.39	–.13	–.14	.16	.11	–.06	–.12	–.09	–.08	.00	–.05	.13	–.17	–.01	–.09	.03	–.21	–.03	.13	–

Notes: [a]N = 799; [b]Correlations above .07 are significant at p < .05.

214 *The Effect of Customer Service Encounters*

lower job satisfaction ($r = -.14$) as did those who worked full-time ($r = -.14$). If we turn to emotional exhaustion it can be seen that it was more likely to be associated with the presence of high workloads ($r = .55$) and pressure to reduce wrap-up time ($r = .40$) while it was negatively associated with promotional opportunities ($r = -.47$); distributive justice ($r = -.39$); training ($r = -.37$); supervisory support ($r = -.36$); skill use ($r = -.34$); autonomy ($r = -.32$); and social interaction ($r = -.29$). Not unlike job satisfaction, emotional exhaustion was related to both tenure and employment status being higher among longer-serving call centre staff ($r = .26$) and full-time workers ($r = .16$).

An analysis was conducted of the determinants of both job satisfaction and emotional exhaustion amongst staff in both organizations (see Table 9.3). The demographic variables (age, female, education, tenure and full-time) along with the organizational variable (Flightco) were

Table 9.3 Multiple regression for job satisfaction and emotional exhaustion

	Job satisfaction	Emotional exhaustion
Demographics		
Age	.10**	−.02
Female	−.04	.04
Education	.03	−.03
Tenure	−.05	.11***
Full-time	−.04	.03
Organization		
Flightco	.01	−.08**
Job design		
High workload	−.00	.33***
Autonomy	−.01	−.02
Skill use	.14***	−.01
Work environment		
Co-worker support	−.01	.05
Supervisory support	.08*	−.09**
Respect	.04	.05
Social interaction	.07*	−.04
Pressure on wrap-up time	−.11**	.03
Promotional opportunities	.33***	−.09**
Training	.01	−.10**
Distributive justice	.05	−.08*
Attitudinal outcome		
Job satisfaction	−	−.29***
Adjusted R^2	.34	.57

Notes: $*p < .05$ level; $**p < .01$ level; $***p < .001$ level.

initially entered into the two models. The variable (Flightco) was placed in the models for the purpose of identifying whether the organization for which the CSRs worked (*viz.* Flightco) had an effect on job satisfaction and emotional exhaustion independent of all the other factors. If we first take job satisfaction, it can be seen that age had a positive association ($\beta=.10$) with job satisfaction but that the organizational variable (Flightco) had no impact once all the demographic variables had been controlled for. In terms of the variables relating to job design and the work environment the results show significant relationships between job satisfaction and skill use ($\beta=.14$); supervisory support ($\beta=.08$); social interaction ($\beta=.07$); pressure on wrap-up time ($\beta=-.11$) and promotional opportunities ($\beta=.33$). This indicates that job satisfaction was higher amongst those staff who were encouraged to use their skills, who received greater support from their supervisors and who were more satisfied with the amount of social interaction in their workplace. The results also revealed that job satisfaction was higher amongst those employees who were placed under less pressure from management to minimize their wrap-up time and who considered that they had greater opportunities for promotion and personal development in their organization. The variables explained 34 per cent of variance in job satisfaction.

The level of emotional exhaustion experienced by CSRs was influenced by tenure ($\beta=.11$); the organization (Flightco) ($\beta=-.08$); high workload ($\beta=.33$); supervisory support ($\beta=-.09$); promotional opportunity ($\beta=-.09$); training ($\beta=-.10$); distributive justice ($\beta=-.08$) and job satisfaction ($\beta-.29$). Thus employees who reported higher levels of emotional exhaustion were more likely to have longer tenure in the organization and to occupy a job that required them to work very fast. The results also showed that employees at Flightco were significantly less likely to suffer from emotional exhaustion than those at Telco. Supervisory support had the effect of reducing emotional exhaustion as did the presence of promotional opportunities. Where employees considered that they received sufficient training to deal with the requirements of their job and where they believed that they were fairly recognized and rewarded they were also less likely to experience emotional exhaustion. Finally, as we predicted, job satisfaction was associated with significantly lower levels of emotional exhaustion. The explained variance for emotional exhaustion was 57 per cent.

Discussion

The purpose of this study was to establish whether there was any evidence of a relationship between the character of the service interaction, the design of the work arrangements and the level of worker well-being in the two organizations' call centres. As we showed, there has been some research to suggest that the work regime will indeed reflect the nature of the service provided and the needs and requirements of the customer (Batt, 2000; Gutek, 1996; Macdonald and Sirianni, 1996). In our case studies we saw that service interactions at Flightco were variable and unpredictable and that call centre workers were required to exercise judgement and use their discretion in dealing with customers. Employees could be called upon, for example, to book a round-the-world ticket and plan a full travel itinerary for a disabled customer or organize an end-of-the-year excursion for a football team or a resort holiday for a family. Flightco expected them to satisfy existing customers, cultivate good relationships with new ones and generate a healthy revenue flow for the organization. In terms of the service encounter, Flightco's objective was to optimize the conversion of customer calls into sales.

At Telco, interactions were less variable, less unpredictable and more constrained by conversational rules and operating procedures. This was not to say, however, that customer enquiries did not necessitate extensive product knowledge or information system skills or require employees to demonstrate an ability to solve quite difficult problems. The organization simply did not obtain the same potential pay-off from an encounter with a customer as Flightco did. Consequently it sought to process customers more uniformly and with greater speed. Its overarching aim was to optimize operational efficiency. It wanted to provide good customer service but not at the cost of customer throughput. Indeed the import-ance attached to the statistics relating to the completion of calls within a specified time period encouraged many call centre workers to transfer customers to other providers before the servicing of the enquiry was fully complete. This created confusion for the customer and rework for other staff. It both impeded service quality and impaired operational efficiency. As one Telco employee observed:

> There is [sic] at least two to three calls per week that require a lot of time and patience for a solution – these customers are often at their wits end to get a solution – sometimes it is a total mess created by others and needs unravelling – sometimes it is a logistical problem in [Telco]...I believe in customer service and I dislike being punished for attempting to fulfil the obligation of service to customers.

There was another important difference between the service encounters at the two organizations. This related to the norms of social interaction between the service providers and the service recipients. At Flightco the interactions were generally conducted in a civil and polite manner. Arranging air travel and planning holidays was normally a pleasant experience for customers and this tended to be reflected in the nature of the service encounter. Flightco staff reported few abusive calls or particularly vexatious interactions with customers. On the other hand, at Telco the employees were often targets for abuse. Invariably they were the subject of customer irritation when they were neither the cause of the problem nor in a position to remedy the customer's complaint. Service operators frequently had to confront customers who were hostile about telephone accounts that were incorrect or higher than expected; telephones that were disconnected because of non-payment of bills; slow installation of telephone equipment; and computer difficulties and systems failures that sometimes impeded the location of relevant customer data or information. A Telco worker noted that in these circumstances: 'Constantly dealing with customers is mentally and emotionally draining', while another stated:

Sometimes people need time out. This is because of stress which can be directly attributed to the attitude of management to staff and the constant monitoring of every minute of every day. I find this very unprofessional, quite demeaning and very stressful.

The distinctions between the nature of the service encounters and the character of the work arrangements were reflected in the attitudes of the workers to their job and to their organization. As we saw in Table 9.1 the call centre staff at Telco were significantly less satisfied with their jobs and reported significantly higher levels of emotional exhaustion. They worked faster and were given less autonomy and received less encouragement to use their skills. Overall they perceived lower levels of distributive justice and less fair organizational outcomes. These results were confirmed by the comments that were received from the employees in the two organizations. For example, one staff member at Telco stated rather colourfully: 'We are the cockroaches at the bottom of the company', while a further employee observed that 'staff are made to feel they are nothing but "battery hens"'. Holding a similar opinion, another respondent complained that employees at Telco were 'treated as process factory line workers ... [yet] at the same time expected to give silver service to our customers'. In contrast to these sentiments, workers at Flightco were more complimentary about their organization's practices. One stated:

218 The Effect of Customer Service Encounters

I am enjoying working with [Flightco] and find them a very fair company to work for. At times it can be stressful but there is always someone on hand to help you. I hope I will be around for a long time working for [Flightco].

Another employee expressed similar views: 'I am extremely happy and proud to work for [Flightco] as I have never worked in such a professional call centre. Everyone is happy to be here and to do this job unlike my previous call centre experience.' There were, however, some discordant voices particularly in relation to issues of managerial respect and commitment to employees and to the availability of opportunities for social interaction. This is shown in the following comments from two employees:

Although I genuinely love working for [Flighto], I cannot help thinking that the company would 'sell me down the river' in an instant if they could save some money from this. I also have the impression that Telephone Sales are viewed as a bunch of parasites, even though we are responsible for bringing in massive amounts of direct, commission-free revenue into the company.

Call centre work is mentally unstimulating and physically slothful. Being 'clamped' into a headset for eight hours is physically abusive and socially isolating. The 30 minutes lunch break allows little time for social interaction ... to enable stress relief.

Table 9.3 provides further insights into the factors that shaped job satisfaction and emotional exhaustion amongst the customer service workers. The three most important determinants of job satisfaction were promotional opportunities, skill use and pressure on wrap-up time. Thus, those employees who believed that they had chances to get ahead in the organization were significantly more likely to enjoy their job. In addition, employees who were encouraged to use their skills and abilities tended to express greater satisfaction with the job while management efforts to minimize wrap-up time had a negative impact on workers' job satisfaction. These results were not unexpected and were consistent with findings in both call centre environments and in other work settings (see Deery, Iverson and Walsh, 2002; Holman, this volume; Saxton, Phillips and Blakeney, 1991; Spector, 1997). It should be pointed out that job satisfaction was not affected by the organization for which the employees worked once we had controlled for the demographic variables. Therefore, in terms of proposition 1, the results did not provide support for the contention that job satisfaction would be lower in a work environment that was designed to maximize customer throughput (Telco) than in one that sought to emphasize service quality (Flightco). Although the mean scores for job satisfaction at Telco were significantly lower than those recorded at Flightco (see Table 9.1) once we employed multivariate analysis and controlled for the demographic characteristics of the two workforces we were unable to detect a statistically significant organizational effect on job satisfaction (see Table 9.3).

In contrast, emotional exhaustion was strongly associated with the call centre for which the employee worked. Those CSRs who worked for Flightco were significantly less likely to suffer burnout than those who worked for Telco. On the other hand, employees who experienced high workloads and reported that their job required them to work very fast were significantly more likely to report emotional exhaustion. Indeed, high workload was the most important factor in explaining emotional exhaustion. The second most important determinant of emotional exhaustion was job satisfaction. As expected there was an inverse relationship between the two variables. These results were consistent with our second research proposition which stated that employees who were less satisfied with their jobs and had higher workloads could be expected to experience higher levels of emotional exhaustion.

The results in Table 9.3 also revealed that tenure was positively associated with burnout. Longer-serving employees were thus more likely to report exhaustion and emotional strain irrespective of the organization they worked for or the type of employment regime under which they were employed. In this context, however, it should be pointed out that supervisors appeared to play an important part in worker well-being. Not only was supervisory support related to higher job satisfaction it was also associated with lower emotional exhaustion. These results suggest that those supervisors who had good interpersonal skills and who were willing to listen to and assist their staff with work-related issues could help raise levels of job satisfaction and reduce levels of burnout. Table 9.2 enables us to explore this issue a little further. It can be seen from the table that supervisory support was associated with perceptions of greater autonomy ($r = 0.20$, $p < 0.05$) and skill use by staff ($r = 0.32$, $p < 0.05$). It was also related to higher satisfaction with the amount of social interaction in the call centre ($r = 0.25$, $p < 0.05$), less pressure to minimize wrap-up time ($r = -0.30$, $p < 0.05$) and perceptions of greater opportunities for personal development and promotion ($r = 0.32$, $p < 0.05$). This indicates that variations in the management

220 The Effect of Customer Service Encounters

style of first line supervisors can have quite important effects on employee attitudes and perceptions of their emotional well-being. The final observation that may be made from Table 9.3 pertains to the important effect of promotion on emotional exhaustion. In both call centre environments employees who believed that they had dead-end jobs and poor prospects for advancement were more likely to experience burnout.

Conclusion

Most service organizations exercise some choice over the way in which they structure interactions with their customers. Some purposefully seek to circumscribe the nature and form of the encounter, restrict the autonomy of both the service recipient and the service provider and standardize the exchange in order to maximize throughput and minimize cost. Under these circumstances it is likely that the tasks will be highly repetitious, the conversations tightly scripted and the work closely monitored. Alternatively, other organizations may aim to provide a more customized or individualized service and allow greater variation in the form and content of the interaction between the employee and the service recipient. Here, interpretive skills and employee discretion will be more highly valued, conversational rules will be more relaxed and quantitative measures decidedly less visible. There would also be greater normative and less technical control over worker behaviour. These types of arrangements are more likely to take root where customer requirements are more complex and highly personalized while the earlier relationships that we described are more prone to emerge where the service is simpler and more routine and offers smaller margins. Of course these choices are not unconstrained. The encounter system and work regime that ultimately takes shape will be influenced by a range of other factors including the competing objectives of employees and their unions, the individual styles of managers, and supply and demand pressures in both the product and labour markets.

The two organizations in this study chose to construct quite different relationships with their customers. Their systems of service delivery were also dissimilar. Flightco encouraged its employees to build relationship-style contacts with customers in order to create sales and generate return business. Staff were expected to use their skills and demonstrate their initiative. In contrast, Telco sought to standardize interactions with their customers. Although their staff were highly trained and were also expected to be knowledgeable and skilful their encounters with customers were judged on the number that they handled rather than the quality of the exchange. The organization's objective was to maximize throughput and operational efficiency. The evidence indicated that this type of service delivery system was associated with inferior outcomes for workers. They had higher workloads, had less autonomy and were significantly more likely to suffer emotional exhaustion.

References

Baron, J. N., D. M. Burton and M. T. Hannan (1996) 'The road taken: Origins and evolution of employment systems in emerging companies', *Industrial and Corporate Change*, 5(2), pp. 239–75.

Batt, R. (1999) 'Work organization, technology and performance in customer service and sales', *Industrial and Labour Relations Review*, 52(4), pp. 539–64.

Batt, R. (2000) 'Strategic segmentation in front-line services: matching customers, employees and human resource systems', *International Journal of Human Resource Management*, 11(3), pp. 540–61.

Batt, R. (2002) 'Managing Customer Services: Human resource practices, quit rates and sales growth', *Academy of Management Journal*, 45(3), pp. 587–97.

Belt, V., R. Richardson and J. Webster (1999) 'Smiling down the phone: women's work in telephone call centres', paper presented at the RGS-IBG Annual Conference, January, University of Leicester.

Caplan, R. D., S. Cobb, J. R. P. French, R. V. Harrison and S. R. Pinneau (1975) *Job Demands and Worker Health*, Report No. 75–160, Washington, DC: US Department of Health, Education and Welfare.

Cordes, C. L. and T. W. Dougherty (1993) 'A review and an integration of research on job burnout', *Academy of Management Review*, 18(4), pp. 621–56.

Deery, S., R. Iverson, and J. Walsh (2002) 'Work relationships in telephone call centres: Understanding emotional exhaustion and employee withdrawal', *Journal of Management Studies*, 39(4), pp. 471–96.

Fernie, S. (this volume).

Fuller, L. and V. Smith (1996) 'Consumers' reports: management by customers in a changing economy', in C. L. Macdonald and C. Sirianni (eds), *Working in the Service Society*, Philadelphia: Temple University Press.

Gutek, B. A. (1995) *The Dynamics of Service: Reflections on the Changing Nature of Customer/Provider Interactions*, San Francisco: Jossey-Bass.

Hackman, J. R. and G. R. Oldham (1980) *Work Redesign*, Reading, MA: Addison-Wesley. Herzenberg, S. A., J. A. Alic and H. Wial (1998) *New Rules for a New Economy: Employment and Opportunity in Postindustrial America*, Ithaca, NY: Cornell University Press.

Holman, D. (this volume).

House, J. S. (1981) *Work Stress and Social Support*, Reading, MA: Addison-Wesley.

Jackson, S. E., R. L. Schwab and R. S. Schuler (1986) 'Toward an understanding of the burnout phenomenon', *Journal of Applied Psychology*, 71, pp. 630–40.

Kinnie, N. J., J. Purcell and S. Hutchinson (2000) 'Modelling HR Practices and Business Strategy in Telephone Call Centres', paper presented at the AIRAANZ Conference, February, University of Newcastle, Australia.

Korczynski, M. (2002) *Human Resource Management in Service Work: The Fragile Social Order*, Basingstoke: Palgrave.

222 The Effect of Customer Service Encounters

Lee, R. T. and B. E. Ashforth (1990) 'On the meaning of Maslach's three dimensions of burnout', *Journal of Applied Psychology*, 74, pp. 743–7.

Lee, R. T. and B. E. Ashforth (1996) 'A meta-physic examination of the correlates of three dimensions of job burnout', *Journal of Applied Psychology*, 81(2), pp. 123–33.

Leidner, R. (1996) 'Rethinking questions of control: lessons from McDonald's', in C. L. Macdonald and C. Sirianni (eds), *Working in the Service Society*, Philadelphia: Temple University Press.

Lopez, H. (1996) 'The politics of service production: route sales work in the potato-chip industry', in C. L. MacDonald and C. Sirianni (eds), *Working in the Service Society*, Philadelphia: Temple University Press.

Maslach, C. and A. Pines (1977) 'The burn-out syndrome in the day care setting', *Child Care Quarterly*, 6, pp. 100–13.

Macdonald, C. L. and C. Sirianni (1996) 'The service society and the changing experience of work', in C. L. Macdonald and C. Sirianni (eds), *Working in the Service Society*, Philadelphia: Temple University Press.

Price, J. L. and C. W. Mueller (1981) *Professional Turnover: The Case of Nurses*, New York: SP Medical and Scientific.

Price, J. L. and C. W. Mueller (1986) *Absenteeism and Turnover of Hospital Employees*, Greenwich, CT: JAI Press.

Purcell, J. and N. Kinnie (2000) 'Employment Regimes for the Factories of the Future: Human Resource Management in Telephone Call Centres', paper for the National Academy of Management Symposium on 'Employment Relationships, Culture and Work Modes within the Strategic Human Resource Architecture', August, Toronto.

Saxton, M. J., J. S. Phillips and R. N. Blakeney (1991) 'Antecedents and consequences of emotional exhaustion in the airline reservations service sector', *Human Relations*, 44(6), pp. 581–95.

Spector, P. (1997) *Job Satisfaction: Application, Assessment, Causes, and Consequences*, London: Sage.

Tetrick, L. E. and J. M. LaRocco (1987) 'Understanding prediction and control as moderators of the relationships between perceived stress, satisfaction, and psychological well-being', *Journal of Applied Psychology*, 72, pp. 538–43.

Wharton, A. S. (1993) 'The affective consequences of service work', *Work and Occupations*, 20, pp. 205–32.

Wharton, A. S. (1996) 'Service with a smile: understanding the consequences of emotional labor', in C. L. Macdonald and C. Sirianni (eds), *Working in the Service Society*, Philadelphia: Temple University Press.

10
Employee Well-being in Call Centres*
David Holman

Introduction

Currently, call centres appear to be the *bête noire* of organizational types. Call centres have been labelled as 'electronic panopticons', 'dark satanic mills of the 21st century' and 'human battery farms' (Fernie and Metcalf, 1998; Garson, 1988; IDS, 1999). These are hardly the most positive of images. One reason for these poor images is the impact that call centre work is perceived to have on the well-being of customer service representatives (CSRs), that is, front-line phone staff. In particular, attention has focused on the possible effects that job design, performance monitoring, human resource (HR) practices and team leader support may have on employee well-being. However, although such links have been proposed, few empirical studies have examined them in any great depth. The main aim of this chapter is to examine the effects of job design, performance monitoring, HR practices and team leader support on four measures of employee well-being, namely anxiety, depression, intrinsic job satisfaction and extrinsic job satisfaction. Furthermore, given that call centre work has been highlighted as particularly stressful, it is also worth considering whether it is any more stressful than other types of work. As such, the other aim of this chapter is to compare well-being in call centre work to that in other comparable types of work.

---

*This chapter originally appeared in the *Human Resource Management Journal*, 12(4), pp. 35–50.

Call centre work and well-being

A review of the literature suggests that four factors have a significant effect on the well-being of CSRs in call centres. They are job design, performance monitoring, HR practices and team leader support (Frenkel *et al.*, 1998; IDS, 1999; Knights and McCabe, 1998; Taylor and Bain, 1998).

Research on job design has demonstrated that control, variety and the demands placed on employees are important predictors of well-being (Karasek and Theorell, 1990; Spector, 1987; Terry and Jimmieson, 1999). With regard to job control, call centres vary in the extent to which they give CSRs discretion over work tasks. In some call centres, CSRs are required to conduct calls according to a script and have little choice over when to take a call or how long to spend with a customer. In other call centres, CSRs have much greater control of what they say to customers and how long they can talk to a customer. In call centres, as in other forms of work, high job control has been found to be positively associated with job satisfaction (Batt and Appelbaum, 1995), while the use of scripts has shown a positive association with emotional exhaustion (Deery, Iverson and Walsh, 2002).[1]

CSRs' work also has differing amounts of variety. For example, many CSRs have to deal with the same type of call and have little opportunity to do other tasks (for example, administration). Others have more varied and less monotonous work, as they are able to deal with different types of calls and are able to combine their extensive product or service knowledge with their IT and customer service skills to provide a service that is tailored to meet the needs of the customer (Frenkel *et al.*, 1998; Winslow and Bramer, 1994). Deery, Iverson and Walsh (2002) found that routinized CSR work was positively associated with emotional exhaustion. Emotional exhaustion has also been associated with high workload demands (Deery, Iverson and Walsh, 2002) and high emotional demands (Zapf *et al.*, 1999). In summary, low job control, low variety and excessive job demands are likely to cause job-related stress in call centres. It should be noted, however, that research in this area is limited to a few studies and that only a fairly narrow range of job characteristics and measures of well-being have been addressed.

Performance monitoring is one of the most prominent and pervasive of all call centre practices. It is achieved in two main ways. First, information on employees' activity derived from the call management system enables supervisors to examine, for example, an individual's average call time, the time spent taking calls and the type of call taken.

Second, supervisors can listen remotely to a CSR's calls, with or without the CSR's knowledge. The aim of the monitoring is to ensure that CSRs meet the prescribed technical (for example, call time, accuracy of information) and social (for example, friendliness, persuasiveness) performance standards. However, this can be done in either a punitive manner or as part of a wider development system of training, coaching and performance development (Stanton, 2000).

It is argued that employees can benefit from performance monitoring as it enables them to improve their performance and develop new skills (Grant and Higgins, 1989). Well-being is improved as employees derive satisfaction from the knowledge of their improved performance and from being better able to cope with work demands (Aiello and Shao, 1993; Stanton, 2000). To its critics, performance monitoring is intrinsically threatening to employees, as the information gained may affect an employees' remuneration or co-worker relationships (Alder, 1998). Monitoring is also considered to be a demand in itself (Smith *et al.*, 1992). The threat of monitoring and increased demand is thought to impact negatively on employee well-being.

Of the few studies examining the effects of performance monitoring on well-being, only a handful have been conducted in call centres (Aiello, 1993). Chalykoff and Kochan (1989) assessed the impact of a call centre's electronic monitoring system on satisfaction with the monitoring system and on job satisfaction. They discovered that immediacy of feedback, the use of constructive feedback and the clarity of rating criteria were all positively related to satisfaction with the monitoring system, which in turn was related to job satisfaction. Frenkel *et al.* (1998) found that call centre employees generally accepted electronic monitoring when they could see its place within a broader system of appraisal and development. Overall, this suggests that, when performance monitoring is used developmentally rather than punitively, it is positively associated with well-being; and, if performance monitoring is excessive and too frequent, it will have a negative association with well-being.

Research on human resource practices and team leader support has demonstrated that they can have a positive effect on employee well-being. For instance, the perceived fairness of the payment system, the usefulness of performance appraisal and the adequacy of the training have all been linked to job satisfaction (Agho, Mueller and Price, 1993; Blau, 1999; Saks, 1995; Spector, 1987), as has social support from team leaders (Warr, Cook and Wall, 1979). The few studies of HR practices and well-being in call centres report similar findings (Batt and Appelbaum, 1995;

Deery, Iverson and Walsh, 2002; Frenkel *et al.*, 1998), although Batt and Appelbaum (1995) reported no significant association between training and job satisfaction.

Call centre work is often highlighted as particularly stressful and, by implication, more stressful than other comparable forms of work. However, there is a paucity of studies that have examined differences in well-being between call centre work and other forms of work. For example, call centre work in Germany has been shown to have lower job satisfaction, a higher incidence of psychosomatic complaints and a higher rate of emotional exhaustion than care work and hotel service work (Zapf *et al.*, 1999). In the US, Batt and Appelbaum (1995) revealed that job satisfaction in call centre workers was similar to sewing machine operators, but lower than that of craft workers. These studies did not state whether these differences were significant. Only one study, by Frenkel *et al.* (1999), could be found that tested for differences in well-being between call centre work and other forms of work. In this study, call centre workers reported lower satisfaction with the nature of their work than sales workers and knowledge workers (e.g., IT systems designers, money market dealers).[2]

In summary, existing research suggests that the level of employee well-being in call centres is affected by job design, performance monitoring, HR practices and team leader support. However, this research suffers from a number of problems. First, no study has focused directly on two major dimensions of stress, namely anxiety and depression (Daniels, 2000; Warr, 1996, p. 226). Studies have either used other measures (for example, psychosomatic complaints, emotional exhaustion) or they have not defined the term stress with any precision (Belt, Richardson and Webster, 1999; Knights and McCabe, 1998). It would therefore seem imperative that these dimensions of stress are examined in relation to job design, monitoring, HR practices and team leader support.

Second, measures of job satisfaction have contained either a few items or one item, and this is particularly so in those studies looking at its relationship to job design and HR practices (Batt and Appelbaum, 1995; Frenkel *et al.*, 1998; 1999). This precludes the possibility of examining whether job design and HR practices relate differently to intrinsic job satisfaction (features integral to the work itself, for example, variety, autonomy) and extrinsic job satisfaction (features external to the work itself, for example, pay, opportunities for advancement, the way the firm is managed). Indeed, it seems sensible to suggest that job design factors will be associated with intrinsic job satisfaction and that HR practices and team leader support will not. Likewise, HR practices and team leader support should be associated with extrinsic job satisfaction, while job design factors should not. Using a measure of job satisfaction that covers intrinsic and extrinsic satisfaction will allow a more nuanced understanding of the causes of job satisfaction in call centres.

Third, there is a need to examine a wider range of job characteristics. In addition to employing measures that assess the control that CSRs have over methods used and what they say (for example, method control), there is a need to assess the extent of control that CSRs have over the timing of their work and the breadth of tasks engaged in. Addressing job characteristics such as timing control, role breadth, as well as method control, would therefore seem important. CSRs also need to constantly concentrate on their work and deal with customer queries. As such, attention demand and problem-solving demand are also relevant job characteristics for study in call centres (Jackson et al., 1993). Fourth, the lack of comparative work means that there is a need to compare well-being in call centre work with other forms of work.

Given the above, the first aim of this study is to examine, within call centres, the effects of job design, employee monitoring, HR practices and team leader support on four measures of employee well-being, namely anxiety, depression, intrinsic job satisfaction and extrinsic job satisfaction. The expected relationships between the main study variables are shown in Table 10.1. The second aim of this study is to examine differences in well-being between call centre work and other forms of work.

Method

Samples

The main sample consisted of CSRs who were employed in three different call centres of a UK bank. Each call centre dealt with a different type of product, namely, personal and business accounts, mortgages and loans. The sites will be referred to as Bank-Call, Mortgage-Call and Loan-Call. CSRs spent about 80–90 per cent of their time answering incoming calls that were mainly from external customers. The remaining time was spent in team meetings and on off-line administration. Call times and call quality were closely monitored at all three sites. Due to the nature of the product, Mortgage-Call employees required the most extensive product knowledge and Bank-Call employees the least.

To compare call centre work to other similar types of work, we drew on data reported by Mullarkey et al. (1999). When looking at job satisfaction, the comparative samples consisted of 246 clerical workers and

228 Employee Well-being in Call Centres

Table 10.1 Expected relationships between the main study variables

Independent variables	Dependent variables			
	Anxiety	Depression	Intrinsic job satisfaction	Extrinsic job satisfaction
Timing control	−ve	−ve	+ve	−
Method control	−ve	−ve	+ve	−
Attention demand	+ve	+ve	−ve	−
Problem-solving demand	+ve	+ve	−ve	−
Role breadth	−ve	−ve	+ve	−
Level of monitoring	+ve	+ve	−ve	−ve
Monitoring used to punish	+ve	+ve	−ve	−ve
Payment (fairness of)	−ve	−ve	−	+ve
Performance appraisal	−ve	−ve	−	+ve
Training adequacy	−ve	−ve	−	+ve
Team leader support	−ve	−ve	−	+ve

Note: A dash indicates that a significant relationship is not expected.

2,239 manufacturing shop floor workers. When looking at anxiety and depression, the comparative samples consisted of 941 clerical employees and 5,587 manufacturing shop floor employees.

Procedure

Research was conducted by the means of a questionnaire administered on-site. Prior to the survey administration, interviews with 40 CSRs and ten team leaders were conducted and the information obtained was used to inform the wording of items and the choice of measures used in the questionnaire. One month before the administration of the questionnaire all employees received a ten-minute briefing and a pamphlet describing the research and its aims. Participation in the research was voluntary and confidentiality guaranteed. Five hundred and fifty-seven questionnaires were returned: 221 were from Bank-Call, 157 from Mortgage-Call and 179 from Loan-Call. This represented a response rate of 68 per cent, 88 per cent and 81 per cent respectively. The overall response rate was 79 per cent. Of the total sample, 57 per cent were full-time and 31 per cent were male. The mean age was 30 years and ten months (range 17–56). Twenty-one per cent of the sample had college-or university-level qualifications, 76 per cent had school-level qualifications, whereas 3 per cent had no educational qualifications. The average job tenure was 19 months (range 0–120 months). Of the three sites, there were proportionally more male employees at Bank-Call (48.2 per cent) and employees at this site were younger (m = 25 years) and had shorter job tenure (m = 8.25 months). This compares to Mortgage-Call and Loan-Call where the proportion of male employees was, respectively, 29 per cent and 14 per cent and average job tenure was 22.1 and 30.2 months. There were proportionally fewer full-time employees at Loan-Call (42 per cent) than at Bank-Call (71 per cent) and Mortgage-Call (72 per cent).

Measures

The following scales were used to measure the major study variables. Unless stated, all responses were obtained on a five-point scale from 'not at all' to 'a great deal'.

Well-being

Anxiety was a six-item measure developed by Warr (1990). Questions asked about the extent to which the individual had felt tense, calm, relaxed, worried, uneasy and contented at work in the last month ($\alpha = 0.82$). The measure covers both ends of the anxiety-contentment dimension of well-being. It can be labelled 'anxiety-contentment', but for clarity and convenience it is normally referred to by one end, 'anxiety'. Depression was a six-item measure, also developed by Warr (1990), that asked about the extent to which the individual had felt miserable, depressed, optimistic, enthusiastic, gloomy and cheerful at work in the last month ($\alpha = 0.85$). This measure covers both ends of the depression-enthusiasm dimension of well-being and will be referred to as 'depression'. The response scale went from 'never' to 'all the time'. Responses were scored so that, for anxiety, higher values represent greater anxiety and lower contentment. For depression, higher values represent greater depression and lower enthusiasm.

Job satisfaction was assessed using Warr, Cook and Wall's (1979) measures of intrinsic job satisfaction and extrinsic job satisfaction. Intrinsic satisfaction was a seven-item measure that asks about the extent to which individuals are satisfied with features integral to the work itself (for example, variety, opportunity to use one's skills, autonomy) ($\alpha = 0.88$). Extrinsic satisfaction was an eight-item measure that asks about the extent to which individuals are satisfied with features external

230 *Employee Well-being in Call Centres*

to the work itself (for example, pay, opportunities for advancement, the way the firm is managed) ($\alpha = 0.80$). The response scale of seven intervals went from 'I'm extremely dissatisfied' to 'I'm extremely satisfied'.

Job characteristics

Five main job characteristics were measured in the study, namely, timing control, method control, attention demand, problem-solving demand and role breadth. Adapted versions of the Jackson *et al.* (1993) scales were used to measure the first four characteristics. Items were reworded when necessary to reflect a call centre environment. Specifically, timing control was measured by a five-item scale and assesses the extent to which a person has control over the timing of their work (sample item, 'Do you decide how long to spend with a customer?') ($\alpha = 0.81$). Method control was a five-item measure and assesses the extent to which people have control over the methods they use in their work and how they talk to customers (sample item, 'Can you vary how you talk with customers?') ($\alpha = 0.82$). Attention demand consisted of four items and considers the extent to which employees must concentrate on and attend to the work task (sample item, 'Do you have to concentrate all the time to watch for things going wrong?') ($\alpha = 0.72$). Problem-solving demand had five items and considers the level and extent of the problem-solving challenge at work (sample item, 'Do you have to solve problems which have no obvious correct answer?') ($\alpha = 0.75$). Role breadth was a 22-item scale that covered activities outside of the primary task (Pepper *et al.*, 1999). Items include 'To what extent are you involved in organizing break times?' and 'To what extent do you present information to others in your team?' ($\alpha = 0.90$).

Monitoring

The monitoring of CSR performance was measured using two single-item measures that were developed specifically for this study and were based on comments from employee interviews. The first concerned the extent to which CSRs agreed that they were monitored too much, and the second, the extent to which CSRs agreed with the statement 'call monitoring is used to punish you rather then develop you'. The five-item scale ranged from 'disagree very much' to 'agree very much'.

Human resource practices

Payment fairness was a two-item measure that asked about the extent to which CSRs thought the payment and bonus system was fair ($\alpha = 0.76$). Performance appraisal was a one-item measure that asked whether CSRs found their performance appraisal useful. Training was a two-item measure that asked about the perceived adequacy of the training and coaching received ($\alpha = 0.81$).

Team leader support

This was a nine-item measure (Axtell *et al.*, 2000) which asked about the extent to which support is received from one's team leader for example, 'Does your team leader discuss and solve problems with you?' ($\alpha = 0.89$).

Results

Descriptives

Table 10.2 shows the means, standard deviations and correlations of the main study variables. With regard to the dependent variables, the results indicate that CSRs felt anxious ($m = 2.63$) and depressed ($m = 2.62$) occasionally or some of the time in the last month. CSRs also reported that they were moderately satisfied with the intrinsic aspects of their job ($m = 3.98$) and slightly more satisfied with the extrinsic aspects of their job ($m = 4.76$). With regard to the independent variables, CSRs tended to report having relatively little control over the timing of their work ($m = 2.32$) and the methods they could use in their work ($m = 2.74$). The low level of role breadth ($m = 1.85$) indicates that CSRs did little apart from answer calls. The level of job demand was seen to be moderate to high (attention demand, $m = 3.61$; problem-solving demand, $m = 3.19$). CSRs tended to agree that they were monitored too much ($m = 3.42$), but tended to disagree that monitoring was used to punish them ($m = 2.61$). CSRs tended to agree that their performance review was useful ($m = 3.51$) and that they received adequate training ($m = 3.42$). CSRs also reported that they received moderate to high levels of support from their team leader ($m = 3.69$).

Relationships between independent variables and well-being

An exploratory analysis was conducted to establish whether any of the independent variables did not relate significantly to the dependent variables (after control and demographic variables had been accounted for), and could thus be eliminated from subsequent analysis. At step one, the control and demographic variables of job tenure, age, site, gender and full-time/part-time were entered. (The last three variables were dummy coded.)[3] At step two, the independent variable of interest

Table 10.2 Means, standard deviations and intercorrelations (n = 557)

	M	SD	1	2	3	4	5	6	7	8	9	10
1. Bank-Call	0.40	0.49	–									
2. Mortgage-Call	0.28	0.45	–.51***	–								
3. Loan-Call	0.32	0.46	–.56***	–.43***	–							
4. Age	30.10	8.27	–.40***	.19***	.24***	–						
5. Gender (Male = 1)	0.32	0.47	.29***	–.04	–.27***	–.20***	–					
6. Job tenure (Months)	19.25	19.25	–.46***	.09*	.39***	.35***	–.15***	–				
7. Full-time	0.63	0.48	.14***	.12**	–.27***	–.23***	.31***	–.17***	–			
8. Timing control	2.32	0.96	–.34***	.44***	–.06	.07	.09*	.12**	.07	–		
9. Method control	2.74	0.93	–.21***	.38***	–.09*	.07	.11**	.09*	.06	.57***	–	
10. Attention demands	3.61	0.89	–.36***	.09*	.29***	.34***	–.19***	.25***	–.16***	.14***	.09*	–
11. Problem-solving demand	3.19	0.73	–.32***	.15***	.19***	.18***	–.10**	.19***	–.09	.27***	.24***	.59***
12. Role breadth	1.85	0.45	.08	–.04	.12**	–.01	.01	.19***	.07	.24***	.37***	.05
13. Level of monitoring	3.42	1.00	–.07	–.12**	.19***	.04	–.01	.07	–.11*	–20***	–.19***	.11**
14. Monitoring/punish	2.61	1.00	.00	.04	–.04	.00	.07	.03	–.04	–.10*	–.14***	–.03
15. Payment fairness	2.96	0.95	–.31***	.01	.32***	.15***	–.29***	.16***	–.16***	.09*	.02	.07
16. Performance review	3.51	0.94	–.11**	–.20***	.30***	.06	–.15***	.07	–.03	–.00	.03	.16***
17. Training adequacy	3.42	0.82	–.07	.09*	–.02	–.04	–.06	–.03	.05	.13**	.09*	.03
18. Team leader style	3.69	0.71	.04	–.20***	.15***	.02	–.07	–.01	.18	.00	.12***	.02
19. Anxiety	2.63	0.72	–.10*	.06	.05	–.06	.01	.06	.03	–.07	–.14***	.12**
20. Depression	2.62	0.77	.16***	.04	–.21***	–.24***	.16***	.06	.12**	–.15***	–.25***	–.16***
21. Intrinsic job satisfaction	3.98	1.13	–.34***	.16***	.20***	.28***	–.26***	.17***	–.13**	.23***	.34***	.25***
22. Extrinsic job satisfaction	4.76	0.79	–.24***	.05	.20***	.19***	–.24***	.14***	–.15*	.12***	.10*	.14***

	11	12	13	14	15	16	17	18	19	20	21	22
1. Bank-Call												
2. Mortgage-Call												
3. Loan-Call												
4. Age												
5. Gender (Male = 1)												
6. Job tenure (Months)												
7. Full-time												
8. Timing control												
9. Method control												
10. Attention demands												
11. Problem-solving demand	–											
12. Role breadth	.24***	–										
13. Level of monitoring	.07	−.08	–									
14. Monitoring/punish	.01	−.02	.47***	–								
15. Payment fairness	.14	.06	−.07	−.24***	–							
16. Performance review	.12**	.25***	−.19***	−.33***	.31***	–						
17. Training adequacy	.04	.15***	−.07	−.16***	.28***	.21***	–					
18. Team leader style	.05	.23***	−.18***	−.32***	.31***	.43***	.28***	–				
19. Anxiety	.10*	−.11**	.24***	.24***	−.15***	−.13***	−.21***	−.30***	–			
20. Depression	−.13**	−.23***	.24***	.33***	−.30***	−.38***	−.24***	−.41***	−.58***	–		
21. Intrinsic job satisfaction	.21***	.30***	−.25***	−.36***	.40***	.40***	.28***	.40***	−.29***	−.63***	–	
22. Extrinsic job satisfaction	.08	.16***	−.15***	−.35***	.52***	.39***	.37***	.50***	−.29***	−.51***	.67***	–

Notes: *p < .05; **p < .01; ***p < .001; the means and standard deviations for variables 4–22 are for all study participants in all three sites.

234 *Employee Well-being in Call Centres*

was entered. (All variables were standardized prior to analysis.) Table 10.3 shows that most independent variables were significantly related to three or four of the dependent variables. Only problem-solving demand and attention demand were related to two out of the four dependent variables – although a relationship to extrinsic job satisfaction was not expected. On the whole, it can be seen that the independent variables were related to the dependent variables. All independent variables were therefore retained in subsequent analysis. It is also interesting to note that, in addition to most relationships being significant, most are in the expected direction (see Table 10.1).

To assess the unique contribution of each of the independent variables on the four measures of well-being, further hierarchical multiple regressions were conducted. At step one, the control and demographic variables were entered, followed, at step two, by all the independent variables of interest.

The results in Table 10.4 show significant statistical associations between anxiety and method control ($\beta=-.11$, $p<.05$), attention demand ($\beta=.13$, $p<.05$), level of monitoring ($\beta=.14$, $p<.01$), training adequacy ($\beta=-.09$, $p<.05$) and team leader support ($\beta=-.19$, $p<.001$). Depression was significantly associated with method control ($\beta=-.15$, $p<.01$), level of monitoring ($\beta=.12$, $p<.01$), performance review ($\beta=-.14$, $p<.001$), training adequacy ($\beta=-.09$, $p<.05$) and team leader support ($\beta=-.21$, $p<.001$). Intrinsic job satisfaction exhibited significant associations with method control, attention demand, role breadth, performance review (βs from .08, $p<.05$ to .21, $p<001$) and level of monitoring ($\beta=-.09$, $p<.05$). For extrinsic job satisfaction the significant associations were, method control ($\beta=-.15$, $p<.001$), payment fairness ($\beta=.20$, $p<.001$), training adequacy ($\beta=.13$, $p<.001$), team leader support ($\beta=.20$, $p<.001$) and monitoring to punish ($\beta=-.08$, $p<.05$). It can also be noted from Table 10.3 that age was positively associated with depression ($\beta=.20$, $p<.01$) and intrinsic job satisfaction ($\beta=.12$, $p<.01$), and that job tenure was negatively associated with intrinsic job satisfaction ($\beta=-.10$, $p<.05$).

Comparing call centre work to other forms of work

Using a series of t-tests, call centre work was compared to two other comparable forms of work – clerical and shop floor manufacturing work. The means for each of the three call centres and the clerical and shop floor samples are shown in Table 10.5. The results indicate that, in comparison to clerical work, anxiety ($p<.05$) was lower at Bank-Call,

Table 10.3 Hierarchical multiple regressions: initial analysis of independent effects of main study variables on well-being variables

	Anxiety		Depression		Intrinsic job satisfaction		Extrinsic job satisfaction	
	β	r^2	β	r^2	β	r^2	β	r^2
Step 1.								
Demographics and controls								
Mortgage-Call	.13*		.10		−.03		.03	
Loan-Call	.13*		.17**		.19***		−.01	
Age	−.09		.20**		.12**		−.03	
Gender	.04		.09		−.05		−.08	
Job tenure	.04		.10		−.10*		.02	
Full-time/ part-time	.04		.03		.03		−.06	
Extrinsic job satisfaction	–		–		.63***		–	
Intrinsic job satisfaction	–		–		–		.68***	
r^2 for Step 1		.02***		.09***		.53***		.50***
Step 2								
Job design variables								
Timing control	−.16***	.04	−.22**	.04	.13**	.01	−.02	.00
Method control	−.21***	.04	−.31***	.08	.27***	.06	−.13***	.01
Attention demand	.13**	.01	−.08	.01	.10**	.01	−.05	.00
Problem-solving demand	.07	.00	−.10*	.01	.11**	.01	−.06	.00
Role breadth	−.13**	.01	−.25***	.06	.19***	.03	−.03	.00
Monitoring								
Level of monitoring	.24***	.06	.28***	.08	−.16***	.02	−.01	.00
Monitoring/ punish	.24***	.06	.32***	.10	−.17***	.03	−.12***	.01
Human resource practices								
Payment fairness	−.22***	.04	−.25***	.05	.04	.00	.28***	.06
Performance appraisal	−.18**	.03	−.37***	.12	.19***	.03	.12**	.01
Training Adequacy	−.22***	.05	−.25***	.06	.05	.00	.21***	.04
Team leader support	−.31***	.09	−.40***	.16	.15***	.02	.26***	.05

Notes: *p < .05; **p < .01; ***p < .001.

236 *Employee Well-being in Call Centres*

Table 10.4 Hierarchical multiple regressions: unique effects of main study variables on well-being variables

	Anxiety	Depression	Intrinsic job satisfaction	Extrinsic job satisfaction
	β	β	β	β
Step 1				
Demographics and Controls				
Mortgage-Call	.13*	.10	−.03	.03
Loan-Call	.13*	.17**	.19***	−.01
Age	−.09	−.20**	.12**	−.03
Gender	.04	.09	−.05	−.08
Job tenure	.04	.10	−.10*	.02
Full-time/part-time	.04	.03	.03	−.06
Extrinsic job satisfaction	–	–	.63***	–
Intrinsic job satisfaction	–	–	–	.68***
Step 2				
Job design variables				
Timing control	−.03	−.02	−.04	.06
Method control	−.11*	−.15**	.21***	−.15***
Attention demand	.13*	−.03	.10**	−.03
Problem-solving demand	.04	−.03	−.02	−.02
Role breadth	−.01	−.05	.09**	−.03
Monitoring				
Level of monitoring	.14**	.12**	−.09*	.04
Monitoring/punish	−.01	.08	−.05	−.08*
Human resource practices				
Payment fairness	−.07	−.08	.03	.20***
Performance appraisal	.01	−.14***	.08*	.03
Training adequacy	.09*	−.09*	.03	.13***
Team leader support	−.19***	−.21***	−.06	.20***
r^2 for Step 1	.02***	.09***	.53***	.50***
Δr^2 for Step 2	.17***	.28***	.12***	.10***
Total adjusted r^2	.17	.35	.63	.58

Notes: *p < .05; **p < .01; ***p < .001.

but depression was higher (p < .01), and intrinsic job satisfaction (p < .001) and extrinsic job satisfaction (p < .01) were both lower. In comparison to shop floor work, employees at Bank-Call reported lower anxiety (p < .05) and intrinsic job satisfaction (p < .001), higher extrinsic job satisfaction, and no significant difference with depression. At Mortgage-Call, well-being was not significantly different from clerical work on any of the four measures. Also, while anxiety and depression at

Table 10.5 Means and standard deviations for each call centre and for clerical and shop floor manufacturing work (Standard deviations in parenthesis)

	Anxiety	Depression	Intrinsic job satisfaction	Extrinsic job satisfaction
Bank-Call	2.54 (.74)	2.77 (.86)	3.51 (1.14)	4.53 (.86)
Mortgage-Call	2.69 (.74)	2.76 (.67)	4.27 (1.05)	4.83 (.69)
Loan-Call	2.68 (.73)	2.38 (.71)	4.31 (.98)	5.00 (.70)
Clerical	2.69 (.76)	2.56 (.72)	4.48 (1.10)	4.70 (.93)
Shop floor Manufacturing	2.81 (.82)	2.71 (.77)	4.08 (1.13)	4.20 (1.05)

Mortgage-Call were not significantly different from shop floor work, intrinsic job satisfaction (p < *.05)* and extrinsic job satisfaction (p < .001) were higher at Mortgage-Call. At Loan-Call, anxiety and intrinsic job satisfaction were not significantly different from that of clerical workers, but depression was lower (p < .05) and extrinsic job satisfaction was higher (p < .001). Compared to shop floor work, employees at Loan-Call reported less anxiety (p < .05) and depression (p < .001) and more intrinsic job satisfaction (p < .01) and extrinsic job satisfaction (p < .001).

Overall, it is clear that employees at Bank-Call report lower levels of well-being (apart from anxiety) than clerical or shop floor employees. Employees at Mortgage-Call and Loan-Call, report that their well-being was the same if not higher than clerical or shop floor workers.

Discussion

The aims of this paper were to examine the relationship of call centre practices (for example, job design, monitoring and so on) to employee well-being and to compare well-being in call centre work to that in other forms of work.

The results demonstrate that job control has a positive association with well-being (that is, low anxiety and depression, and high intrinsic and extrinsic job satisfaction) and that engagement in a wide variety of tasks also has a positive association with intrinsic job satisfaction. These results are in line with earlier job design research (Parker and Wall, 1998) and, although fairly unsurprising, confirm such relationships in the call centre setting. One unexpected finding was a lack of association between timing control and well-being in the analysis of relative effects (see Table 10.4). However, when the independent effects of variables were analyzed (see Table 10.3), timing control was associated with

238 *Employee Well-being in Call Centres*

anxiety, depression and intrinsic job satisfaction. This suggests that, while timing control is important, other types of job control such as method control may have the greater effect on well-being in call centres. In other words, with regard to well-being, CSR control over how they talk to customers and how they do a work task is more important than control over when a call is taken. Further interesting findings pertained to the relationships between job demand and well-being, which tended to be non-significant or not in the direction predicted. Thus, although attention demand had the predicted positive association with anxiety, it also had an unexpected positive association with intrinsic job satisfaction. This suggests that in a call centre, although the requirement to pay constant attention to one's work may cause feelings of worry and anxiety (for example, about making a mistake), actively attending to and meeting the customers needs and problems may also prove satisfying.

The results additionally reveal that a high level of monitoring has a negative association with well-being. These results are in line with other research findings and confirm the important effect of performance monitoring on well-being in a call centre environment (Chalykoff and Kochan, 1989). Although performance data was not reported, this finding suggests that excessive monitoring may have the opposite effect on performance to the one intended. Excessive monitoring may, over the long term, make employees more depressed and less active. In addition, higher levels of anxiety brought about by excessive monitoring may cause people to devote their cognitive resources to dealing with their anxiety rather than focus on providing a quality customer service (Kuhl, 1992). However, the effect of stress on performance is still a matter of some debate (Jex, 1998) and it also plausible that those who are more anxious and depressed are likely to be monitored more often because of the perceived effect their emotional state might have on performance. Longitudinal research is needed to examine the correct causality.

Employees' evaluations of HR practices (namely, the fairness of the payment system, the usefulness of the performance appraisal and the adequacy of the training) tended to be associated negatively with depression and positively with extrinsic job satisfaction. The reasons why these practices are associated with well-being may vary. For example, if an individual believes their level of pay is unfair (that is, that they do not receive compensation that reflects their level of effort), then they feel less enthusiastic about their current activities. With regard to performance appraisal, getting constructive feedback can be construed as a satisfying experience, while training may decrease a CSR's anxieties about one's ability to do the job. The relationship of HR practices with well-being, and the fact that team leader support had a high positive association with well-being, provides support for existing research demonstrating that a supportive HR and leadership environment has a significant effect on employee well-being.

The results of this study regarding job and organizational factors must also be understood in relation to the results of the demographic factors. Table 10.4 indicates that that age is the second most significant predictor of depression and intrinsic satisfaction. Job tenure also had levels of association equal to other job and organizational factors with regard to intrinsic job satisfaction. However, the strength of relationship between the demographic and dependent variables could be a function of the order in which variables were entered in the regression analysis. To examine this, four hierarchical regressions were conducted (one for each dependent variable) in which the job and organizational characteristics were entered at step 1 and the demographic variables at step 2. The results showed that the order of entry had little effect on the standardized beta coefficients of the demographic variables and that the adjusted r^2 for step 2 (that is, demographic variables) were not dramatically affected.[4] The order of entry therefore had little effect on the strength of relationship between the demographic and dependent variables, indicating that age and job tenure need to be addressed when considering well-being in call centres. It must also be noted that some of the effect sizes are rather small and that for anxiety, intrinsic job satisfaction and extrinsic job satisfaction, much of the variance is unaccounted for by the job and organizational factors variables covered in this study.

In summary, the results revealed that, of the job and organizational factors covered in this study, having high control over work methods and procedures, a low level of monitoring, and a supportive team leader would appear to have the most significant effects on employee well-being. In terms of employee well-being, this suggests that call centres are not radically new or different forms of work organization and that the lessons learnt in other organizations may be successfully applied to call centres. The age of the employee also seems have a significant effect, with older employees tending to be more depressed but more satisfied with the intrinsic aspects of their work.

The findings from this study go some way to challenging the stereotyped image of all call centres as 'electronic sweatshops' or 'human battery farms'. Call centre work compares favourably to shop floor manufacturing work and clerical work with regard to well-being. Indeed, at two call

240 *Employee Well-being in Call Centres*

centres the level of well-being was equivalent to, and in many cases better than, these forms of work. However, as demographic factors were not controlled for in the comparative analysis, the results may be best viewed as providing tentative support for the idea that well-being in certain forms of call centre work compares favourably to that in other forms of work.

The practical implications of this study with regard to well-being are quite evident. Job control should be maximized and practices such as insisting that calls are handled within an exact time and excessive call scripting should be resisted. Job demands and role breadth should be such that they provide a challenging environment and one in which the CSR has a variety of tasks to do. Levels of monitoring should be minimized and there is a need to develop effective performance appraisal and training. Efforts should also be made to ensure that team leaders are skilled in administering performance appraisal and monitoring practices, and have a supportive and facilitative style. The need to invest in the training of team leaders would appear particularly important in call centres, where CSRs are often promoted to this role from within the organization. This can mean that new team leaders are placed in a situation where they have to deal with sensitive issues (such as giving feedback on performance) under demanding conditions, yet are relatively inexperienced and ill equipped to cope with such tasks.

A question that arises from this study is whether employee well-being and performance are compatible aims in call centres. For example, in call centres serving a mass market, the small profit margins of the market served means that there is often a focus on reducing costs, particularly labour costs that can account for up to 60 per cent of total costs in service industries (Batt, 2000), and on high call volumes to maximize customer throughput. These aims are achieved through a variety of means but normally through Tayloristic job designs and low-cost HR practices. Tayloristic job designs mean that less skilled, cheaper labour can be employed and that fewer resources can be devoted to recruiting, training and developing employees (Batt, 2000; Holman, 2002). This implies that, based on the findings reported in this chapter, the practices found in a 'mass service' call centre are unlikely to reduce employee well-being (see also Batt and Moynihan, 2001; Holman and Fernie, 2000 for further evidence to support this assertion). As a consequence, the aims of employee well-being, cost minimization and operational efficiency appear incompatible in 'mass service' call centres.

However, not attending to the causes of employee well-being can also incur costs. Lower levels of well-being may increase absence and turnover rates (Batt and Moynihan, 2001), which in turn can increase staffing, recruitment and training costs. When local labour markets are very competitive, these costs may be exacerbated. Lower well-being may also decrease the quality of customer service and increase errors (Schlesinger and Heskett, 1991). This can lead to lower first-time call resolution and more 'unnecessary' calls. In addition, high levels of performance monitoring to ensure that scripts and call times are strictly adhered to incur greater supervisory costs. As such, low employee well-being may increase total costs. Employee well-being and performance may not be incompatible aims, even in a mass service call centre. Indeed, there is some evidence to suggest that managers in mass service call centres are recognizing this and are introducing empowered job designs (i.e, greater autonomy, more variety) to alleviate the deleterious effects of Tayloristic job designs (Houlihan, 2001).

Finally, some limitations of this study need to be noted. It is a single study of three call centres in one sector. Although there is little to indicate that the call centres studied are atypical, and that the findings will not apply in other call centres, the generalizability of the findings still needs to be tested. Studies focusing on other measures of well-being (For example, emotional exhaustion, psychosomatic complaints) and on emotional labour are also needed. It may be that this study has underestimated the negative effects of call centre work on well-being as it did not cover a wide enough range of measures. In addition, the study was not longitudinal and it is therefore difficult to infer causality with any certainty. Furthermore, this study relies mainly on self-report questionnaire data. Common method variance, halo effects and other forms of response bias present a potential source of invalidity to substantive interpretation. Clearly, longitudinal, multi-method research conducted in other sectors and on a wider range of well-being measures is needed.

Acknowledgement

The support of the Economic and Social Research Council (ESRC) (UK) is gratefully acknowledged. The work was part of the programme of the ESRC Centre for Organization and Innovation.

Notes

1. Zapf *et al.* (1999) found a link between interaction control (that is, the degree to which a CSR can control how they speak to a customer) and job satisfaction, psychosomatic complaints and emotional exhaustion. However, the interaction

242 *Employee Well-being in Call Centres*

control measure had a poor reliability (α=0.51) and so these results must be treated with caution.

2. They also found differences in stress, but the measure used confounded the themes of worrying after work, the ability to unwind after work and feeling used up at the end of the workday. This makes it difficult to interpret the results.

3. When extrinsic job satisfaction was the dependent variable, intrinsic job satisfaction was controlled for; and when intrinsic job satisfaction was entered, extrinsic job satisfaction was entered as a control. These controls were entered as intrinsic and extrinsic job satisfaction are conceptually similar (unlike anxiety and depression which are orthogonally related) and highly correlated (r=.67, p<.001). Controlling for their effect in this way enables a more accurate picture to be obtained of the relationship between the dependent variable and the variable of interest.

4. Full results can be obtained from the author.

References

Agho, A. O., C. W. Mueller and C. J. Price (1993) 'Determinants of job satisfaction: An empirical test of a causal model', *Human Relations*, 46, pp. 1007–27.

Aiello, J. R. (1993) 'Computer-Based Work Monitoring: Electronic Surveillance and its Effects', *Journal of Applied Social Psychology*, 23, pp. 499–507.

Aiello, J. R. and Y. Shao (1993) 'Electronic performance monitoring and stress: The role of feedback and goal setting', in M. J. Smith and G. Salavendy (eds), *Human-Computer Interaction: Applications and case studies*, Amsterdam: Elsevier Science, pp. 1011–16.

Alder, G. S. (1998) 'Ethical issues in electronic performance monitoring: A consideration of deontological and teleological perspectives', *Journal of Business Ethics*, 17, pp. 729–43.

Axtell, C., D. Holman, T. Wall, P. Waterson, E. Harrington and K. Unsworth (2000) 'Shopfloor Innovation: facilitating the suggestion and implementation of ideas', *Journal of Occupational and Organizational Psychology*, 73(3), pp. 265–85.

Bain, P. and P. Taylor (2000) 'Entrapped by the "electronic panoptican"? Worker resistance in the call centre', *New Technology, Work and Employment*, 15(1), pp. 2–18.

Batt, R. (2000) 'Strategic segmentation in front-line services: matching customers, employees and human resource systems', *International Journal of Human Resource Management*, 11(3), pp. 540–61.

Batt, R. and E. Appelbaum (1995) 'Worker participation in diverse settings: does the form affect the outcome, and if so, who benefits?' *British Journal of Industrial Relations*, 33(3), pp. 353–78.

Batt, R. and L. Moynihan (2001) 'The viability of alternative call centre production models', paper presented at Call Centres and Beyond: the Human Resource Management Implications, November, Kings College, London.

Belt, V., R. Richardson and J. Webster (1999) 'Smiling down the phone: women's work in telephone call centres', workshop on call centres March, London School of Economics.

Blau, G. (1999) 'Testing the longitudinal impact of work variables and performance appraisal satisfaction on subsequent overall job satisfaction', *Human Relations* 52, pp. 1099–113.

Chalykoff, J. and T. Kochan (1989) 'Computer-aided monitoring its influence on employee job satisfaction and turnover', *Personnel Psychology* 42, pp. 807–34.

Daniels, K. (2000) 'Measures of five aspects of affective wellbeing at work', *Human Relations*, 53, pp. 275–94.

Deery, S. R. Iverson and J. Walsh (2002) 'Work relationships in telephone call centres: understanding emotional exhaustion and employee withdrawal', *Journal of Management Studies*, 39(4), pp. 471–96.

Fernie, S. and D. Metcalf (1998) '(Not) Hanging on the Telephone: payment systems in the new sweatshops', *Centrepiece*, 3, pp. 7–11.

Frenkel, S., M. Korczynski, K. Shire and M. Tam (1998) 'Beyond bureacracy? Work organization in call centres', *International Journal of Human Resource Management*, 9(6), pp. 957–79.

Frenkel, S., M. Korczynski, K. Shire and M. Tam, (1999). *On the Front Line: Organization of work in the information economy*, Ithaca, NY: Cornell University Press.

Garson, B. (1988) *The Electronic Sweatshop: How Computers are Transforming the Office of the Future into the Factory of the Past*, New York: Simon & Schuster.

Grant, R. A. and C. A. Higgins (1989) 'Computerised performance monitors: Factors affecting acceptance', *IEEE Transactions on Engineering Management*, 38, pp. 306–14.

Holman, D. J. (2002) 'Call Centres', in D. J. Holman, T. D. Wall, C. W. Clegg, P. Sparrow, and A. Howard (eds) *The New Workplace: A guide to the human impact of modern working practices*, Chichester: Wiley.

Holman, D. and C. Fernie (2000) 'Can I help you? Call centres and job satisfaction', *CentrePiece*, 5(1), pp. 2–5.

Houlihan, M. (2001) 'Control and commitment in the call centre? More evidence from the field', paper presented at Call Centres and Beyond: the Human Resource Management Implications, November, Kings College London.

Incomes Data Services (IDS) (1999), *Pay and Conditions in Call Centres*, London: Income Data Services.

Jackson, P., T. D. Wall, R. Martin and K. Davids (1993) 'New measures of job control, cognitive demand, and production responsibility', *Journal of Applied Psychology*, 78(5), pp. 753–62.

Jex, S. M. (1998), *Stress and performance: Theory, research and implications for managerial practice*, London: Sage.

Karaseck, R. A. and T. G. Theorell (1990) *Healthy Work: Stress, Productivity and the Reconstruction of Working Life*, New York: Basic Books.

Knights, D. and D. McCabe (1998) 'What happens when the phone goes wild? Staff, stress and spaces for escape in a BPR telephone banking call regime', *Journal of Management Studies*, 35(2), pp. 163–94.

Kuhl, J. (1992) 'A theory of self-regulation: Action versus state orientation, self discrimination, some applications', *Applied Psychology: An International Review*, 41, pp. 97–129.

Mullarkey, S., T. D. Wall, P. Warr, C. W. Clegg and C. B. Stride (1999), *Measures of Job Satisfaction, Mental Health and Job Related Wellbeing: A Bench-Marking Manual*, Sheffield: Institute of Work Psychology, University of Sheffield.

Parker, S. K. and T. D. Wall (1998), *Job and Work Design*, London: Sage.

Pepper, K., C. M. Axtell, C. W. Clegg, P. H. Gardner and T. D. Wall (1999), *Measures of Role Breadth*, Sheffield: Institute of Work Psychology, University of Sheffield.

244 *Employee Well-being in Call Centres*

Saks, A. M. (1995) 'The relationship between amount and helpfulness of entry training and work outcomes', *Human Relations*, 49, pp. 429–51.

Schlesinger, L. and J. Heskett (1991) 'Breaking the cycle of failure in services', *Sloan Management Review*, 32, pp. 17–28.

Smith, M. J., P. Carayon, K. J. Sanders, S. Y. Lim and D. LeGrande (1992), 'Employee stress and health complaints in jobs with and without monitoring', *Applied Ergonomics*, 23, pp. 17–27.

Spector, P. E. (1987) 'Interactive effects of perceived control and job stressors on affective reactions and health outcomes for clerical workers', *Work and Stress*, 1, pp. 155–62.

Stanton, J. M. (2000) 'Reactions to employee performance monitoring: Framework, review and research directions', *Human Performance*, 13, pp. 85–113.

Taylor, P. and P. Bain (1998) 'An Assembly Line in the Head', 16th International Labour Process Conference, 30 March–1 April, UMIST, Manchester.

Terry, D. and N. Jimmieson (1999) 'Work control and wellbeing: A decade review', in C. Cooper and I. Robertson (eds), *International Review of Industrial and Organizational Psychology*, 14, London: John Wiley and Sons, pp. 95–148.

Warr, P. B. (1990) 'The measurement of wellbeing and other aspects of mental health', *Journal of Occupational Psychology*, 63, pp. 193–210.

Warr, P. B. (ed.) (1996) *Psychology at Work*, 4th edition, Harmondsworth: Penguin.

Warr, P. B., J. D. Cook and T. D. Wall (1979) 'Scales for the measurement of some work attitudes and aspects of psychological well-being', *Journal of Occupational Psychology*, 52, pp. 285–94.

Winslow, C. D. and W. L. Bramer (1994). *Futurework*, New York: Free Press.

Zapf, D., C. Vogt, C. Seifert, H. Mertini and A. Isic (1999) 'Emotion work as a source of stress: the concept and development of an instrument', *European Journal of Work and Organizational Psychology*, 8(3), pp. 371–400.

11
All Talk But No Voice: Non-union Employee Representation in Call Centre Work*

Paul J. Gollan

Introduction

Although there have been a growing number of studies on employment relations in call centres (Bain and Taylor, 1999; Batt, 1999; Fernie and Metcalf, 1998; Frenkel *et al.*, 1998; 1999; IDS, 1997, 1998, 1999, 2000, 2001; Kinnie, Purcell and Hutchinson, 2000; Knights and McCabe, 1998; Korczynski *et al.*, 1996; Korczynski, 1999; Simms, 1999; Taylor and Bain, 1999a, 1999b; 2001), it is apparent from existing research that little is known about the effectiveness of employee consultation and representation in non-unionized call centres. In particular, we know very little about how such non-union employee representation and consultation structures are composed, their independence from managerial influence, the 'representativeness' of such bodies, and their accountability (Gollan, 2001). In addition, little has been documented about the impact and influence of such structures on managerial decision-making.

Furthermore, the general literature on employee participation and representation thus far has taken little account of the high concentration of female employees and part-time workers and the high staff turnover often found in call centre operations. It can be argued that the growth of such employment may have major implications for the effectiveness

---

*This chapter is based on an article, 'All talk but no voice – employee voice at the Eurotunnel Call Centre', published in the *Economic and Industrial Democracy Journal*, 24(4). Copyright: Sage Publications.

245

246 *All Talk But No Voice*

of employee consultation and representation, in that many of these employees may slip through the participative and consultation net because of their working time arrangements.

The purpose of this research is to examine non-union consultation and representative arrangements at a call centre at Eurotunnel in the United Kingdom and assess their effectiveness in representing the needs of employees. The chapter attempts to address a number of research questions. First, why do some organizations choose non-union employee representation[1] as an HRM strategy and are such structures appropriate in a call centre environment? Second, what factors do organizations consider when choosing the type of non-union employee representation strategy? Third, how effective are non-union employee representation structures at representing the interests and providing voice of call centre employees?

The structure of the chapter is as follows. First, the chapter addresses the current theoretical debates concerning non-union employee representation arrangements. This section examines the conceptual issues of non-union employee representation forms addressing the question whether they are a 'substitute' for unions or are in some way a 'complement' to current union forms, by examining the relationship to unionism, and the strategies involved in non-union employee representation from an employer perspective. The second section reviews the current evidence in the UK, examining previous survey and case study research into non-union employee representation and briefly highlighting the available research and debates on consultation and representation in call centres. This section attempts to identify some important themes from the existing research on non-union employee representation. The third section introduces the Eurotunnel case study presenting a background to the company and to the company council structure. A brief review of the call centre operations is also provided. The fourth section makes an assessment of an employee survey at Eurotunnel and reports on the initial findings. It also gives some indication of the important representation and consultation issues from the perspective of employees at the Eurotunnel call centre operations. Finally, a discussion is undertaken of the major findings of the study and the implications for non-union consultation and representation in call centres are examined.

Current debates

Current debates on non-union employee representation structures can be divided into two main themes: first, the influence of non-union employee representation arrangements and their relationship to unionism and second, management strategies and approaches to non-union employee representation.

Freeman and Medoff (1984) have argued, that although unions can provide an effective method of collective employee 'voice', there may be an incentive for employers to provide some alternative voice mechanism where workplace union organization is weak or absent. The academic literature has identified the important role of unions in giving employees a voice, enabling them to express dissatisfaction with the working environment without fear of management retaliation. Thus, it is suggested, where unions are weak or non-existent this voice effect will be absent, or alternatively an employee may exercise voice through the exit option, although Freeman and Medoff (1984) also argue that the exit option represents a less than optimal form of voice.

Can non-union employee representation approximate 'voice' as represented by traditional union structures? Interestingly, as Freeman and Medoff noted, the efficacy of voice depends on the way in which labour and management interact, rather than whether unions exist or not (Sako, 1998; Freeman and Medoff, 1984). As such, commentators have argued that from a social perspective, the role of non-union employee representation as bargaining agents (thus similar to traditional trade union forms) may be desirable for power equality or ethical industrial democracy reasons. Advocates state that this can only be achieved by legal enactment, for example mandated works councils, because employers will be reluctant to introduce bodies that challenge managerial prerogative and potentially reduce profit due to the additional costs involved.

This proposition, however, is dependent on the wider institutional context. Organizations may create such bodies for the purposes of bargaining to reduce the likelihood of outside involvement by trade unions in organizational decision-making, thus ensuring that bargaining processes are contained within the organization. This may be due to the perception that an outside influence may distort internal processes and structures and have a negative impact on employee behaviour and organizational performance.

Others have argued that structures representing the interests of employees through collective bargaining (legally enforced or not) may give more legitimacy and efficacy to the decision-making process (Hyman, 1997a; Hyman, 1997b), ensuring greater organizational commitment. In addition, Hyman (1997a) also suggests that non-union employee representation forms have the capacity to assist unionism in workplaces where they are given many responsibilities and especially when enforced

248 *All Talk But No Voice*

through statutory rights. Others have suggested that 'the question is not whether works councils will weaken unions, but rather whether unions will be prevented from developing a strong presence where there is a works council'. As Fishman (1995, p. 7) has stated, 'There is surely no inherent reason why a works council should inhibit union growth.'

In contrast, other commentators have suggested that works councils have 'consolidated a more recent shift to non-unionism' (Kelly, 1996, p. 56). This rationale is premised on the belief that employer-initiated structures are based on employers' terms and cannot be effective in providing a true voice for employees' issues and concerns because they institutionalize worker co-operation, thus limiting scope for trade union action (Kelly, 1996; Lloyd, 1999). In addition, these commentators also state that such structures are packed with 'hand-picked cronies' or, in the cases where employees can elect representatives (including union representatives), it will not be fully independent of the company and will not have the backing of national union organizers to enforce action or outcomes. 'Without union backing, staff councils would simply be quisling bodies' (*The Guardian*, 2000, p. 33).

In general, these debates have focused on the functions of non-union employee representation forms and their outcomes. Two fundamentally different approaches have been taken: first, non-union representation structures are seen as an inherent 'win–lose' or 'zero sum' game. This is based on the premise that an individual employee is inherently at a disadvantage in the employment relationship due to the monopoly power of the employer. Alternatively, non-union representation structures have been viewed as an instrument through which both sides realize a 'win–win' outcome in the employment relationship. This perspective highlights the notion of a common interest between employers and employees and a unitarist approach based on shared beliefs and goals.

Previous research

Recent survey research has suggested that there has been limited growth in alternative collective mechanisms for employee voice to trade union representation and collective bargaining. The Workplace Employee Relations Survey 1998 (WERS98) indicates that the presence of workplace-level joint consultative committees was stable at 29 per cent from 1990 to 1998, with a further quarter of workplaces operating a committee only at a higher level in the organization. Over two-thirds of employees were covered by these arrangements. In addition, the evidence from WERS98 suggests that over half of workplaces with between 25 and 50 employees did not operate any joint consultative committees, and that 80 per cent of organizations with fewer than 100 employees had no consultative body. Millward, Bryson and Forth's (2000) analysis of WERS98 data highlighted the importance of the views of employees towards consultation. The researchers found a clear link between how often consultation occurs and its perceived value – with a lack of consultation contributing to perceptions of poor management among employees. Millward, Bryson and Forth (2000, p. 129) also found that:

> Employees with some type of non-union voice arrangement generally felt that managers were better at keeping them up-to-date with proposed changes at the establishment than did those employees in workplaces without any formal voice mechanism. This was true whether non-union arrangements were found in isolation or together with union channels of voice.

In terms of employees' perceptions of 'fair treatment' the combined presence of a recognized union and union representation on a consultative committee was found to be decisive in delivering fair workplace outcomes. Although non-union or direct voice mechanisms were seen to be useful in enhancing the responsiveness of management to specific employee issues they appeared to be less effective than unions at promoting fair treatment for employees in general (Millward, Bryson and Forth, 2000).

Case study research by Gollan (2000; 2002) and Terry (1999) has reinforced these findings. It suggests that most non-union firms seek to install structures of collective consultation in order to increase information and communication, rather than for negotiation or bargaining purposes. Most of these companies see non-union representative and consultation as providing a more effective channel of communication than unions, stressing more 'harmonious' and less conflictual relations with the workforce. It would seem from their stated objectives that management view non-union representation as a means of increasing company productivity and efficiency rather than as an effective forum of collective representation for the interests of employees. One of the few studies that has explored the impact of non-union representation in a call centre (Korczynski, 1999) concluded that such structures had very little influence on management decision-making. The study suggested that management frequently sought to predetermine the decision-making process and undermine the influence of employees.

Overall, a number of important conclusions can be drawn from the available research. First, non-union collective consultation structures

250 *All Talk But No Voice*

generally have limited access to resources which reduces their ability to evaluate effectively the issues discussed at meetings and to represent the views of employees. Second, management is usually the party that controls the structure and agenda of meetings and occupies the position of chair. Third, most bodies are only given powers of recommendation to management or the chair has the right of veto over its decisions. Fourth, unlike unions, few committees have negotiation and bargaining rights over pay and conditions. Finally, few of these bodies in practice fulfil the traditional trade union role of conflict resolution.

Case study: Eurotunnel (UK) call centre operation

Background

Eurotunnel has a 50-year lease to operate the Channel Tunnel link between Britain and France. It has full operational and management control of all rail traffic through the Channel Tunnel for this period. In addition, it operates a train shuttle service between Folkestone (UK) and Calais (France). The Eurotunnel group has a complex structure consisting of two legal entities to meet requirements in the UK and France. Eurotunnel employs a total staff of 2,300, with approximately 1,300 based in Britain on UK contracts. The UK head office is in Folkestone (Longport). This chapter will focus on Eurotunnel UK operations because all its call centre operations are based in Folkestone.[2]

Until June 2000, Eurotunnel (UK) only recognized the company council for negotiation purposes. As part of an early policy choice to integrate its two workforces, the company council for UK-contracted employees was established in December 1992. This is broadly similar to the enterprise committee (or *comité d' entreprise*) under French legislation. In June 2000, a recognition and partnership agreement was signed between Eurotunnel (UK) and the Transport and General Workers Union (T&GWU) to cover all non-managerial staff.

According to management, the company's human resource (HR) policy systematically takes into consideration its bi-national status, whether regarding staff allocation or the fixing of salaries and benefits. The 1999 annual report states:

> National differences are taken into account when creating personnel management policies, especially as far as labour laws are concerned, the main objective always being to ensure as far as possible equal status for the personnel of each country. Salaries are competitively fixed in

Paul J. Gollan 251

line with the current market conditions of each country, with most of the associated salary benefits (paid holiday, retirement pension, medical insurance) being either identical or directly comparable.

Eurotunnel 1999 Annual Report, p. 23

The Eurotunnel (UK) company council was established in 1992 as the sole channel of employee representation. The company council consists of employees who are democratically elected every two years.[3] Importantly, it is the company's communications forum and has three main aims: to give information and consult on matters of common concern to employees; to manage the social and welfare budget equal to 1 per cent of payroll (approximately £250,000–£350,000 per year); and to represent all employees at Eurotunnel (before June 2000, this included bargaining and negotiation over pay and conditions). All representatives must be permanent employees with at least one year's service, and on permanent rather than temporary contracts. They may, however, be full-time or part-time employees. This is an issue in the call centre operations where many employees are agency workers on limited contracts of employment.

With the introduction of the 'Fairness at Work' legislation, a key issue discussed at the company council has been union recognition. A recognition and partnership agreement was signed by Eurotunnel management and the T&GWU in June 2000, which recognized negotiation rights, confirmed the acceptance of the existing consultation framework and established a joint management trade union forum. As a result, the agreement created two representation structures. A modified company council with eight representatives meets six times a year and represents all employees at Eurotunnel including the call centre staff. The joint trade union forum represents union members at Eurotunnel covering all issues of concern, including negotiations over company-wide pay levels.

In addition to the formal company council meetings, agenda meetings for employee representatives only are also held about one week before full company council meetings. As stated in the company council information letter: 'The company council meeting is where the questions and issues that have been raised at the agenda meetings are answered by the Eurotunnel management.'

The company council consults on all matters and issues of concern to employees. These issues include: operational changes; shift rosters; workplace change; investment strategy; terms of employment; and financial and performance data, including but not limited to profits. These data may incorporate future financial and market strategies, commercial

252 *All Talk But No Voice*

policy and profit figures. In addition, each representative can provide personnel representation on individual issues. However, in general, personal issues and grievances are excluded from discussion, unless they raise issues that have implications for the workforce as a whole. Until union recognition, wages and conditions were also discussed by representatives at separate annual wage forums.

Call centre operations

The call centre operations are located near the main Eurotunnel UK base at Folkestone (Longport). At peak times, the call centre is operated by nine teams each with about 16 members (144 operators overall). In total, there are 175 employees based in the call centre (including agency staff). The call centre is divided into target zones for the UK and Europe. From Monday to Friday, the UK operation is open from 7 am to 11 pm and for Europe it is open from 7 am to 6.30 pm. There are rolling shifts each lasting eight to ten hours. At the weekends, both operations are open from 8 am to 6 pm.

The call centre workforce consists of 26 per cent male and 74 per cent female employees. Eighty-two per cent work full-time and 18 per cent part-time. Overall, some 71 per cent of operators (124 staff) are Eurotunnel employees and on average 29 per cent are agency staff. The call centre operation has a mix of nationalities and cultures, to reflect its language requirements. There are five main nationalities working in the call centre – British, French, Dutch, Belgian and German. Approximately 50 per cent of calls are in English. The average length of service in the call centre is 21 months (for permanent staff). All recruits must go through two weeks' training.

The call centre staff take on average 280,000 calls a year (inbound) with around 120,000 bookings. All telephone calls are processed by an automatic call distribution (ACD) system. There may be approximately 80 calls in progress at any one time but during periods of high demand, this figure can rise to 150 calls. These peak periods centre around Christmas, Easter and summer holiday periods in July and August. In addition, an average of 8, 300 insurance policies a year are sold. About 65 per cent of customers buy their tickets through the call centre and the remainder buy tickets at the office on-site. Each call centre operator generates an average of £5,000 revenue a day for Eurotunnel.

Eurotunnel pays higher salaries for bilingual agents. The premium for additional language skills ranges from £400 to over £2,000 (see Table 11.1 for details). Pay progression through the pay scales is based on individual performance. Shift or unsocial hours premiums are paid although there

Paul J. Gollan   253

Table 11.1   Pays rates for Eurotunnel call centre staff, 1999 and 2000

Job title	Minimum £pa		Midpoint £pa		Maximum £pa	
	1999	2000	1999	2000	1999	2000
Telesales level 1 – English only	9,791	10,025	11,420	11,700	13,050	13,375
Telesales level 1 – bilingual	11,081	11,025	12,720	12,700	14,350	14,375
Telesales level 2 – English only	10,661	10,927	–	–	13,050	13,050
Telesales level 2 – bilingual	11,961	12,260	–	–	–	–
Telesales level 3 – English only	12,110	12,412	14,055	14,406	17,300	16,400
Telesales level 3 – bilingual	13,410	13,745	14,710	15,738	17,300	17,732
Team leader	17,060	17,486	20,525	21,037	23,990	24,589
Team leader/ Supervisor	18,360	18,819	21,825	21,345	23,290	23,872

Source: IDS, *Pay and Conditions in Call Centres*, 1999 and 2000.

is no provision for overtime premiums. In addition to these, bonus and commission payments can be paid. Monthly bonuses are paid as fixed amounts depending on the sales threshold being reached. Bonuses are non-pensionable and variable, and do not exceed 30 per cent of base salary and shift allowances. Commission payments are also made on selling insurance policies to UK customers. Full-time weekly hours are 37.5 with a holiday entitlement of 25 days a year. Other staff benefits include: pension, subsidized meals, health insurance, staff travel discount, recognition awards and Sharesave scheme.

Research strategy

The research was conducted over a period of appropriately three-and-a-half years (December 1998 to June 2002) and involved case study analysis, interviews, company documents, employee surveys, focus groups and observation. The rationale for using Eurotunnel as a case study was the culturally and functionally diverse nature of its workforce both within the call centre operations and in the workforce as a whole located in Folkestone. The case study also highlighted the complexity of operating a uniform consultation structure for a highly diverse workforce.

254 *All Talk But No Voice*

In order to assess employees' responses prior to union recognition, an employee survey was undertaken in the period December 1999 to January 2000. The objective was to assess employee attitudes to the company council and to the role a trade union might play at Eurotunnel's call centre and in the organization more generally. In addition, an issue analysis of company council meetings was also made to ascertain the most important matters raised by call centre representatives (CSRs).

The survey involved a self-completion questionnaire consisting of 27 questions and was distributed to almost half of the Eurotunnel call centre workforce (60 employees) by company council representatives and deputies.[4] In order to gain a representative sample of all workers, instructions were given to employee representatives to ensure they were distributed to shift workers, part-timers and foreign nationals. Of these, 30 useable responses were obtained from call centre operations, giving a response rate of 50 per cent. As such, the survey covered just over 24 per cent of the total Eurotunnel call centre workforce (excluding agency staff). In order to compare the call centre findings with those of other employees at Eurotunnel, a survey was also conducted of the other sections at Eurotunnel. In total 93 useable responses were obtained. The findings in this chapter focus on the responses from the call centre operations. The issues covered in the questionnaire included: work involvement; personal involvement in the consultation process; information received from management; the extent of voice and influence; union relations; company council effectiveness; and management relations. In addition, three focus groups were used to highlight and discuss themes raised in the completed questionnaires. A series of four interviews were conducted with the representatives of the call centre operations on the company council over a period of 12 months. In addition, six interviews were conducted with the manager for the call centre operations and the HR director of Eurotunnel.

Research findings

Employment tenure and gender

There was a high proportion of staff who had worked for the call centre for less than 12 months. According to the survey, just under a quarter (24 per cent) of those call centre staff responding to the survey had worked at Eurotunnel for a year or less. Some 76 per cent of call centre staff had been at the call centre for two to five years with no respondents indicating they had worked longer than five years. Sixty per cent of the call centre respondents were female. This is in contrast to other sections at Eurotunnel where only 13 per cent of respondents were female.

Information and consultation

Over 60 per cent of call centre respondents indicated that they were either not well informed or not informed at all about workplace issues at Eurotunnel. In terms of those workplace issues, staff saw pay and basic conditions, shift rosters and working hours as the most important (see Table 11.2).

Overall, the respondents in the call centre operations were generally positive about how helpful the different consultation methods were, with notice boards, word of mouth, company council representatives and meetings of managers cited as the most helpful. Some 40 per cent of call centre staff indicated that company council representatives were not helpful. Lower on the list in terms of helpfulness were the external media, the workplace newsletter and e-mail messages. Respondents from the other sections of Eurotunnel overwhelmingly stated that e-mail messages were the most helpful in keeping up-to-date about Eurotunnel, with nine out of ten respondents suggesting e-mail was very helpful (39 per cent) or helpful (50 per cent). This was an interesting contrast compared to the call centre operators – less than six in every ten respondents suggested this. This could suggest that while call centre operators have greater access to e-mail, they also have little time to access information.

The vast majority of call centre respondents were dissatisfied with the amount, type and timing of information from management. Seventy-six

Table 11.2 Most important call centres issues

Issue	Which of the following are the most important issues in your area or section? (%)			
	Very important	Fairly important	Not so important	Not important at all
Job security	57	33	10	–
Line management relations	40	47	13	–
Pay and basic conditions	77	23	–	–
Working hours	60	27	13	–
Shift rosters	67	20	13	–
Health and safety	50	30	17	3

256   *All Talk But No Voice*

Table 11.3   Satisfaction with management information

Issue	In regards to information management gives you, how satisfied are you with: (%)			
	Very satisfied	Satisfied	Not so satisfied	Not satisfied at all
Amount of information	3	20	53	23
Type of information	3	37	47	13
Timing of information	3	7	60	30

Table 11.4   The amount of information given on workplace issues

Issue	How much information do you receive on the following? (%)				
	None	A little	Some	A lot	A great deal
Pay and benefits	17	47	27	10	–
Introduction to new technology	27	37	23	10	3
Working practices	23	27	27	20	3
Staffing issues, including recruitment and redundancies	60	27	10	3	–
Employee grievances	43	37	10	10	–

per cent were not satisfied with the amount of information they received from management while 90 per cent expressed dissatisfaction with the timing of the information they received (see Tables 11.3 and 11.4).

One of the CSRs referred to problems of timing and access:

> We have good information here although there are still some things missing. The problem is that communication lags between managers and the different departments. The real problem in the call centre is that many people work part-time or are casual. Thus it is hard to get in contact and to maintain that contact with people, although we do have a newsletter 'talk-talk' which gets published every month and gets general information on the call centre. We also have a company council notice board.

When asked the question, 'Typically when management communicates with you, to what extent do you believe the information you are given?', some 84 per cent of call centre respondents indicated 'not at all' or 'a little' or 'some'. This attitude was reflected in an interview with one of the call centre representatives, who argued, workers

Take it [information] with a pinch of salt. They bend the truth a little, but we also do the same. The problem is that managers normally have more information than the company council. The amount of information is not adequate nor the timing of the information. I think it has to do with the structure of the company.

Representation

Only 10 per cent of call centre respondents indicated that they very often or fairly often talked to their section representative. Some 45 per cent stated they never talked to their representative. Less than 14 per cent of the call centre respondents indicated that they had frequent contact with their work representatives, 55 per cent stated that they had occasional contact, and some 21 per cent suggested they never had contact. More worrying was the 10 per cent who did not even know their call centre worker representatives.

One CSR highlighted the problem:

Everyday, we try to stop work when someone wants to raise an issue. The problem of walking around at call centres is that people are on the phone most of the time, and you are waiting around wasting time. This means money especially in commissions and bonus payments. Better to wait for a break or let people come to you.

Company council

In terms of the importance of the company council as a method of communications respondents in the call centre rated it more highly on matters relating to employee grievances and staffing issues than they did on pay and benefits and the introduction of new technology (see Table 11.5).

One respondent from a call centre focus group argued:

The company council do a reasonable job considering the difficulties they have with conditions and unapproachable management. The social side is well organized. However, the lack of communication and changes in procedures of work, which are very contradictory, are

258 *All Talk But No Voice*

Table 11.5 The importance of the company council in communicating on workplace issues

Issue	How important is the company council in communicating on the issues below? (%)			
	Very important	Important	Not so important	Not important at all
Pay and benefits	10	45	10	35
Introduction to new technology	3	35	24	38
Changes to working practices	21	31	21	28
Staffing issues, including recruitment and redundancies	28	14	21	38
Employee grievances	35	21	24	21

a great problem. Management seem unaware that we all have a life outside Eurotunnel, what a pity!

One of the representatives explained:

> I see the company council as a guardian body to ensure the communication is passed on correctly. It could be a lot more effective but the company would have to give it a lot more power than now. We [company council] are not a negotiating body but a consultation body. Although we could organize in a similar form to a union, the problem is the legal framework in that the company council is a 'trust' under regulations. We are a consultation and welfare and social body for employees only.

Very few call centre respondents stated that they had an opportunity to influence management decision-making on any issue, with between 70 and 90 per cent stating they had no opportunity to influence such issues. This was especially the case regarding pay and benefits, the introduction of new technology and staffing issues. As one focus group respondent stated, 'There is no chance to voice opinion on day-to-day issues which may affect future business of Eurotunnel.' Another focus group respondent stated, 'Due to the nature of a "call centre"...the actual communication between the management and employees is pretty much a one-way thing.'

Representation

On the question of who would best represent staff on major workplace issues, the overwhelming majority of respondents said a trade union. The strongest support for a trade union was related to the issue of pay (see Table 11.6).

The *Eurotunnel Company Council Recognition Survey*[5] also reported little support for the company council as it existed. Only 9 per cent of call centre respondents to the survey supported the existing company council. However, there was more support for the company council having powers to negotiate as well as to consult. Some 33 per cent of call centre respondents in the recognition survey supported a company council with negotiating rights.

Company council effectiveness

Nearly two-thirds of call centre respondents stated that the company council was not effective in representing general employee interests or the interests of employees in the section or area in which they worked.

The view of Eurotunnel employees was voiced by one call centre respondent, who suggested that:

> Company council does well regarding social activities but is unable, through no fault of their own, to influence management decisions. Sadly the company does not do enough to ensure a stable, pleasant environment. Things are constantly changing and pressure to achieve

Table 11.6 Type of representation on workplace issues

Issue	Ideally, who do you think would best represent you in dealing with managers here at Eurotunnel about the following issues? (%)		
	Company council	Union	Individually
Increases in pay	21	64	14
Making a complaint	36	46	18
If a manager wanted to discipline me	25	43	32
Changes to my immediate workplace	36	32	32

260   *All Talk But No Voice*

targets is constant. There is room for a great deal of improvement to working conditions.

In contrast one of the CSRs argued:

> Overall, the company council is very good considering the power we have and what access we have regarding influence and information. As an example we have had a major influence on the design and implementation of the new bonus pay structure and the new health and safety policy. It depends on how you handle different issues. Another is the pay rise, where the management wanted to give us a pay rise of 1.7 per cent and in the end we agreed to an across the board rise of 3.5 per cent. I doubt a union would have done much better and the union would have gone on strike. On a road show [of the call centre], we had many people come to say we were doing a good job and they did not want people from the outside to deal with our issues because they do not work here.

Trade unions

None of the respondents from the call centre were union members, nor was there any active union presence or contact with other union members or representatives. However, over 71 per cent of the respondents in the call centre indicated that management should recognize a trade union.

These findings were also reflected in the *Eurotunnel Company Council Recognition Survey* which found that 52 per cent of the call centre respondents were in favour of trade union representation. In terms of call centre employees' willingness to join a trade union, the recognition survey found some 58 per cent of the respondents stated they were willing to join. However, one of the CSRs was cautious about the impact of trade union recognition. He argued:

> I do not think management should recognize trade unions because I think it would be quite harmful for the company due to the different unions with different agendas and interests. The fear is that you will get a lot of outside conflicts with unions because unions also represent people outside Eurotunnel. Internalizing industrial relations here is more effective because such outside influence would divide views and we would be divided. The best option would be to give the company council more power rather than bringing in outside conflicts. We see

what happens over in France where they have a number of unions and how this affects things like bonuses. Also greater union influence would reduce company council influence. We also need to represent those that do not belong to a union. I would rather have a combined company council with the same power as a union. There must be co-operation and a partnership between employees and management.

The majority of call centre respondents suggested that a trade union would improve their position over pay and benefits, work conditions, health and safety and employee grievances (see Table 11.7). Interestingly, nearly two-thirds of call centre respondents believed that trade unions would increase their job security while more than 70 per cent felt that their working conditions would be improved.

The vast majority of call centre respondents suggested that if trade unions were recognized at Eurotunnel, the company council should retain a consultation role (see Table 11.8). This view was strongest in relation to pay and benefits and employee grievances. However, on three issues – the introduction of new technology, changes to working practices and staffing issues – call centre respondents were more evenly divided. Few call centre respondents believed that the company council should have no role.

One call centre respondent suggested,

The idea of the council is a good one. They want the same benefits as anyone else, but they don't have the power to achieve a great deal.

Table 11.7 Trade unions would improve the following workplace issues

Issue	Do you believe trade unions would improve your position over the following issues? (%)	
	Yes	No
Pay and benefits	68	32
Work conditions	71	29
Health and safety	57	43
Training	36	64
Employee grievances	68	32
Job security	64	36

262 *All Talk But No Voice*

Table 11.8 The role of the company council if trade unions were recognized

Issue	If trade union were recognized at Eurotunnel what role should the company council have? (%)			
	No role	Information role	Consultation role	Don't know
Pay and benefits	19	15	56	11
Introduction to new technology	19	33	37	11
Changes to working practices	19	30	37	11
Staffing issues, including recruitment and redundancies	22	30	37	11
Employee grievances	19	12	54	15

They need to evolve with the company and be given more power on certain issues. Management need to accept them and inform them more than they do now. Work with them not against them.

Management

Between 70 and 80 per cent of call centre respondents thought that managers were not good at keeping everybody up-to-date about proposed workplace changes, providing a chance to comment on such changes, responding to suggestions from employees, and dealing with work problems. In response to the question 'In general, how would you describe relations between managers and employees at Eurotunnel?' 53 per cent stated either 'not so good' or 'not good at all'. Over half of call centre respondents stated that managers were not good at treating employees fairly.

Towards recognition and partnership

A union recognition and partnership agreement was signed between Eurotunnel and the T&GWU in 2000. Taylor and Bain (2001, p. 41) have argued that 'call centres are fertile soil for trade union recruitment and organization, and that the intensity with which workers in many locations were being driven would inevitably produce collectively organized responses'. Recent events at Eurotunnel seem to have confirmed this view. In June 2000, union membership was estimated by a T&GWU regional organizer to be no more than 'two or three' people in the call centre. By June 2002 the director of HR conceded that 'nearly all of the call centre staff belonged to the T&GWU'. In addition, there were union representatives in all of the eight sections at Eurotunnel, including a representative in the call centre.

Discussion and conclusions

The call centre operations at Eurotunnel provided an opportunity to explore the impact of consultative structures on certain management practices, such as communication and participation, and to assess employees' attitudes towards the company council and their views on trade unions. In terms of information from management, the vast majority of call centre employees were not satisfied with the amount, type and timing of the information they received. They were also negative towards the level of information they received, particularly regarding staffing issues and employee grievances. In addition, the majority of respondents were unlikely to believe the information they were given by management. Call centre workers were not positive about the level of influence they had over management decisions and just over half of the respondents believed that managers were not good at treating employees fairly. In terms of the company council, relatively few call centre workers had communicated or even had contact with their representative, with some staff at the call centre not even knowing who he or she was.

There was strong support for trade unions in the call centre. In particular, the majority of workers suggested that a trade union would improve their position over pay and benefits, work conditions, health and safety and employee grievances. The vast majority of call centre employees suggested that the company council should retain a consultation role even with union recognition. However, nearly two-thirds of employees in the survey sample stated that the company council was not effective in representing general employee interests.

These findings would suggest that the company council was seen as an ineffective substitute for union representation due to the very limited role it played in the bargaining and decision-making process. Its prime focus was on information-sharing related to performance and 'business' issues (improving quality, productivity, customer service and/or sales) rather than issues pertaining to workers' wages and employment conditions. Managers had seen the company council as a means of communicating the benefits of change and as a mechanism for persuading employees of the need for change. The results also highlighted the

264 *All Talk But No Voice*

council's lack of effective power with representatives handicapped by insufficient training and inexperience in negotiations.

This assessment is consistent with the *Eurotunnel Company Council Recognition Survey* which concluded:

> The majority of respondents are in favour of a trade union as the way they wish to be represented...What is clear is that people do not believe the company council, as it is currently constituted, is an effective body on these matters. The alternative, to have union representatives on the council, is supported by more than a third of respondents.

Many employees and representatives at the call centre felt that the company council lacked the effectiveness and influence necessary to fulfil its representative requirements. In this sense, the case highlighted the potential limitations of non-union representation as an alternative to union voice. The right to be heard clearly and effectively was as important to workers in this call centre as it was in any other commercial or industrial context.

Notes

1. Non-union employee representation structures can also be referred to as union-independent forms of employee representation or alternative forms of employee representation.
2. It was considered appropriate to base call centre operations at Folkestone since the vast majority of calls into the call centre are UK-based.
3. In addition, a European company council (ECC) was created in November 1998, chaired by the managing director. It is made up of 16 members, eight British and eight French. The ECC meets at least twice a year and is 'informed or consulted on all matters of general bi-national interest within the Company, without encroaching in any way on the autonomy of the national Committees, which preserve all their prerogatives'. The representatives are drawn from the national committees.
4. It was considered appropriate to exclude agency staff from the survey since they were not Eurotunnel employees and often worked for only limited periods at the call centre.
5. The *Eurotunnel Company Council Recognition Survey* was carried out in November 1999 by the Industrial Society on behalf of the Company Council to ascertain employees' views on trade union recognition.

References

Bain, P. and P. Taylor (1999) *Call Centres in Scotland: An Overview*, Glasgow: Scottish Low Pay Unit.

Batt, R. (1999) 'Work organization, technology and performance in customer service and sales', *Industrial and Labour Relations Review*, 52(4), pp. 539–64.

Demaret, L., P. Quinn and S. Grumiau (1998) 'Call Centres and Trade Union Strategy', ICFTU press release, 7 September.

Eurotunnel (1999) *1999 Annual Report.*

Eurotunnel Company Council Recognition Survey (1999) November, London: The Industrial Society.

Fernie, S. and D. Metcalf (1998) '(Not) Hanging on the Telephone: payment systems in the new sweatshops', Discussion Paper no. 390, Centre for Economic Performance.

Fishman, N. (1995) 'TUC Consultative Document: Collective Representation at Work – Practical Political Considerations', unpublished, London.

Fiorito, J., P. Jarley and J. T. Delaney (1996) 'Planning for Change: Determinants of innovation in US national unions', *Industrial and Labour Relations Review*, 49(4), pp. 597–614.

Freeman, R. B. and J. L. Medoff (1984) *What Do Unions Do?*, New York: Basic Books.

Frenkel, S., M. Korczynski, K. Shire and M. Tam (1998) 'Beyond Bureaucracy? Work organization in call centres', *International Journal of Human Resource Management*, 9(6), pp. 957–79.

Frenkel, S., M. Korczynski, K. Shire and M. Tam (1999) *On the Front Line: Organization of work in the information economy*, Ithaca, NY: Cornell University Press.

Gollan, P. (2000) 'Non-union forms of employee representation in the United Kingdom and Australia', in B. E. Kaufman and D. G. Taras (eds), *Non-union Employee Representation: History, Contemporary Practice, and Policy (Issues in Work and Human Resources)* Armonk, New York: M. E. Sharpe.

Gollan, P. (2001) 'Tunnel vision: non-union employee representation', *Employee Relations*, 23(4), pp. 376–400.

Gollan, P. (2002) 'Faces of non-union representation in the UK – Management strategies, processes and outcomes', paper presented at BUIRA conference, 4–6 July, University of Stirling.

The Guardian (2000) 29 January, p. 33.

Guest, D. (1995) 'Human resource management, trade unions and industrial relations', in John Storey (ed.), *Human Resource Management: A Critical Text*, London: Routledge.

Hyman, R. (1997a) The Future of Employee Representation, unpublished discussion paper, Warwick University.

Hyman, R. (1997b) 'The Future of Employee Representation', *British Journal of Industrial Relations*, 35(3), pp. 309–36.

Income Data Services (IDS) (1997) *Pay and Conditions in Call Centres*, London: Income Data Services.

Income Data Services (IDS) (1998) *Pay and Conditions in Call Centres*, London: Income Data Services.

Income Data Services (IDS) (1999) *Pay and Conditions in Call Centres*, London: Income Data Services.

Income Data Services (IDS) (2000) *Pay and Conditions in Call Centres*, London: Income Data Services.

Income Data Services (IDS) (2001) *Pay and Conditions in Call Centres*, London: Income Data Services.

Kelly, J. (1996) 'Works Councils: union advance or marginalisation?', in Aileen McColgan (ed.), *The Future of Labour Law*, London: Mansell.

266 *All Talk But No Voice*

Kelly, J. (1998) *Rethinking Industrial Relations: Mobilisation, Collectivism and Long Waves*, London: Routledge.

Kinnie, N., J. Purcell and S. Hutchinson (2000) "Fun and Surveillance": the paradox of high commitment management in call centres', *International Journal of Human Resource Management*, 11(5), pp. 967–85.

Knights, D. and D. McCabe (1998) 'What happens when the phone goes wild? Staff, stress and spaces for escape in a BPR telephone banking work regime', *Journal of Management Studies*, 35(2), pp. 163–94.

Kochan, T. A., H. C. Katz and R. B. McKersie (1986) *The Transformation of American Industrial Relations*, New York: Basic Books.

Korczynski, M. (1999) 'What a difference a union makes: the impact of partnership unionism on the work organisation of call centres', Workshop on call centres, March, London School of Economics.

Korczynski, M., K. Shire, S. Frenkel and M. Tam (1996) 'Front line work in the "new model service firm": Australian and Japanese Comparisons', *Human Resource Management Journal*, 6(2), pp. 72–87.

Lloyd, C. (1999) 'What do Employee Councils do? Representation in non-union firms', BUIRA Conference, 1–3 July, De Montfort University.

Milkman, R. and K. Wong (1998) 'Organizing Immigrant Workers: Case Studies from Southern California', paper presented at 'The Revival of the American Labor Movement' Conference, 16–17 October, Cornell University.

Millward, N., A. Bryson and J. Forth (2000) *All Change at Work?*, Routledge: London.

Sako, M. (1998) 'The nature and impact of employee "voice" in the European car components industry', *Human Resource Management Journal*, 9(1), pp. 5–13.

Simms, M. (1999) 'Trade Union Organising in Call Centres: The Communication Workers' Union campaign at TalkCo', Cardiff Business School, *mimeo*.

Taylor, P. and P. Bain (1999a)'"An assembly line in the head": work and employee relations in the call centre', *Industrial Relations Journal*, 30(2), pp. 101–17.

Taylor, P. and P. Bain (1999b) 'Working in a Call Centre: Entrapped by the "electronic panoptican"', paper presented to the BSA Conference, 6–9 April.

Taylor, P. and P. Bain (2001) 'Trade unions, workers' rights and the frontier of control in UK call centres', *Economic and Industrial Democracy*, 22, pp. 39–66.

Terry, M. (1999) 'Systems of collective representation in non-union firms in the UK', *Industrial Relations Journal*, 30(1), pp. 16–30.

Walton, R. E. (1985) 'From control to commitment in the workplace', in *Harvard Business Review*, March–April, 64(3), pp. 77–84.

12
Call to Arms? Collective and Individual Responses to Call Centre Labour Management

Diane van den Broek

Introduction

Industrial restructuring, technological change and a greater interest in new management practices have focused attention on the shift from an industrial to 'post-industrial' or 'knowledge economy'. Within this broader rubric of organizational and social change, there has been considerable debate about how labour is managed and the causes, nature and implications of these changes. An extensive literature has analyzed shifts from traditional control-based labour management to a commitment-based human resource (HR) approach (Bell, 1974; Walton, 1985; Drucker, 1993). This debate, which is particularly relevant to call centre operations, pivots on the relevance of post-industrial and, more recently, postmodern models of managerial control (Frenkel *et al.*, 1999; Thompson and Warhurst, 1998).

This chapter analyzes how customer service representatives (CSRs) have responded to call centre management within the Australian telecommunications industry. It focuses on call centres within major telecommunications players, Optus and Telstra as well as Stellar, an outsourced call centre jointly owned by Telstra and Excell Global Services, and TeleTech International, a US-based outsourcing call centre operation. By relocating labour as active agents in these workplaces, this chapter concurs with similar findings that call centre management does not represent the post-industrial commitment model of labour management. However, neither does management assert total or 'omnipotent' control over their employees. Because employees contest managerial policies and practices, call centres do not represent the 'last frontier' of managerial control, but rather are contested sites of resistance and negotiation (Thompson and Ackroyd,

268 *Call to Arms?*

1995; Taylor and Bain, 1999). As indicated below, this resistance and negotiation is manifested in a range of responses to the call centre labour process, including peer pressure and individual opposition to managerial objectives, to more formal collective alliances through trade unionism.

The research utilized a case study interview approach involving a combination of semi-structured taped interviews, telephone interviews and written structured interviews with CSRs, union officials and managerial staff. The following sections provide a brief background to the Australian call centre and telecommunications industry and to the debates about labour control within the industry. The subsequent sections analyze the issues of peer pressure and work intensification and how employees responded to their working conditions. The final section considers the future of the industry and suggests that while these call centres heavily monitored CSRs activities, various forms of employee resistance emerged and will continue to emerge as the industry matures.

Technology, control and resistance

Research has now looked at various aspects of call centre operations, including the (over) use of technology and managerial surveillance (Fernie and Metcalf, 1998; Taylor and Bain, 1999), recruitment within the industry, and the use of teamwork structures within routine call centres (Callaghan and Thompson, 2002; van den Broek, Callaghan and Thompson, forthcoming). Houlihan (Chapter 4 in this volume) has looked at job satisfaction, while Batt (2000) highlights varying degrees of workflow control and worker discretion between different types of call centre workers within the same firm.

While the industry is renowned for high turnover and absenteeism, there is also some research on unionism in the industry. Taylor and Bain (2002) looked at the process of mobilization within several call centres operating in the United Kingdom, Canada and the United States, while Gall *et al.* (2001) focused on Britain and Scotland. These studies have provided important analysis of the material conditions which generate collectivism and the nature and content of union policies, inter-union rivalry and environmental conditions which lead to recognition clauses in workplace agreements.

Since the early 1990s there has been a multitude of media reports which illustrate the stark nature of call centre work. In 1996 Long reported in a major Australian newspaper how computer technology at Telstra monitored 'how long each employee took for each meal break; how long it took when someone stopped work to go to the toilet'. Such stories have become quite common in the popular press, as have the recognition that employees might be resisting such conditions (Long, 1996, p. 16; Lebihan, 2003; Priest and Lebihan, 2003). This chapter takes up these issues by looking at how employees have been responding, both individually and collectively, to the working conditions they face. Increasingly graphic descriptions of how contemporary technology might monitor worker output have led researchers like Zuboff (1988), Fernie and Metcalf (1998) and Barker (1993) to claim unprecedented and uncontested levels of managerial control. The development of more sophisticated monitoring technology, led Zuboff (1988, pp. 322, 323) to propose the limitless potential of information technology where:

> information systems can alter many of the classic contingencies of the superior–subordinate relationship . . . they can transmit the presence of the omniscient observer and so induce compliance without the messy conflict-prone exertions of reciprocal relations.

Fernie and Metcalf compare developments with previous systems of labour control, conceptualizing 'the tyranny of the assembly line . . . [as] . . . a Sunday school picnic compared to the control management exercise in computer technology'. Within 'call centres the agents are constantly visible and the supervisors' power . . . rendered perfect' – via the computer monitoring screen – and therefore its actual use unnecessary (Fernie and Metcalf, 1998, pp. 3, 10). Drawing on Weber's imagery of the 'iron-cage' of bureaucracy, Barker also concluded that concertative control at ISE Communications represented a system of value-based normative rules that controlled employees' actions 'more powerfully and completely than the former system' (Barker, 1993, pp. 408–37). Believing that workers 'have put themselves under their own eye of the norm', he argued that the system of self-managing teams at ISE Communications harnessed employees 'into a rational apparatus out of which they truly cannot squirm' (Barker, 1993, pp. 433–6). Such perceptions of seemingly limitless, or omnipotent, managerial power located 'everywhere and nowhere' result in perceptions that employees were unable to contest its impact.

While there is no doubt that management may be well placed to pace employees' work, the inevitability or success of such compliance/commitment strategies can never be guaranteed. Scholars such as Zuboff (1988), who attribute managerial control to technological innovation, and others like Fernie and Metcalf (1998), who remove internal managerial contradictions, depict the employment relationship as a more coherent and rational process than it may typically be. Indeed propositions which

270 *Call to Arms?*

suggest total managerial control both run the risk of viewing management as an homogeneous entity and ignoring management's need to gain a degree of commitment from their employees. For instance, while many call centres utilize extensive surveillance and monitoring systems, they often do so in combination with worker involvement schemes designed to elicit commitment (Armstrong, 1989, pp. 307–22; van den Broek, Callaghan and Thompson, forthcoming). Several of the companies researched here encouraged commitment through teamwork and worker-involvement schemes. For instance, Telstra and Optus introduced various rewards and incentives to staff that achieved above-average targets on qualitative or quantitative issues. Senior management also undertook regular visits to regional customer service centres, to reward individual CSRs and teams for exceeding productivity targets. However, empowerment techniques such as these, and tight monitoring systems which characterize the call centre industry, may not be incongruous labour management strategies.

McKinlay and Taylor propose that empowerment and emasculation are not mutually exclusive concepts of labour management. Their research on PhoneCo indicated that '[t]eam-based work organization and an empowerment ideology [did] not eliminate the control imperative from the workplace', as employee opposition was articulated through empowerment ideology (McKinlay and Taylor, 1996, pp. 200, 289). The transnational organization emphasized 'total customer satisfaction' and the psychological contract they attempted to create with their employees reinforced corporate commitment. 'Psychological types' were identified and human resource management (HRM) techniques were emphasized (McKinlay and Talyor, p. 285). However, despite high-commitment strategies, their study indicated that worker involvement schemes did not eliminate employee resistance to managerial directives. PhoneCo employees resisted peer review, and although endorsing teamwork, resisted the disciplinary objectives associated with such structures. Moreover, Taylor's research of telephone sales employees suggested that 'employee internalization of attempted normative and discursive controls must not be assumed even when worker behaviour may indicate "consent"' (Taylor, 1998, p. 100).

Structural change, deregulation and privatization have underscored both the shift away from pluralist notions of workplace conflict and a significant reduction in the growth of trade union membership. As Thompson and Ackroyd (1995) also suggest, another reason it has been 'all quiet on the workplace front' has been due to the shift in managerial and academic interest in HRM and the influence of Faucauldian and post-structuralist perspectives. Indeed, post-structuralist perspectives have been particularly pervasive in call centre research (Knights, Calvey and Odih, 1999; Knights *et al.*, 1999). However, focusing on the fundamental continuities of managerial activity and the labour capital relationship, Thompson and Ackroyd (1995, p. 629) counter that:

> Whether it be the establishment of Taylorism, bureaucracy, human relations or new technology, extravagant claims as to the rationality and effectiveness were made by managerial advocates and too often believed by academics. We now know that workers learned to bend the bars in these particular iron cages. Why should the current crop of new management practices be any different?

This research in telecommunications call centres indicates that CSRs found numerous ways to 'bend the bars' in their respective cages. It suggests that the extensive use of employee surveillance and monitoring may have increased management's ability to pace and measure employee output; however, these developments could not be viewed as the totalization of labour control, or the end of employee voice. As indicated below, despite tight monitoring of output, employees are not demobilized by managerial directives, but rather respond within the mechanisms available to them.

Background to the Australian call centre industry and Australian communications

The exponential growth of call centre operations in Australia reflects similar developments overseas. Within Australia there are just under 4,000 call centres which employ approximately 220,000 employees, or 1.4 per cent of the Australian workforce. This represents the second largest percentage of a country's workforce behind the United States which is 1.7 per cent (Budde, 2002a, p. 1). Call centres, of various sizes, operate in industries such as banking, public utilities, airlines, information technology and telecommunications. In 2003, Australian companies are set to boost their A\$9.7 billion expenditure on telephone call centres as they track links between efficient call centre operations and customer satisfaction. Indeed, call centre operations are now regarded as the major revenue raiser within firms, with as much as 70 per cent of company contracts filtering through their call centres (Nicholas and Crowe, 2002). Average salaries for operators are around A\$35,000 but can be between A\$60,000 to A\$80,000 for those in the IT areas. While

272 *Call to Arms?*

call centre transactions have increased by more than 30 per cent over the previous year, call centre employment has only grown by 10 per cent. This means that while the industry has grown, those working in the industry are working harder and faster. Indeed average call answer speed has reduced from 32 seconds in 2001 to 27 seconds in 2002 (Budde, 2002b, p. 3).

During 1991 Telstra's monopoly ended when the Federal Labor government issued Optus Communications a licence to compete with Telstra. It commenced operations in 1992. By June 1997 the Australian telecommunications industry had been further deregulated to facilitate full competition. Given the onset of competition and deregulation, Telstra restructured and downsized in the 1990s. During the 1990s staff numbers dropped from around 85,000 to 65,000, while Optus employed just under 6,000 staff by 1996. At the time of writing, around 280 people worked at the Moe TeleTek site in Victoria and just under 400 staff at the Wollongong Stellar site in New South Wales (Budde, 1996/1997, p. 54; Internal company documents).

Unionization rates differed widely between the organizations. Because of its background as a government department, Telstra's union membership has been historically strong although it had slipped to around 40 per cent by 2000. In contrast Servo constructed a virtual greenfield operation and union membership rates have remained below 5 per cent throughout the research period. TeleTech and Stellar sought union-free worksites initially; however, membership had grown to 40 per cent in the former site and to 10 per cent in the latter site by 2002 (van den Broek, 2001).

The telecommunications industry restructure, which allowed new service providers to build their own communications links, progressively undermined Telstra's market dominance particularly in the provision of mobile and long-distance services. Since deregulation and the partial sale of Telstra, a multitude of telecommunications firms have established call centre operations in Australia. The emergence of TeleTech and Stellar reflect the type of competition which has developed. While these firms are fiercely competitive, they all express the dual concern for customer satisfaction and service provision in combination with efficiency and cost minimization. Intense competition also brought with it the relocation of call centres to regional areas. As has been evident elsewhere, the decision to shift operations to less developed towns or countries has given firms considerable cost savings in wages and other overheads (Richardson and Belt, 2001). Stellar's decision to establish a call centre in regional New South Wales and TeleTech's decision build one in regional Victoria was influenced by above-average unemployment rates, lower labour costs and the potential to reduce turnover rates.

The CSRs employed within the firms studied provide services such as selling, marketing, account management, preparation of billing information, acceptance of customer complaints and requests for service within the generic term of 'customer service'. Customer complaints were an important aspect to the job and CSRs were expected to expend 'emotional labour' while performing these tasks (Hochschild, 1983; Telecommunications Industry Training Advisory Board, 1994, p. 15). Young women make up the bulk of the industry and much of the training is in-house. Generally, CSRs work within self-managed teams that specialize in a particular product or service, and are required to remain at their workstations logged into their computer for the majority of the day. Working within a highly competitive environment, the organizations emphasize high-quality service provision whilst at the same time focusing on efficient and economic output targets. Tasks are subdivided into inbound and outbound sales with telemarketing departments handling high-volume outbound selling solicitation. CSRs' jobs have become more specialized and repetitive while at the same time becoming increasingly more demanding. Through the spread of electronic monitoring and automatic call distribution (ACD) systems, calls are automatically fed into CSRs headsets with management well placed to measure CSR performance by sales volume and achievement quotas.

Inside these call centres, the scene is a familiar one. The open plan office design provided clear vision and easy access for management to assess the pace of CSR work. Motivational mobiles and electronic boards displaying performance statistics dominate the ceilings and walls. However, augmenting direct observation were various other ways management could monitor employee output. CSRs were expected to take calls on the first minute after arriving at work and, apart from break times, to be at their desk and available to take calls for the majority of the working day. CSRs were expected to reach benchmarked time periods when answering calls and daily reports, listing the number of calls taken by each CSR. Also the average time taken to complete the call, how many outgoing calls the CSR made, and how long these calls took were measured (Internal company document; Interview with employees and team leaders, 1996).

The ACD system was designed to predict the number of CSRs needed to process customer demands on a daily basis. It allocated workloads and compared daily output to chart future workload allocation and analyzed employee performance. The data included the teams' 'talk'

274 *Call to Arms?*

time, 'wrap' time and overall branch wrap time. It also listed team availability as compared to branch availability, team adherence to schedules as compared to branch adherence to schedules as well as the calls contribution to overall revenue as a percentage. Centre availability for each team within the branch was also listed (Interview with team leader, 1997).

Whilst on their shifts, CSRs are required to enter a code outlining the reason for absences from their workstations, thereby enabling the measurement of unproductive time. Various expectations about performance are established for CSRs including swift response times to calls and minimum abandoned calls. For example, at Stellar CSRs were expected to complete calls in 18.9 seconds and were allotted daily 'health breaks' which allowed each CSR nine minutes to use the toilet facilities. CSRs were expected to remain at their workstations with a card system determining their status for moving. A 'red card' indicated the need for a toilet break, while a 'yellow card' indicated the need for a supervisor to assist a call. CSRs in other call centres were required to raise their hand to move from their stations (Interview with union organizer, 2001).

Work intensification and peer pressure

The motivation for using team structures within Optus appeared to serve the dual purpose of strengthening unitarist ideology while at the same time reinforcing 'positive peer relations on the office floor' (Barker, 1993; Korczynski, 2001, p. 94). Although the issue of peer pressure would not always arise, one Optus manager stated this is where the 'team dynamics kicked in'. She observed that in such a situation colleagues might say to an employee who was under-performing, 'come on, you're letting the side down or your having too much sick leave' (Interview with team leader, 1995; Interview with middle manager, 1995).

Team leaders observed how team members themselves could assess whether an employee 'fitted in' to corporate goals (Interview with team leader, 1995). One team leader recalled how a CSR reacted to another's time-wasting. It involved an incident where a CSR was playing 'Solitare' on their computer whilst in the 'not ready' mode. A fellow employee, noticing that he was 'slacking off' sarcastically remarked that once he had finished the game they could play another one together. The attention this generated from his peers was enough to encourage the 'time-waster' to resume taking calls immediately. As the team leader noted:

> the environment we've created is that your performance will affect the team so it's a natural reaction that the team works together ...

[My job is]... not to address them for not pulling their weight but to encourage them to pull their weight.

Interview with team leader, 1996

Work intensification and peer pressure also existed within Telstra. One CSR stated that:

> It's a team effort, you don't want the team to be let down. They [team leaders] have eight teams and they keep showing these bits of paper and they say 'this team got so much' and you think 'I've tried so bloody hard and you just can't get those extra points.' If they said work at your own place to make these sales, I wouldn't care. I don't particularly want the $20 coupon that they're offering. I'd say forget it, but because it's a team thing you tend to work a little harder because you want the others to benefit. Some of them are keen as mustard to get there so you don't want to be the one dragging the chain.

Interview with employee, 1997

Another more contemporary recruit responded that:

> I'm probably the 'keen as mustard' sort of person. I respect people who do try but also in my case I find that it gets frustrating because you get some people who just can't be bothered. Even though it is a team effort, they're just not trying. So we even approached our manager and said 'we're trying hard'. I feel like I'm doing a lot better and I want to go back to individual because you can get some teams where 80 per cent of them do the work and 20 per cent of them are relaxing. Whereas that 20 per cent could go to someone who deserves it.

Interview with employee, 1997

This evidence indicates that there were considerable, and quite targeted, managerial policies to generate peer pressure and to encourage employees to take 'ownership' of work tasks. However, managerial emphasis on sales and performance output made CSRs very cynical about managerial rhetoric associated with customer service. Many CSRs believed that the heavy use of statistics was encouraging a 'worse service' and this is reinforced by quantitative research. One study of Telstra call centres revealed that while 98 per cent of CSRs thought customer service was important, 72 per cent did not believe that management had a high regard for service quality and 66 per cent thought they were inadequately rewarded for customer service (Employee interviews, 1996; Deery and Iverson, 1998, pp. 12, 13). So while there was considerable managerial and peer pressure to meet and exceed output targets, many CSRs were more concerned about their inability to deliver quality customer service.

Some CSRs felt that pressure on call volume compromised the occupational health and safety of workers. Common health complaints in the industry included eye damage from over-exposure to computer screens and back problems from sitting in one position all day (Employee interviews, 1995; 1997). More recently acoustic shock has emerged within the industry. This condition results from a sudden, loud or piercing noise delivered over a phone line caused from electronic feedback, sudden interference, or from loud noises emitted from those on the other end of the phone line, leading to temporary or permanent damage to the recipient's inner ear (Frankland, 24 September 2001).[1] Given such intense working conditions it is not surprising that there have been varying levels of CSR unrest in the industry. While peer pressure may be one response to the call centre working environment, there were many other ways in which CSR's responded, ranging from informal individual responses to managerial directives, to more collective campaigns to mobilize workers into trade unions.

Individual and collective non-union responses

Although not informed about when their calls were being monitored, CSRs 'learnt when to recognize' when monitoring was being undertaken and adjusted their behaviour accordingly. By identifying when team leaders were absent from the floor, and when monitoring was occurring, CSRs were tacitly foiling managerial directives. Others did their own form of monitoring. For example, one Optus CSR, who believed that 'everyone was intimidated by their stats', maintained a regular diary noting why he was unavailable at particular times of the day, so that it could be produced to management on request.

Such issues as workload could prompt individuals to informally join together to contest managerial directives. While unionization was negligible and collective employee response rare at Optus call centres, the issue of increased workloads and managerial pressure did prompt CSRs to form alliances on occasions. For example, one group of Optus CSRs openly voiced their resistance to the introduction of 'call forcing', that is the automatic distribution of waiting calls, by confronting management and signing a petition registering their opposition. The petition, largely co-ordinated by an active union member, indicated their belief that customer queues developed from under-staffing, rather than unsatisfactory employee performance of existing staff (Interview with employee, 1995; Internal company correspondence; Interview with union organizer, 2001). The Australian call centre industry is characterized by extremely high levels of absenteeism and turnover. A study of 3,681 Australian call centres revealed that call centre staff took an average of 8.74 days of sick leave per annum, compared to the national workforce average of 5.2 days (Nixon, 2002, p. 1). Specific industry studies, such as those in the telecommunications industry, reveal that absenteeism within firms such as Telstra totalled around 12 sick days during 1998 (Deery and Iverson, 1998, p. 6).[2] ACA Research reports that more than 36 per cent of CSRs in the industry admitted taking time off from work due to stress which the research association assesses costs the call centre industry around $34 million. Average national turnover in the industry is also estimated to be around 22 percent, although it can be as high as 60 per cent in some centres (ACA Research, 2001).

Employees have found an array of methods to cope with their working conditions. Perhaps the most pervasive action taken by many CSRs is that of hanging up on customers or redirecting calls to other areas of the corporation or other firms. One Telstra employee suggested that 10–20 per cent of calls were 'flicked' daily, while redirecting was said to occur 'all the time' at Stellar. (Employee interviews, 1995; 1996; 1997; ABC Radio National, 2000; Interview with union organizer, 2001). Other examples of misbehaviour might include CSRs doing 'just enough' work or redirecting their frustrations about their work conditions onto customers. A common example of this would be intentionally misinforming and lying to customers (Interview with union organizer, 2001). Therefore, in call centres where there are few other avenues for CSRs to articulate grievances, there may be more incidences of such action.

Formal and collective responses

There are various reasons why call centre operations are relatively hard workplaces to unionize. These include the newness of the occupation and the lack of union history. Furthermore, limited career paths in addition to the intense pace of work and high labour turnover are not conditions under which unionization might flourish (Bibby, 2000, p. 5). However, of the over 200,000 employees in the call centre industry, the Australian Council of Trade Unions (ACTU) assesses that around 15–20 per cent are unionized. This is compared with a 19.1 per cent unionization

278 *Call to Arms?*

in the Australian private sector overall. Not surprisingly, the most union-ized call centres are those that operate in the public or ex-public sector such as the airlines. Government or ex-government utilities are reasonably well unionized while others, including telecommunications and banking, are considerably less organized. The contract call centres are by far the least unionized and prove to be the most difficult to organize (Interview with ACTU organizer, 2001; ABS, 2000). As indicated below, unions' difficulty in organizing this industry has been exacerbated by the fact that, until recently, there has been no award coverage for many employees in the industry.

Nationally the ACTU has formed a Call Centre Unions Group to provide support for call centre employees and to provide a Code of Practice for interested parties. Unions covering public servants, finance and other service workers and other parties involved in this initiative include employer groups and call centre industry associations keen to see investment in education and skills development to improve industry standards.

As part of a combined union initiative to organize the industry, the ACTU established 'Call Central' in 2000. The Call Central website provides information about minimum standards in the industry and is designed to provide a resource for call centre workers. The initiative was intended to overcome the financial limitations that confront individual unions in their organizing efforts and to minimize potential coverage disputes between the unions. The 6,000 call centre workers who have joined unions since November 2000 are, in part, the result of this initia-tive (Interview with ACTU organizer, 2001). Within the four call centres that are the subject of this study union membership varies widely. Membership within Telstra, the largest of the firms, stands at around 40 per cent. By contrast, CSRs in established or newly established green-field call centres have been the least interested in seeking collective representation. The combination of elaborate HR strategies and a non-union enterprise agreement at Optus has combined to keep the firm a virtual greenfield site since it established in 1994. Membership within the firm was less than 5 per cent in 1994 and it remains at no more than 8 per cent (van den Broek, 2001; Interview with union organizer, 1996; 2001).

Many of the newly established call centres have been successful in keeping their operations union-free by requiring their staff to sign non-union individual contracts known as Australian workplace agreements (AWAs). Stellar and TeleTech staff are under such contracts where wages and conditions were inferior to those operating at Telstra and Optus.

At Stellar, staff were required to sign a three-year AWA and because there has been no industry award the responding union, the CPSU, have until recently had no right of entry. The situation is similar at TeleTech. Despite these obstacles, the union has managed to secure delegates at Stellar and union membership within the Wollongong site has grown from one member to 10 per cent of its 400 staff between 2000 and 2002. Similarly at TeleTech membership has grown from nought to 40 per cent between 2001 and 2002. Again this is despite the anti-union stance of management and the discrimination against union activists which has occurred within both organizations (Interview with union organizers, 2001; 2002).

Union growth in these two firms has been assisted by a number of successful industrial campaigns. For example, at Stellar it was only through union action that the 'card system', which required staff to put up a coloured card to use toilet facilities, was abandoned. Similarly, at TeleTech union organizers and activists secured improved wages and conditions for staff under their AWAs. Small victories such as these, based around common grievances felt by many CSRs, encouraged others to join in collective action at the workplace and to exhibit that activism more vigorously than in the past (Interview with union organizers, 2001; 2002).

Within the telecommunications industry, unionization is obviously not as strong as it was when Telstra operated as a monopoly. Although unions in the past have enjoyed widespread coverage, it has not been easy for them to maintain membership amid anti-union management policies or to organize the new greenfield players in the industry. Many firms have turned to the use of labour hire companies and outsourcing operations. Similarly changes to federal government industrial relations legislation, which now restricts union organizers' access to workplaces, and the managerial push for individual contracts have also contributed to the patchy union membership within the industry. However, as elaborated below, a significant breakthrough for unions has been the recent granting of an award in the industry. This will give unions right of entry into some worksites and in the case of Stellar and TeleTech has led to a more nuanced management style which has been less antagonistic to union representation.

Cyber spanners or sitting ducks? Discussion and conclusion

Call centres within the Australian telecommunications industry contain a mixture of unionized and non-unionized firms. As such the pattern of

280 *Call to Arms?*

collective employee response varies considerably. For instance, CSRs at Telstra have a history of collective representation and formal avenues to process their grievances, while at Optus CSRs rarely access collective voice mechanisms. The research at Stellar and TeleTech suggests that CSRs at these former greenfield sites are beginning to form collective alliances based on common grievances. As the secretary of the South Coast Labour Council stated (Interview, 2001):

> workers are going to respond whatever way they can to put a halt to the line...Workers are going to be as creative as they were 100 or 200 years ago. There's going to be cyber spanners – the cyber spanners will take different forms...I think the smarter call centre operators are starting to realize that.

The ability of employees to resist managerial directives is influenced by a number of factors. Employment security and bargaining arrangements, managerial attitudes towards unions, government legislation which excludes or encourages union activity and the ideological persuasions of call centre workers themselves all play a part in influencing the way employees might respond to managerial directives. However, issues such as authoritarian managerial styles, excessive workloads, inflexible break times and unreasonable rosters have prompted some forms of collective and formal resistance. As Taylor and Bain's (2002) research indicates, adverse working conditions can lead to collective interest identification and action. However, these developments often depend on the activities of workplace unionists and their ability to engender a 'culture of solidarity'. Meaningful collectivism may be hard to sustain unless workers are able to establish the legitimacy of their grievances across the workplace (Taylor and Bain, 2002; Gall *et al.*, 2001, p. 15). Part of the success in establishing isolated union presence within some of the call centres studied here has also been the targeted strategy of peak union bodies such as the ACTU. The greater desire by some unions to create active delegate structures, which promote a grassroots activism of organizing rather than servicing members within the workplace, may also contribute to increased collective representation within the industry (Cooper, 2001). The establishment of the ACTU's 'Call Central' in 2000 has assisted in the growth in overall union membership in Australian call centres from 10 per cent in 2000 to 30 per cent by 2002. Moreover, the granting of a new Telecommunications Service Industry Award in 2002 which covers 25 of the largest telecommunications firms will also allow for greater union access and potential coverage within that sector.

The pace and repetition of work has increased within call centres. Technical control, in the form of ACD systems has reduced CSRs' influence over the pace of their work, and the use of VDU telephone technology has facilitated management's ability to monitor daily output. However, while more sophisticated technology has increased the ability of the organization to monitor CSR output, managerial control is not total. CSRs can adopt various forms of action to resist increased workloads and monitoring. This research indicates that while there is considerable employee compliance with managerial directives, employee resistance is by no means marginal. Employee responses range from peer pressure and individual opposition to managerial objectives to more formal collective alliances through trade unionism.

Notes

1. Confined almost exclusively to call centres, acoustic shock, or 'the industrial injury of the twenty-first century' has led to a steady stream of claims from affected staff. Now the Australian Services Union is planning a compensation test case which, if successful, could potentially open the door for a flood of legal claims. But just as the physical noise causes acoustic shock damage, the level of stress that the individual agent is under at the time will dictate the severity of the injury. 'The one thing that seems to be common in acoustic shock injury is that there is a stress factor involved. It is a startle reflex and the more you're stressed, the greater the chance of being startled', Neil Frankland, available at http://www.callcentres.net/static:news/week62art1.html, accessed 24 September 2001.
2. A 1998 absenteeism survey of all Telstra state centre consultants, which had a response rate of 88, noted that central determinants of absenteeism included job satisfaction, management of wrap time and lack of job variety. Deery and Iverson, 1998.

References

ABC Radio National (2000) *Background Briefing*, 25 June.
ABS (Australian Bureau of Statistics) (2000) Trade Union Membership, cat. no. 6310.0, Canberra: Australian Bureau of Statistics.
ACA Research (2001) 'The 2001 Australia and New Zealand Call Centre Industry Benchmark Study', Sydney.
Armstrong. P. (1989) 'Management, Labour Process and Agency', *Work, Employment and Society*, 3(3), pp. 307–22.
Bain, P. and P. Taylor (1999) 'Employee relations, worker attitudes and trade union representation in call centres', unpublished paper, Department of Human Resource Management, University of Strathclyde and Department of Management and Organization, University of Stirling.
Bain, P. and P. Taylor (2000) 'Entrapped by the "electronic panopticon"? Worker resistance in the call centre', *New Technology, Work and Employment*, 15(1), pp. 2–18.
Barker, J. (1993) 'Tightening the Iron Cage: Concertative Control in Self-Managing Teams', *Administrative Science Quarterly*, 38.

282 Call to Arms?

Batt, R. (2000) 'Strategic segmentation and front-line services: matching customers, employees and human resource systems', *International Journal of Human Resource Management*, 11(3), pp. 540–61.

Bell, D. (1974) *The Coming of the Post Industrial Society*, London: Heinemann.

Bibby, A. (2000) 'Organising in financial call centres', a report for UNI, 30 March.

Budde, P. (1996/7) *Telecommunications Strategy Report*, Sydney: Paul Budde Communications.

Budde, P. (2002a) 'Global-VAS-Call Centres and CIT', Sydney: Paul Budde Communications.

Budde, P. (2002b) 'Australia-Call Centres', Sydney: Paul Budde Communications.

Callaghan, G. and P. Thompson (2002) '"We Recruit Attitude": the selection and shaping of routine call centre labour', *Journal of Management Studies*, 39(2), pp. 233–54.

Cooper, R. (2001) 'Getting Organized? A White Collar Union Responds to Membership Crisis', *Journal of Industrial Relations*, 43, p. 4.

Deery, S. and R. Iverson (1998) 'An Examination of the Causes of Absenteeism at Telstra', University of Melbourne.

Drucker, P. F. (1993) *Managing for the Future: The 1990s and Beyond*, New York: Truman Tally Books/Plume.

European Foundation for the Improvement of Living and Working Conditions (1999) 'Strike at BT highlights union concern over conditions in call centres', available at http://www.eirofound.ie/1999/12/inbrief/UK991243h. html.

Fernie, S. and D. Metcalf (1998) '(Not) Hanging on the Telephone: payment systems in the new sweatshops', Discussion Paper no. 390, Centre for Economic Performance.

Frenkel, S. and L. Donoghue (1996) 'Call Centres and Service Excellence: Design and Management Challenges to Support a Service Excellence Strategy: A knowledge worker case study', paper no. 006, Centre for Corporate Change.

Frenkel, S., M. Korczynski, K. Shire and M. Tam (1999) *On the Front Line: Organization of work in the information economy*, Ithaca, NY: Cornell University Press.

Gall, G., P. Bain, K. Gilbert, G. Mulvey and P. Taylor (2001) 'Worker Mobilisation, Collectivism and Trade Unionism in Four Call Centres in Britain', Employment Research Unit 16th Annual Conference, 10–11 September, Cardiff Business School, Cardiff University.

Hochschild, A. (1983) *The Managed Heart: Commercialization of Human Feeling*, Berkeley: University of California Press.

International Labour Office (1993) 'Conditions of Work Digest', 12, p. 1.

Knights, D., D. Calvey, and P. Odih (1999) 'Social Managerialism and the Time Disciplined Subject: Quality-Quantity Conflicts in a Call Centre', paper to the 17th Annual International Labour Process Conference, March, School of Management, Royal Holloway, University of London.

Knights, D., Noble, F., Willmott, H., Vurdubakis, T. (1999) 'Constituting the CSR: consumption, production and the labour process in call centres', paper to the 17th Annual International Labour Process Conference, March, School of Management, Royal Holloway, University of London.

Korczynski, M. (2001) 'The contradictions of service work: call centre as customer-oriented bureaucracy', in A. Sturdy, I. Grugulis and H. Willmott (eds), *Customer Service: Empowerment and Entrapment*, Basingstoke: Palgrave.

Lebihan, R. (2003) 'Call centres fail to lose sweatshop reputation', *Australian Financial Review*, 7 February.

Long, S. (1996) 'Work: Why it just gets HARDER', *Australian Financial Review*, 24 September.

McKinlay, A. and P. Taylor (1996) 'Power, Surveillance and Resistance Inside the Factory of the Future', in P. Ackers, C. Smith and P. Smith (eds), *The New Workplace and Trade Unionism*, London: Routledge.

Nicholas, K. and D. Crowe (2002) 'Companies realise value of call centres', *Australian Financial Review*, 9 August.

Nixon, S. (2002) 'Sick or not, we just can't shake the Mondayitis', *Sydney Morning Herald*, 10 February.

Priest, M. and R. Lebihan (2003) 'Unions Run for Coverage in Call Centres', *Australian Financial Review*, 15 February.

Richardson, R. and V. Belt (2001) 'Saved by the Bell? Call Centres and Economic Development in Less Favoured Regions', *Economic and Industrial Democracy*, 22, pp. 67–98.

Taylor, P and Bain, P. (1999) '"An assembly line in the head": work and employee relations in the call centre', *Industrial Relations Journal*, 30(2), pp. 101–17.

Taylor, P. and P. Bain (2002) 'Call Centre Organizing in Adversity: From Excell to Vertex', in Gall, G. (ed) *Union Organising*, Routledge, London.

Taylor, S. (1998) 'Emotional labour and the new workplace', in P. Thompson and C. Warhurst (eds), *Workplaces of the Future*, Macmillan: London.

Telecommunications Industry Training Advisory Board (1994) *Telecommunications Industry Mapping Project*, May.

Thompson, P. and S. Ackroyd (1995) 'All Quiet on the Workplace Front? A Critique of Recent Trends in British Industrial Sociology', *Sociology*, 29(4), November, pp. 615–33.

Thompson, P. and C. Warhurst (eds) (1998) *Workplaces of the Future*, London: Macmillan.

van den Broek, D. (1997) 'Human Resource Management, Cultural Control and Union Avoidance: An Australian Case Study', *Journal of Industrial Relations*, 3(3), pp. 332–48.

van den Broek, D. (2001) 'Crossed Wires: Cultural Change and Labour Management in the Australian Telecommunications Industry', unpublished PhD thesis, University of New South Wales.

van den Broek, D. (2002) 'Monitoring and Surveillance in Call Centres: Some Responses From Australian Workers', *Labour and Industry*, 12(3), pp. 43–58.

van den Broek, D., G. Callaghan and P. Thompson (forthcoming) 'Exploring the Team Paradox', *Economic and Industrial Democracy*.

Walton, R. E. (1985) 'From control to commitment in the workplace', *Harvard Business Review*, March–April, 64(3), pp. 77–84.

Warhurst, C. and P. Thompson (1998) 'Hands, Hearts and Minds: Changing Work and Workers at the End of the Century', in P. Thompson and C. Warhurst (eds), *Workplaces of the Future*, London: Macmillan.

Zuboff, S. (1988) *In the Age of the Smart Machine: The Future of Work and Power*, New York: Basic Books.

Name Index

ABC Radio National 277, 281
ACA Research 146, 150, 277, 281
Ackroyd, S. 267, 270, 271, 283
Adler, P. 79, 100
Agho, A. O. 225, 242
Aiello, J. R. 225, 242
Alder, G. S. 225, 242
Alferoff, C. 132, 150
Alic, J. 3, 20, 204, 205, 221
Allscheid, S. 33, 52
Alvesson, M. 187, 195
Appelbaum, E. 30, 31, 47, 49, 58, 71, 225, 226, 242
Argote, L. 36, 51
Argyris, C. 83, 100
Armstrong. P. 270, 281
Arnold, J. 191, 195
Arthur, M. B. 191, 195
Ashburner, L. 169, 171
Ashforth, B. 4, 9, 10, 19, 206, 222
Ashkanasy, N. 9, 11, 19
Australian Bureau of Statistics 278, 281
Axtell, C. 61, 71, 73, 231, 242, 243

Bachmann, R. 126
Badigannavar, V. 71
Bailey, D. 32, 34, 50
Bailey, T. 27, 49
Bain, P. 3, 6, 9, 13, 19, 22, 26, 52, 57, 73, 77, 88, 100, 101, 126, 130, 144, 150, 151, 153, 171, 173, 174, 195, 197, 224, 242, 244, 245, 262, 264, 266, 268, 280, 281, 282, 283
Baldry, C. 88, 100
Barker, G. 8, 19
Barker, J. 269, 274, 281
Barney, J. 30, 49
Baron, J. N. 204, 221
Bass, B. M. 71
Batt, R. 5, 8, 11, 14, 19, 35, 36, 37, 38, 43, 44, 45, 49, 51, 57, 58, 71, 75, 76, 77, 82, 95, 100, 125, 130, 148, 149, 150, 153, 171, 202, 203, 204, 205, 208, 216, 221, 224, 225, 226, 240, 241, 242, 245, 264, 268, 282

Beardshaw, V. 164, 171
Beaumont, P. 103, 104, 125, 126
Becker, B. 30, 49
Becker, M. C. 148, 150
Bell, D. 267, 282
Belt, V. 8, 9, 17, 19, 71, 135, 150, 176, 195, 201, 221, 226, 242, 272, 283
Berbeke, W. 33, 52
Berg, P. 49
Bibby, A. 277, 282
Billing, Y. D. 195
Birch, K. 169, 171
Blakeney, R. N. 206, 218, 222
Blau, G. 225, 242
Bolton, S. 146, 150
Borys, B. 79, 100
Boudreau, J. 53
Bowen, D. E. 5, 19, 22, 33, 52, 55, 73
Boxall, P. 129, 151
Bramer, W. 57, 74, 224, 244
Braverman, H. 162, 163, 165, 171
Breathnach, P. 174, 195
Bristow, G. 175, 195
Brockbank, A. 175, 184, 192, 197
Brown, J. S. 29, 49
Bryson, A. 249, 266
Buchanan, R. 174, 196
Budde, P. 271, 272, 282
Bunzel, D. 152
Burton, D. M. 204, 221
Button, G. 21

Call Centre Research 146, 150
Callaghan, G. 6, 7, 8, 14, 16, 20, 22, 75, 77, 81, 82, 93, 100, 125, 131, 132, 144, 147, 150, 151, 153, 171, 268, 270, 282, 283
Calnan, M. 173
Calveley, M. 168, 172
Calvey, D. 271, 282
Cameron, D. 75, 80, 82, 100
Campion, M. A. 35, 49
Cannon-Bowers, J. A. 35, 36, 50, 51
Cant, S. L. 173
Caplan, R. D. 211, 221

286 Name Index

Cappelli, P.   40, 50
Carayon, P.   33, 50, 244
Cassar, V.   72
Cassell, C.   184, 188, 196
Chagnon, M.   167, 172
Chalykoff, J.   58, 72, 225, 238, 243
Charter of the French Language
   168, 173
Chase, R. B.   29, 50
Chissick, C.   33, 51
Clegg, C. W.   73, 243
Coates, S.   21
Cobb, S.   221
Cockburn, C.   184, 196
Cohen, S. G.   32, 34, 35, 50
Communications Workers Union
   (CWU)   174, 196
Converse, S. A.   35, 36, 50
Conway, N.   55, 56, 67, 72
Cook, J.   21, 60, 74, 225, 229, 244
Cook, P.   21
Cooper, C.   244
Cooper, R.   73, 280
Cordes, C. L,   206, 221
Cotton, J. L.   32, 50
Cox, J.   33, 52
Coyle, A.   190, 192, 196
Coyle, J.   173
Crouch, C.   131, 150
Crowe, D.   271, 283

Daniels, K.   226, 243
Datamonitor   1, 20, 25, 50
Daus, C.   9, 11, 19
Davids, K.   73, 243
Deery, S. J.   10, 12, 17, 18, 20, 33,
   50, 55, 72, 80, 82, 100, 141, 146,
   147, 150, 206, 218, 221, 224,
   226, 243, 276, 277, 281, 282
Delaney, J. T.   265
Delery, J.   31, 50
Demaret, L.   265
Donnelly, L.   170, 172
Donoghue, L.   20, 282
Department of Health (DoH)   155,
   156, 172
Doré, C.   156, 172
Doty, D.   31, 50
Dougherty, T. W.   206, 221
Drucker, P. F.   267, 282
Dubinsky, A. J.   34, 53
Duddleston, A.   191, 196
Duguid, P.   29, 49
Dyer, L.   53

Eagleson, G.   7, 22, 75, 77, 80, 81, 82,
   98, 99, 101, 146, 152
Edwards, P.   126
Edwards, R.   20
European Foundation for the
   Improvement of Living and
   Working Conditions   282
Eurotunnel   259, 260, 264, 265

Feldman, D.   10, 21
Fernie, S.   3, 6, 14, 15, 20, 54, 55, 56,
   57, 72, 125, 204, 221, 223, 240,
   243, 245, 265, 268, 269, 282
Fiedler, F.   71, 72
Finegold, D.   131, 150
Fineman, S.   13, 22
Fiorito, J.   265
Fishman, N.   248, 265
Flecker, J.   131, 150
Forth, J.   249, 266
Freeman, R. B.   247, 265
French, J. R. P.   221
Frenkel, S.   3, 6, 7, 8, 12, 18, 20, 21,
   33, 52, 57, 58, 72, 75, 76, 77, 78,
   79, 80, 81, 82, 83, 87, 91, 95, 99,
   100, 103, 122, 125, 126, 129, 151,
   153, 154, 172, 224, 225, 226, 243,
   245, 265, 266, 267, 282
Fuller, L.   2, 201, 203, 221

Gall, G.   19, 171, 268, 280, 282, 283
Gardner, P. H.   73, 243
Garson, B.   3, 20, 223, 243
Gerhart, B.   30, 49
Gilbert, K.   282
Gladstein, D. L.   34, 50
Godard, J.   32, 50
Goffee, R.   175, 191, 192, 196,
Gollan, P.   18, 245, 249, 265
Goodwin, G. F.   51
Goolsby, J.   33, 52
Grant, R. A.   225, 243
Green, A.   187, 191, 196
Green, E.   184, 188, 196
Greenword, L.   172
Gripaios, P.   175, 195
Grumiau, S.   265
Guest, D.   55, 56, 64, 67, 72, 79,
   98, 100, 265
Gutek, B.   2, 20, 29, 50, 202, 216, 221

Hackman, R. J.   3, 35, 50, 206
Hakim, C.   179, 194, 196
Halbrook, R.   53

Name Index   287

Hales, C. 147, 151
Halford, S. 175, 185, 189, 193, 196
Handy, C. 168, 172
Hannan, M. T. 221, 224
Hardill, I. 191, 196
Harley, B. 32, 52
Harrington, E. 71, 242
Harrison, R. V. 221
Hart, G. 155, 172
Heery, E. 72
Heffner, T. S. 51
Hénault, M.
Herzenberg, S. 3, 20, 204, 205, 221
Heskett, J. 32, 50, 241, 244
Hicks, C. 164, 172
Higgins, C. A. 225, 243
Higgs, C. A. 35, 49
Hill, S. 22
Hinsz, V. R. 35, 50
Hochschild, A. 9, 10, 20, 54, 72,
    146, 151, 273, 282
Hofbauer, J. 131, 150
Holman, D. 18, 33, 50, 51, 55, 58,
    67, 71, 72, 205, 218, 221, 240,
    242, 243
Holtgrewe, U. 4, 22, 148, 150, 151,
    154, 172
Hoque, K. 56, 67, 72
Hoskins, G. 189, 196
Houlihan, M. 15, 58, 132, 144, 149,
    151, 241, 243, 268, 282
House, J. S. 211, 221
Houseman, S. 37, 51
Humphrey, R. 4, 9, 10, 19
Hunter, L. 103, 104, 125, 126
Huselid, M. 31, 51
Hutchinson, S. 4, 7, 20, 21, 30, 51,
    57, 73, 75, 76, 77, 79, 81, 82, 95,
    96, 97, 98, 100, 125, 126, 153,
    172, 204, 221, 245, 266
Huws, U. 1, 21
Hyman, J. 22, 173
Hyman, R. 247, 265

Ichniowski, C. 30, 51, 56, 72
Income Data Services 1, 20, 72,
    196, 243, 245, 253, 265
Inkson, K. 191, 195
International Labour Office (ILO) 282
Isic, A. 74, 244
Iverson, R. 10, 12, 17, 18, 20, 33, 50,
    55, 72, 80, 82, 100, 141, 146, 150,
    206, 218, 221, 224, 226, 243, 276,
    277, 281, 282

Jackson, P. 60, 73, 206, 221, 227,
    230, 243
Jarley, P. 265
Jex, S. M. 238, 243
Jimmieson, N. 67, 73, 224, 244
Johnson, J. 33, 51
Johnson, R. 33, 52

Kalleberg, A. L. 49
Kanter, R. M. 175, 196
Kaplan, R. 32, 51
Karaseck, R. A. 243
Katz, H. C. 266
Keenoy, T. 100
Kerst, C. 4, 22, 148, 150, 151, 154, 172
Key Note 1, 11, 20
Kinnie, N. 4, 7, 15, 20, 21, 30, 51,
    57, 58, 73, 75, 76, 77, 79, 81, 82,
    95, 96, 97, 98, 100, 103, 123, 124,
    126, 147, 150, 153, 172, 203, 204,
    221, 222, 245, 266
Klimoski, R. 36, 51
Knights, D. 13, 21, 57, 58, 73, 80,
    100, 132, 150, 151, 224, 226,
    243, 245, 266, 271, 282
Knowles, E. 173
Kochan, T. 51, 58, 72, 225, 238,
    243, 266
Koch-Schulte, S. 174, 196
Kohl, G. 28, 51
Korczynski, M. 1, 2, 4, 6, 12, 20, 21,
    67, 72, 73, 75, 99, 100, 101, 125,
    126, 131, 151, 172, 204, 205, 221,
    243, 245, 249, 265, 266, 274, 282
Kuhl, J. 238, 243

Lacy, C. 136, 151
Lamming, R. 104, 126
Lane, C.
Lankshear, G. 13, 21
LaRocco, J. M. 211, 222
Lasaosa, A. 54, 73
Lawler, E. 5, 19, 31, 51
Ledford, G. E. 35, 50
Lee, R. T. 172, 206, 222
Legge, K. 87, 97, 101
LeGrande, D. 244
Leidner, R. 4, 6, 9, 21, 27, 29, 51, 55,
    73, 82, 99, 101, 204, 222
Leprohon, J. 157, 172
Levine, D. 51, 72
Levitt, T. 29, 51
Liang, D. W. 36, 51
Lim, S. Y. 244

288 Name Index

Locke, E. 32, 52
Lockyer, C. J. 99, 152
Long, S. 196, 268, 269, 283
Lopez, H. 201, 222
Loveman, G. W. 33, 51

MacDonald, C. L. 3, 4, 9, 10, 13, 20, 21, 73, 222
MacDuffie, J. P. 31, 37, 47, 51, 79, 101
Maddock, S. 175, 196
Mahoney, T. 55, 56, 73
Malo, D. 157, 172
Marshall, J. N. 21, 22, 174, 196
Martin, R. 73, 243
Maslach, C. 206, 222
Mason, D. 21
Mathews, B. P. 131, 151
Mathieu, J. E. 36, 51
Maurice, M. A. 154, 170, 172, 173
McCabe, D. 13, 21, 57, 73, 80, 100, 224, 226, 243, 245, 266
McDowell, L. 175, 177, 184, 196
McKersie, R. B. 266
McKinlay, A. 270, 283
McMahon, J. 103, 126
Meder, D. 53
Medoff, J. L. 247, 265
Medsker, G. J. 35, 49, 50
Menezes, L. de 7, 22, 54, 73
Mertini, H. 74
Metcalf, D. 3, 6, 20, 54, 56, 57, 72, 73, 125, 223, 243, 245, 265, 268, 269, 282
Milkman, R. 266
Milkovich, G. 53
Millward, N. 249, 266
Mitial 174, 196
Miozzo, M. 2, 5, 6, 21
Mohammed, S. 36, 51
Moreland, R. 36, 51
Morris, J. 10, 21
Moynihan, L. 14, 44, 45, 51, 53, 57, 71, 95, 148, 149, 240, 241, 242
MSSS 155, 156, 166, 167, 173
Mueller, C. W. 210, 211, 222, 225, 242
Mullarkey, S. 227, 243
Mulholland, K. 2, 4, 13, 21
Mulvey, G. 19, 22, 171, 173, 282
Munday, M. 175, 195
Munro, J. 169, 173

National Audit Office 156, 161, 173
Neumark, P. 46, 50
Nicholas, K. 271, 283

Nicholl, J. 173
Nixon, S. 277, 283
Noble, F. 151, 282
Norton, D. 32, 51

O'Neil, M. 173
Odih, P. 271, 282
Oldham, G. R. 31, 50
Olson, C. 51, 72
Organisation for Economic Co-operation and Development (OECD) 175, 196
Orr, J. 35, 51, 50

Papper, E. M. 35, 50
Parker, S. K. 237, 243
Paul, J. 1, 10, 16, 21, 33, 52
Pearce, J. A. 51
Peccei, R. 8, 21, 22, 56, 64, 72
Pepper, K. 60, 73, 230, 243
Pfeffer, J. 79, 101
Phillips, J. S. 206, 218, 222
Pine, B. J. 30, 52
Pines, A. 206, 222
Pinneau, S. R. 221
Plain Software Company Limited 162, 173
Poynter, G. 129, 130, 151
Price, C. J. 225, 242
Price, J. L. 210, 211, 222
Priest, M. 269, 283
Pringle, J. K. 191, 195
Purcell, J. 4, 7, 20, 21, 30, 51, 57, 73, 75, 76, 77, 79, 81, 82, 95, 97, 98, 100, 101, 104, 124, 125, 126, 153, 172, 203, 204, 221, 222, 245, 266

Quilter Wheeler, S. 173
Quinn, P. 265

Rafaeli, A. 34, 52
Rainnie, A. 103, 126
Ramirez, M. 2, 5, 6, 21
Ramsay, H. 32, 52
Rathwell, T. 155, 173
Ravlin, E. C. 51
Rayton, B. 125, 126
Redman, T. 131, 151
Rhoads, G. 33, 52
Richardson, R. 8, 9, 19, 21, 22, 71, 174, 195, 196, 201, 221, 226, 227, 242, 272, 283
Robinson, R. 164, 171, 173
Rosener, J. B. 175, 196

Name Index

Rosenthal, P. 8, 13, 21, 22
Rothwell, S. 126
Rutherford, S. 175, 184, 192, 196
Ryan, A. M. 33, 52

Sabin, M. 168, 169, 173
Sako, M. 150, 247, 266
Saks, A. M. 225, 244
Salas, E. 35, 36, 50, 51
Salvadge, J. 164, 173
Sanders, K. J. 244
Sanders, T. 162, 169, 173
Sargent, A. 33, 52
Sasser, W. E., Jr 32, 50
Savage, M. 175, 185, 189, 193, 196
Saxton, M. J. 206, 218, 222
Scarbrough, H. 103, 123, 126
Scase, R. 126, 175, 191, 192, 196
Schacht, J. 28, 52
Schlesinger, L. 32, 50, 52, 241, 244
Schmit, M. 33, 52
Schneider, B. 11, 22, 33, 52, 55, 73, 129, 151
Scholarios, D. 32, 52, 152
Schon, D. 83, 100
Schweiger, D. M. 32, 51
Seifert, C. 74, 244
Sellier, F. 154, 170, 173
Sewell, G. 22
Shackleton, R. 187, 196
Shamash, J. 169, 173
Shao, Y. 225, 242
Shelley, S. 172
Shire, K. 4, 20, 21, 22, 72, 100, 125, 126, 148, 150, 151, 154, 172, 243, 265, 266, 282
Silvestre, J.-J. 154, 170, 173
Simms, M. 245, 266
Sinclair, D. 103, 104, 125, 126
Singh, J. 33, 52
Sirianni, C. 3, 4, 9, 10, 13, 20, 21, 73, 203, 216, 221, 222
Smith, C. 154, 172, 173, 283
Smith, M. J. 225, 242, 244
Smith, P. 283
Smith, V. 2, 20, 201, 203, 221
Spector, P. 67, 73, 206, 219, 222, 224, 225, 244
Spreitzer, G. 35, 50
Stanford, P. 175, 197
Stanton, J. M. 225, 244
Stanworth, C. 130, 151, 174, 175, 196
Stasser, G. 36, 52
Storey, J. 82, 101, 265

Strauss, G. 51, 72
Stride, C. B. 243
Stuchlik, M. 53
Sturdy, A. 13, 21, 22, 75, 101, 283
Sutton, R. I. 34, 52
Swart, J. 125, 126

Tam, M. 20, 21, 72, 100, 125, 126, 151, 172, 243, 265, 266, 282
Taylor, P. 2, 3, 6, 9, 11, 13, 19, 22, 57, 73, 77, 88, 100, 101, 126, 130, 144, 150, 151, 173, 174, 195, 197, 224, 242, 244, 245, 262, 264, 266, 268, 270, 280, 281, 282, 283
Taylor, S. 22, 101, 130, 151, 283
Telecommunication Industry Training Advisory Board 273, 283
Terry, D. 67, 73, 224, 244
Terry, M. 126, 249, 266
Tetrick, L. E. 211, 222, 224, 243
Thompson, P. 6, 7, 8, 14, 16, 20, 22, 75, 77, 81, 82, 93, 100, 101, 125, 129, 131, 132, 133, 135, 137, 141, 143, 144, 145, 147, 150, 151, 152, 153, 154, 172, 173, 177, 197, 267, 268, 270, 271, 282, 283
Thorpe, S. 53
Tijdens, K. 195
Tindale, S. 35, 50
Titus, W. 36, 52
Tomlinson, F. 175, 184, 192, 197
Tornow, W. W. 32, 52
Totterdell, P. 33, 51
Trades Union Congress (TUC) 67, 73, 175, 179, 197
Traves, J. 175, 184, 192, 197
Trottier, L.-H. 157, 173
Turnbull, P. 97, 101

United Kingdom Central Council for Nursery, Midwifery and Health Visiting (UKCC) 164, 173
Ulrich, D. 32, 53
Unison 190, 197
Unsworth, K. 71, 242

Van den Broek, D. 16, 19
Van Klaveren, M. 195
Vogt, C. 74, 244
Vollrath, D. 35, 50
Vurdubakis, T. 151, 282

290 Name Index

Wajcman, J. 175, 191, 192, 194, 195, 197
Walby, S. 179, 197
Waldersee, R. 7, 22, 75, 77, 80, 81, 82, 98, 99, 101, 146, 152
Wall, T. 60, 71, 73, 74, 225, 229, 237, 242, 243, 244
Wallace, C. M. 7, 22, 75, 77, 80, 81, 82, 98, 101, 146, 152
Walsh, J. 10, 12, 17, 18, 20, 55, 72, 80, 82, 100, 168, 206
Walton, R. E. 98, 101, 266, 267, 283
Warhurst, C. 8, 22, 100, 101, 131, 150, 151, 267, 283
Warr, P. 60, 73, 74, 225, 226, 229, 243, 244
Wass, V. 97, 101
Waterson, P. 71, 242
Watson, A. 19, 55, 56, 73, 130, 148, 152, 171
Webster J. 8, 9, 19, 71, 154, 173, 175, 177, 195, 197, 201, 221, 226, 242
Wegner, D. M. 36, 53

Wharton, A. 10, 22, 201, 211, 222
Wheeler, J. 33, 52
White, S. 33, 52
Wial, H. 3, 20, 204, 205, 221
Wiley, J. W. 32, 52, 53
Williams, A. 164, 169, 173
Williams, S. J. 169, 173
Willmott, H. 21, 22, 101, 151, 282, 283
Windt, J. H. 155, 166, 173
Winslow, C. 57, 74, 224, 244
Witz, A. 157, 164, 169, 173, 175, 185, 189, 193, 196
Wong, K. 266
Wood, S. 7, 22, 54, 73, 79, 101
Wright, P. 31, 53

Yammarino, F. J. 34, 53
Yukl, G. 74

Zapf, D. 58, 74, 224, 226, 241, 244
Zornitsky, J. 32, 52
Zuboff, S. 269, 283

Subject Index

absenteeism 10, 12, 19
ACTU 277–81
airline industry 207–21
alleviation model 81, 87–90
anxiety 9, 15, 18, 33, 60, 223, 226, 229, 231–41
ASDA 56
assembly line in the head 3
AT&T 28
attitudes, of employees' 4, 6, 9, 11, 12–14, 18, 133–9, 208–21, 231–41
Australia, call centres in 12, 16, 19, 132–50, 207–21, 268–74, 277–81
authoritarian 15, 19, 55–6, 61–3, 66–71
Automatic Call Distribution (ACD) 5, 29, 252, 273
automation 161, 163–4
autonomy 5, 10, 18, 31, 33–4, 160, 162–5, 211
see also discretion

back office staff 28
balanced score card 32, 89
'Bank-Call' 59, 61–71, 227–9, 231–41
banking industry 54–71, 205, 223–41
Barclays Bank 56
best fit 16, 104
best practice 104, 169
black box 31
British Telecom 28
bureaucracy 79–80
    customer-oriented 6–7
    mass customized 6–7, 76
bureaucratic control 268
burnout, of employees, 7, 9–12, 16, 33, 207, 210–11
see also stress
business strategy 7, 16, 26, 77, 117

call centre managers 7–8, 11, 16, 102, 107–8, 110, 186–95
call centres
    in Australia 12, 16, 19, 132–50, 207–21, 268–74, 277–81
    in Canada 153, 155–60, 165–8, 170–1
    commercial 15–16, 102–5

customer attitudes towards 11, 48–9
    in Germany 148
    growth of 1–2, 25, 174, 239–40
    images of 3–4, 18, 129, 223
    in Ireland 17, 176
    and other forms of work 18, 223, 234–41
    outsourced 91, 102, 176–95
    in Scotland 130, 132–50
    types of 57–8, 77–100
    in the USA 169–70
calls
    length of 28, 39–42
    'Call Centre Bureau' 83–4, 90–3, 96–100
capital social 30
careers
    limits to 181, 186–95
    mobility 183–95
    of women 2, 17, 177–95
    occupational 191
    opportunities 185, 187
    progression 2, 107, 183–95
centralisation, of service provision 2
Chartered Institute of Personnel and Development 104
child care
    commitments 177–9
    facilities 81
clerical work 18, 234–7
client contracts
    award of 111–12
    management of 15, 114–20
clients, effect of 15–6, 102–24
    direct effects 107–11, 114–15
    indirect effects 111–13, 115–18
collective bargaining 56, 63–5
    in Eurotunnel 18, 250–2
commitment, of employees 60, 79–100
communication 257–60
Communications Workers of America 48
company council 18, 251–2, 263–4
competitive advantage, sources of 2, 25–7, 54, 105–6, 133

292 Subject Index

compliance model 80–2
conflict 13, 15, 62, 65
consultative structures 18, 248–50, 255–60
Contact 24, 105–24
containment model 80–2, 85–7
contingency approach 16, 104, 122–4
control
  cultural 89–90, 117, 144–50
  forms of 25–49, 55–7, 66–71, 77–100, 139–50
  normative 13, 16, 139–50
  over workers 2–9, 12, 15, 37–8, 267, 270, 274
  systems 25–49, 55–7, 66–71, 77–100, 139–50
co-worker support 211
costs
  minimisation of 4–8, 14, 27–9, 106
culture 89–90, 117, 144–50
customer service representative 85–100, 118–22, 133–50, 211–21, 224–41, 273–81
  bilingual 252
  demands on 103
customers
  attitudes toward call centres 4, 10–11, 48–9, 54

depression 11, 18, 33, 60, 223, 226, 229, 231–41
deskilling 148
development, of employees 2, 5, 7, 17, 81, 90–3, 189–95
dialogue, with customers 4, 9
discipline 5, 18
discretion, exercise of 15, 37, 75, 77–100

'Education Line' 83–4, 93–100
efficiency, tension with service 4, 13, 16, 25–6, 75, 96, 204
electronic, monitoring 3, 13, 18, 37–46, 57, 165, 224–5, 231–41
embeddness 165
emotional
  effort bargain 16, 146
  exhaustion 9–12, 17–18, 33, 206–7, 209–21, 224
  labour 9–11, 13, 130, 146
emotions
  negative 11
  positive 12

employees
  attitudes 4, 6, 9, 11, 12–14, 133–9, 208–21, 231–41
  burnout 7, 9–12, 16, 33, 207, 210–21
  effects of call centre work on 10–14, 207–21, 231–41
  in Eurotunnel 255–64
  recreational activities 16, 142–3, 145
  representation of 13, 18–19, 257–64
  responses of 12–14, 68–71, 141, 276–81
  socialisation of 16, 139–44
  voice 2, 264
  wellbeing 2, 205–7, 223–7, 229, 231–41
  withdrawal 12, 19
employment
  growth of 1–2, 25, 174, 239–40
  Europe 25
  France 1
  Germany 1
  of graduates 130–1, 180
  UK 1, 25
  USA 1, 25
  of women 87–90, 174, 273
empowerment, approach 5–8, 57–8, 270
Eurotunnel 18, 246, 250–64
Excell Global Services 267
exhaustion, emotional 9–10, 12, 17–8, 33, 206–7, 209–21, 224

fatigue 11
  see also burnout; stress
female, employment in call centres 9–10, 17, 87–90, 174–5, 177–95, 273
female ghettos 17, 175, 177
financial services sector 12–13, 35, 58–9, 148, 176–95
flexibility 10, 109, 114, 116
'Flightco' 207–21
front office, automation 29
front line workers 3, 129, 201
fun, working practices 7, 13, 81, 87, 142–3

gender 21, 135–6, 177–83, 185
  inequality 175, 192–5
governance, workplace 55–7, 66–71
greenfield sites 19
grievances, of employees 18

Subject Index 293

health, occupational 276
hierarchy, layers of 7
high commitment management 7,
15, 66–71, 75–100
high involvement work practices
14–5, 26–7, 30–2, 36–46, 56, 203–4
hiring, criteria 7–8, 77, 108
hours, opening 10
Human Resource Management
Journal 2
Human Resource Systems, types
of 5–8, 36–49
human resources
policies 5–8, 114–15
practices 14–15, 18, 36–49, 58,
60, 66–71, 77–100, 223, 225–6,
230–41
strategy 132–50

identification, with customers 6, 16,
134–5
induction 6, 16, 114, 131, 136–9, 189
information and communication
technologies 2
information panoptican 3, 57, 223
information sharing 18
information systems, design of 5, 269
information technology industry
176–95
investment, in training 5
involvement
of customers 4
of employees 31–2, 56, 82, 93–6
Ireland 17, 176
ISE Communications 268

job
control 18, 25–49, 55–7, 66–71,
77–100, 139–50
descriptions 9
design 15, 27–32, 60, 66–71, 75,
224–7, 230–41
satisfaction 12, 17–18, 60,
205–7, 210–21, 223, 225,
226, 229–41
job rotation 35
jobs
part time 87–90, 109, 176,
189–90

Key Note 1, 11, 20
King's College 2
knowledge sharing 14, 42–6
knowledge worker 29–30, 93–6, 153–6

labour
turnover 7, 12, 14, 19,
114, 146
labour market characteristics of 5,
17, 114, 146
labour process 154, 156–65, 202
managing 17
tensions in 15
language 4, 13
lean production model 4
learning by employees 43–6
'Loan-Call' 59, 65–71, 227–9, 231–41
low discretion high commitment
model 15, 76–100, 149

mail order 176–95
management
approaches 5–8, 15
high commitment 7, 15, 66–71,
75–100
strategy 2, 75
manufacturing 18, 35, 124
market, segmentation 14, 148–9
mass customisation model 14, 26,
30–1, 76, 148–9
effects of 36–49
spread of 6–7
mass production model 57–8, 61–3,
75, 148, 203, 208
effects of 68–71
measurement, of calls 28, 39–42
models of service delivery 25–49
monitoring, performance 3, 13, 18,
37–8, 57, 60, 66–71, 85–90,
112–13, 224–5, 231–41
'Mortgage-Call' 59, 63–71, 227–9,
231–41

negotiation 18
NHS Direct 153, 155–6, 160–5,
168–71
non-unionism 15, 43, 61–3, 136
non-union representation 18–19,
246
normative control 13, 16, 139–50
nurses 17, 154–71
nursing, methodology 17, 156

occupations 153–4, 191
Optus 267, 272, 274, 276, 278–81
organisation structure 181
outsourced call centres 91, 102,
176–95
ownership, influence of 110–11

294 *Subject Index*

panoptican 3, 57, 223
part time working 87–90, 109,
176, 189–90
partnership
agreement 56, 63–6, 68–71,
251, 262–3
pay
structures 108, 115, 252–3
systems 115
peer pressure 143, 274–6
performance management 61–2,
90–3, 139–50, 230–41
performance monitoring 12, 18,
224–5, 231–41
performance outcomes 14, 38–46, 66–71
indicators of 14, 38, 85–7, 209–11
improvements in
personality
of the firm 8
traits 8
personnel management 55, 58, 60–71
PhoneCo 270
phone rage 11
product market 121, 207
segmentation 8
production line, model 5–8, 25–9,
36–49, 61–3, 68–71, 148
professional services model 26,
29–30, 36–49, 148
professional work 17, 153–4, 166–71
promotion 17, 177–86
psychological types 270
public sector 153

quality 4, 8, 11, 13–14, 16, 25–6, 75,
96, 204
Quebec Health Info CLSC 153,
155–60, 165–8, 170–1, 17
quit rates 36–49
'Quotes Direct' 83–7, 96–100

RAC 7
recognition, of unions 251, 262–3
recreational activities 16, 142–3, 145
recruitment, strategies 7–8, 16, 28,
77, 108, 114, 131–9, 178, 208–9
red card 274
representation 13, 18–19, 257–64
resistance 12–14, 19, 144–6, 267,
270–1, 279–81
collective 14, 141, 277–9
by individual employees 13, 276–7
reward systems 59–61, 107–8, 227–9
Ryder Truck 32

sacrificial HR strategy 7, 77, 81, 146
sales
growth 36–49
work 37–49, 63–6, 85–90, 207–9,
227–9, 234–7
satisfaction, job 12, 17–18, 60,
205–7, 210–21, 223, 225, 226,
229–41
scientific management 5
scripting of tasks 6, 9, 13, 93–6
Sears 32
segregation, gendered 135–7,
174–5, 184–95
selection
of employees 7–8, 16, 28, 77,
108, 131–9
of managers 107
service
climate 33
models of delivery 2, 25–49
profit chain 32
tension with efficiency 4, 13, 16,
25–6, 75, 96, 204
service quality 16–17, 29–31,
94–6, 110
rhetoric of 10
'Servo' 16, 132–50, 272
'Shopping Line' 83–4, 87–90,
93–100
skills 7–8, 37–42, 133–9
development of 7, 139–43
social 8
use of 156–71
social capital 131
socialisation of employees
16, 139–44
staff association 13
Stellar 267, 272, 274, 277, 281
stress
of employees, 7, 10–12, 17–18,
33, 205–7, 211–21, 226
see also burnout, anxiety,
depression
strike action 13, 62, 65
supervision
of employees 6, 57–8, 210–21
surveillance 7
sweatshops, electronic 3, 18, 223,
239–40
systems
of control 25–49, 55–7, 66–71,
77–100, 139–50
of reward 59–61, 017–8,
227–9

Subject Index 295

Taylorism, see also Scientific
Management 3, 14, 27–8, 57,
149, 162, 170, 240–1
team leaders 183–90, 223, 225–7,
231–41, 274–6
teams, self-managed 32, 34–5
teamwork 14, 36–46, 142–3, 223, 274–6
'Telco' 207–21
'Telebank' 16, 77, 132–50
telecommunications industry 12, 18,
34–46, 205, 207–21, 271–2, 277
tele-health 167
tele-nursing 17, 156, 160, 161, 169
telephone operators 28–9
'Teletech' 267, 272, 278–81
Telstra 267, 268, 272, 275–6, 277–81
Trade Unions 63–5
attitudes towards 136
in Eurotunnel 18, 251, 259, 264
membership 13, 18–19, 249
training 16, 59–61, 107–8, 131,
139–44, 208–11, 227–9
Transport and General Workers
Union 18, 250–1, 262–3
turnover, labour 7, 12, 19, 114, 146

unionisation 13, 15, 18–19, 26
in Australia 19, 272, 279–81
in Eurotunnel 260–4
obstacles to 277

voice
growth and development of
employee 2, 264
tone of 8, 139

women
in call centres 9–10, 17, 87–90,
174–5, 177–95, 273
career advancement 2, 17,
177–95
work
control over 2–9, 12, 15, 37–8,
267, 270, 274
design 5–8, 31–2, 36–46, 77–100,
205–21, 230–41
environment 88–90, 184–6
intensification 274–6
organisation of 109, 205–7
segmentation 27–31, 36–42, 95
workers
burnout 7, 9–12, 16, 33, 207,
210–11
satisfaction 12, 17–8, 60, 205–7,
210–21, 223, 225, 226,
229–41
speech of 8, 139
well-being 9–10, 17–18, 32, 205–7,
223–7, 229, 231–41
working hours 10–11
working time, arrangements for
10–11
work-life balance 10–11,
189–90
workplace governance 14, 55–7,
66–71
Workplace Employee Relations
Survey 104, 109
works councils 248

yellow card 274